LEARNING MS-WORD AND MS-EXCEL

Rohit Khurana

A.P.H. PUBLISHING CORPORATION
4435-36/7, ANSARI ROAD, DARYA GANJ
NEW DELHI-110 002

Published by
S.B. Nangia
A P H Publishing Corporation
4435-36/7, Ansari Road, Daryaganj
New Delhi 110002
Ph.: 23274050
E-mail : aphbooks@gmail.com

2026

Rs. 3995/-

Printed at
Balaji Offset
Navin Shahdara, Delhi 110032

Editor's Note

Dear Students,

It is often said that success in life can be attributed to goal setting. Setting and reaching apparently unreachable targets or goals has been a part of **ITLESL's (ITL Education Solutions Ltd.)** philosophy from day one. **ITLESL is a dream of people who have dedicated themselves to the ever-changing world of IT.**

Most of the students today have a dream of becoming an IT professional. We are committed to turn that dream into a reality. With **eAcademy**, we take another step to improve the quality of IT education in India. **eAcademy** is increasing its network of centres and is established as a premium IT education solutions provider.

We understand people's growing appetite for newer technologies. Considering such preferences, we make sure that only the latest technologies are chosen. To add to that, we're working with highly qualified professionals and content developers for quality course materials, which is used in all our education centres.

As an organisation we have started to build many new relationships, which will help us in business generation, customer contact, new technology absorption and will also help expose our technologies, work processes and services to the market place.

I would like to thank all my team members without whom a mission like this would have been almost impossible to achieve.

All the very best to all our readers.

Company Profile

eAcademy is a division of ITL Education Solutions Ltd, which is a quality IT career education solutions provider managed by top-notch professionals with vast experience in the IT education industry.

ITL Education Solutions Ltd, is a part of the Rs. 200 crore ITL Group. The group has operations in software development and ERP unit for the domestic SME segment and a state of the art set up for Medical Transcription in association with C Bay of California. ITL Group has keen interest in the education field. We have two-Senior Secondary Schools in Delhi, providing the best of education to the students.

eAcademy has been a pioneer in introducing new Concepts and Methodologies for imparting IT education. The implementation of these concepts has led to the success of the most comprehensive IT career course, the market has to offer to the industry today. At **eAcademy** we believe in providing Quality Education to our students. This quality reflects both in our courseware as well as in the people who develop it. The course is designed after taking a feedback from the user industry on their requirement of skills in the next few months and technical gurus of the IT industry have also been consulted for the designing of the courseware.

At **eAcademy,** our mission is to deliver to the Global market, the best and highly skilled trained IT professionals who can develop software applications and set new trends in this ever-changing world of IT.

Preface

Microsoft Office 2000 is a suite of programs that lets you create and manage written materials, publications, databases, spreadsheets, and Web pages for use with your students or on your own. When you need to create a test, make a research presentation, help students collect data, or schedule resources, Office 2000 gives you tools to work more productively.

The following components of Office 2000 are covered in this book:

Microsoft Word 2000 provides everything you need to produce professional-looking documents, communicate your ideas, and share information with others. Features covered in the chapters include Developing ideas and content, Producing drafts, Organizing documents, Revising writing, Formatting papers, publishing.

Microsoft Excel 2000 makes it easy for you to build spreadsheets and then use, share, and analyze the data, as well as provide reports and present the data graphically. Features covered in the chapters include Gathering and entering data, Formatting data, Working with numbers, Formulae and Functions, Use of proofing tools, Charts.

The content flow of the book has been made in a very simple, yet explanatory manner. All the chapters in the book are well supported by Illustrations and Hands on exercises for the student to get a complete understanding of all the topics covered.

We hope you enjoy reading this book. Please feel free to send in your suggestions and queries at **feedback@itlesl.com**.

TRADEMARKS

DISCLAIMER

COPYRIGHT NOTICE

Designed, developed and Published by the Research & Development Wing, ITL EDUCATION SOLUTIONS LTD., C-88, South Extension - II, New Delhi - 110 049, India.

Part No.: MS200002

Product Line: e Academy

Contents

Chapter 1: Getting Started with Word 1

Chapter 2: Formatting Text and Paragraphs 57

Chapter 6: An Introduction to Excel 181

Chapter 7: Formatting and Customizing Data 219

Chapter 8: Formulas and Functions 247

Getting Started with Word

Objectives

- Introduction
- Start Microsoft Word
- The Office Assistant
- Introduction to Word Window
- Things you need to know
- Opening, Creating and Saving Documents
- Print

Introduction

Microsoft Word is a word processing program that produces professional documents quickly and efficiently. Microsoft Word 2000 is an advanced Windows-based processor. Word 2000 is based on Windows 95/98/NT, rather than Windows 3.x, it can make better use of your PCs memory and disk resources. As Windows 95/98/NT is a multitasking system, you can run your Word 2000 program at the same time as other programs such as Excel, Powerpoint. You also have the ability to exchange information with other Windows-based programs. Thus, you can produce a spreadsheet in Excel and then copy the information into a Word 2000 document for inclusion in a report. It is an extremely versatile tool, ideal for creating short documents, like letters and memos with enough layout and graphics-handling capabilities to also make it suitable for sophisticated publishing.

Word has always had a three-layered architecture consisting of application, template and document layers. Functionality can be contained in any of these three layers. There is the built-in functionality of the application layer, and customized functionality that can be stored in a template or document. Every new document is based on a template. Templates can be very simple, providing consistent formatting for a particular type of document, or very complex, such as an application that creates proposals or quarterly reports. If the user does not choose a specific template, the document is based on the default template, *Normal.Dot.* Templates can be stored on the local hard drive and stored in a workgroup template location anywhere on your network. Storing workgroup templates on the server makes it easier to distribute and update templates.

This section briefly describes the architecture and possibilities with Word 2000. Understanding the architecture will help you make decisions as to whether it is better to convert, archive, or re-engineer your documents in Word.

Start Microsoft Word

Before creating or opening a document in Word, first you will have to load / open MS-Word in memory.

1. Click on **Start** → **Programs** → **Microsoft Office** → **Microsoft Word** or click on the shortcut icon as shown in figure 1.1.

2. The Word opening screen will appear as shown in figure 1.3. The default name of the blank document is document1. The extension of a Word file is *.doc.*

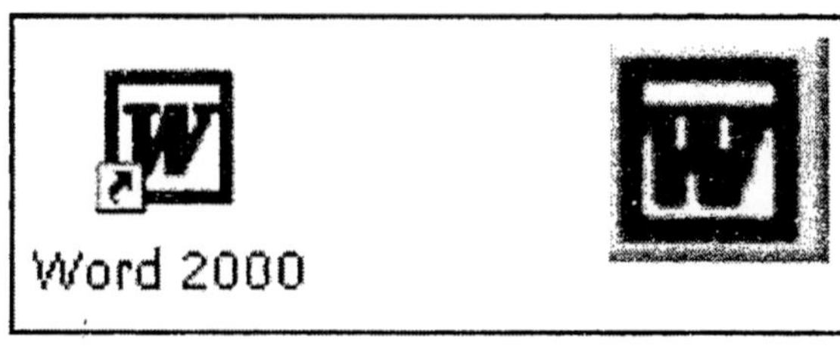

Figure 1.1: MS-Word Icon

If you are using Word for the first time, the Office Assistant welcome will appear. To Start using Word, click the suitable option in the Assistant window.

The Office Assistant

By default Word 2000 will display a *"tip of the day"* each time you start Word. If you take the time to read these as they are displayed, then you will soon find that you are on the way to becoming a Word 2000 expert.

By default this friendly little creature, will watch what you do and offer tips on how to work more productively. You can also ask questions in plain English.

Occasionally the Office Assistant will display information on the screen. Office Assistant gives you simple and quick entry to Help's Answer Wizard and keyword searches. To search for help on a topic, click the Office Assistant, type your question or keyword relevant to your topic, and click Search. Assuming there are six or more "hits" associated with your query, the Assistant presents five answers in the first dialog box, with a See More.... Button.

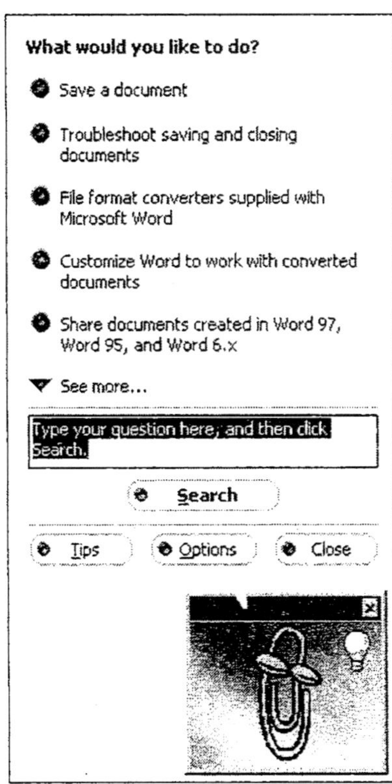

Figure 1.2: Office Assistant dialog box

Introduction to Word Window

The Word screen displays several bars to help you perform tasks efficiently. The following figure explains the different parts of the window.

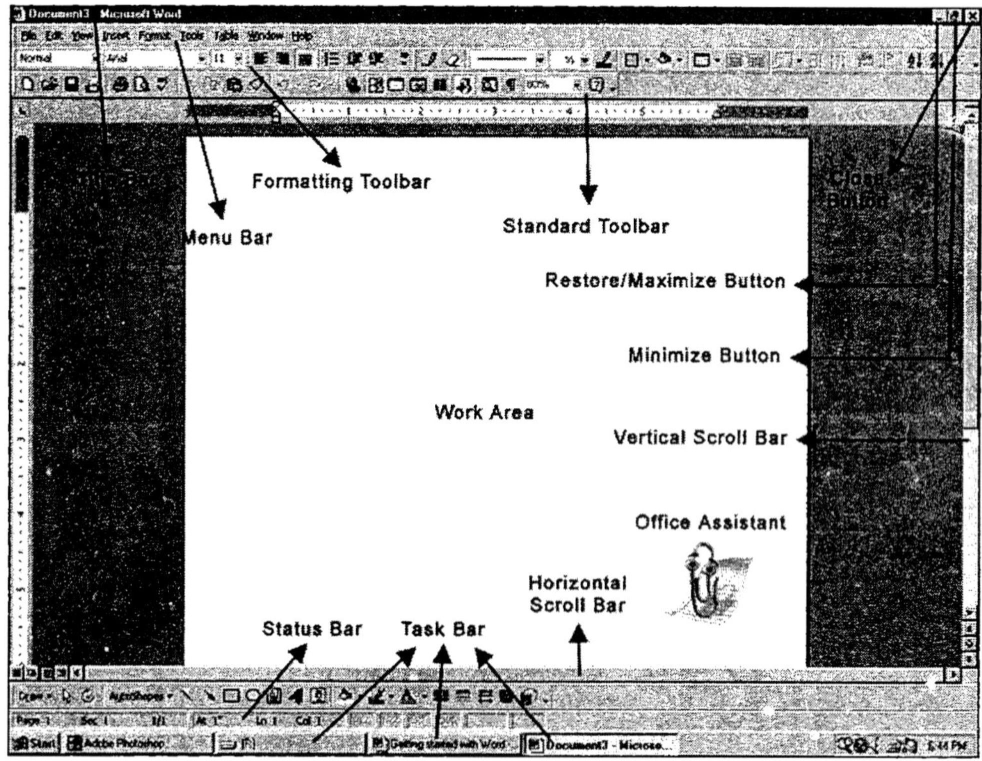

Figure 1.3: Getting familiar with MS-Word Interface

The Title Bar

Figure 1.4: Title Bar

The Title bar, is located at the very top of the screen. On the Title bar, Microsoft Word displays the name of the document you are currently using. At the top of your screen, you should see *"Microsoft Word - Document1"* or a similar name.

The Menu Bar

Figure 1.5: Menu Bar

The Menu bar is directly below the Title bar and it displays the menu. The menu begins with the word File and continues with Edit, View, Insert, Format, Tools, Table, Window and Help. You use the menu to give instructions to the software. Point with your mouse to the menu option and click the left mouse button to open a drop-down menu.

You can now use the left and right arrow keys on your keyboard to move left and right across the Menu bar options. You can use the up and down arrow keys to move up and down the drop-down menu. To select an option, highlight the item on the drop-down menu and press Enter. An ellipse after a menu item signifies additional options; if you select that option, a dialog box will appear.

The Status Bar

The status bar contains several separate items of information. In one block it shows the current page, the current section, and the current page relative to the total number of pages in the document. In the next block it contains the absolute page location of the current cursor. The next two numbers contain the current line number and the current column. These are relative values and can change based on the font used as well as the font size. The last block consists of five toggles. Normally all these toggles will be off and their text will be barely visible, as in the figure below.

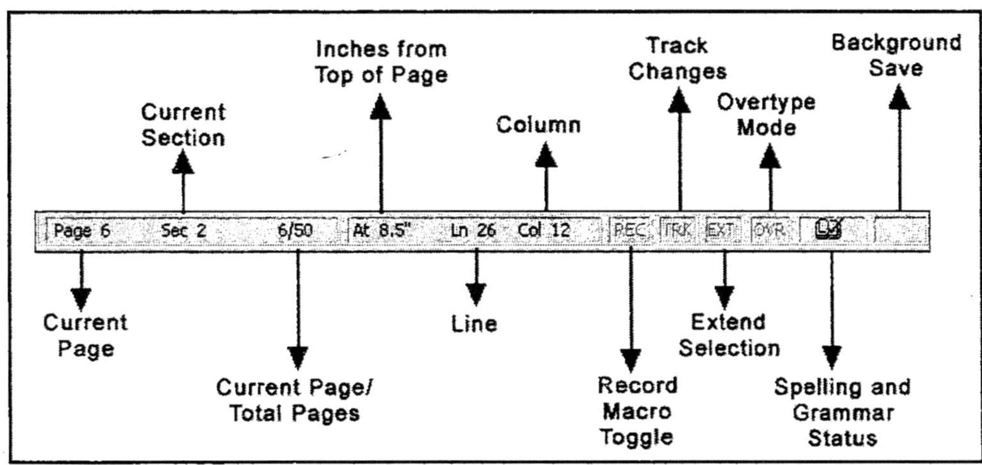

Figure 1.6: Status Bar

The Status bar appears at the very bottom of the screen and provides. The four items are:

Item	Action Signalled
REC	Macro recording is in progress.
TRK	Revision Marking has been turned on.
EXT	The F8 key has been pressed and extended (keyboard) selection is on.
OVR	Overstrike mode is on. Word defaults into insert mode. If you press the insert key, word will type new characters over existing ones--if any are present.

Table 1.1: Status Bar Options

The Ruler Bar

Figure 1.7: Ruler

The ruler is generally found below the main toolbars. The ruler is used to change the format of your document quickly. To display the ruler:

1. Point to View on the Menu bar.
2. Click your left mouse button.
3. The option Ruler should have a checkmark next to it. If it has a checkmark next to it, press Esc twice to close the menu. If it does *not* have a checkmark next to it, continue to the next step.
4. Press the down arrow key until Ruler is highlighted.
5. Press the Enter key. The ruler should display below the toolbars.

Toolbars

Toolbars provide shortcuts to menu commands. Toolbars are generally located just below the Menu bar. Toolbars contain small pictures called tool icons which, when clicked on, provide a shortcut method of performing a Word 2000 action.

For instance, clicking on the **Spelling** tool icon will cause Word 2000 to spell checker is to click on the **Tools** drop down menu and then to select the **Spelling** command from the drop down list displayed.

Word 2000 has a number of distinct toolbars, but then only the Standard and Formatting toolbars are displayed. You can customize Word 2000 so that other toolbars are displayed by default.

- From the **View** drop down menu, click on the **Toolbars** command that displays the Toolbars sub-menu.
- Click on the required toolbar.
- Right click on any toolbar to display a list of other toolbars that may be displayed.

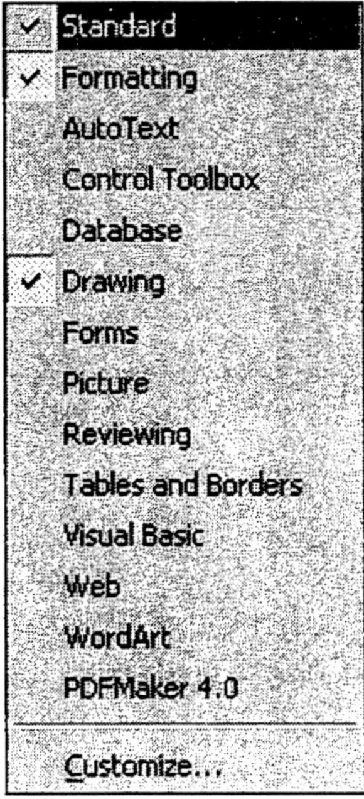

Figure 1.8: Toolbar Menu Options

The toolbars are not fixed to a certain part of the Word 2000 window - they can float which means the toolbars can be moved around on your screen.

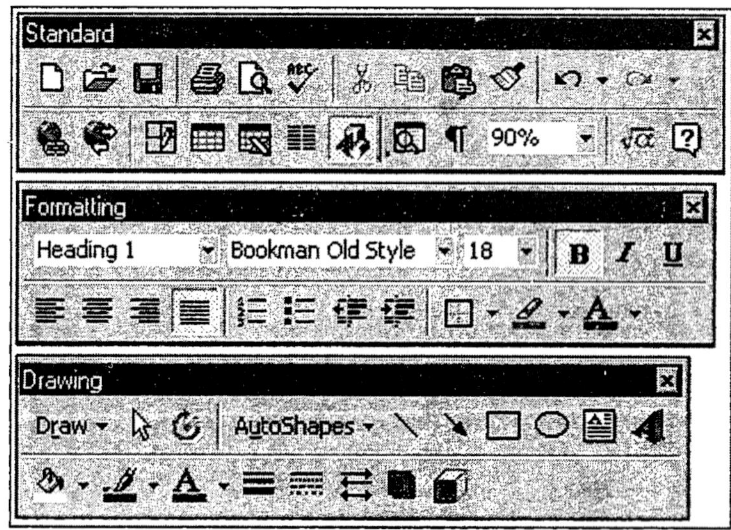

Figure 1.9: Floating Toolbars (Standard, Formatting and Drawing)

The Scroll Bar

Scroll bars are used to view different areas of the active window. You can do so by moving the elevator along the scroll bar or by clicking on the buttons with the arrows marked on them, to move up and down a page.

The Workspace

The workspace is the area in the document window wherein you enter the text of your document.

Document View

With word, you can display your document in one of four views: Normal, Web Layout, Print Layout Outline.

- **Normal View:** Normal view is the most often used and shows such formatting as line spacing, font, point size and italics. Multiple-column text is displayed in one continuous column.

- **Outline View:** Outline view displays the document in outline form. Headings can be displayed without the text. A heading can be moved and the accompanying text moved with it.
- **Print Layout View:** The Page Layout view shows the document as it will look when it is printed.
- **Web Page Layout View:** The Online Layout view optimizes the document for online viewing (viewing the document in a browser).

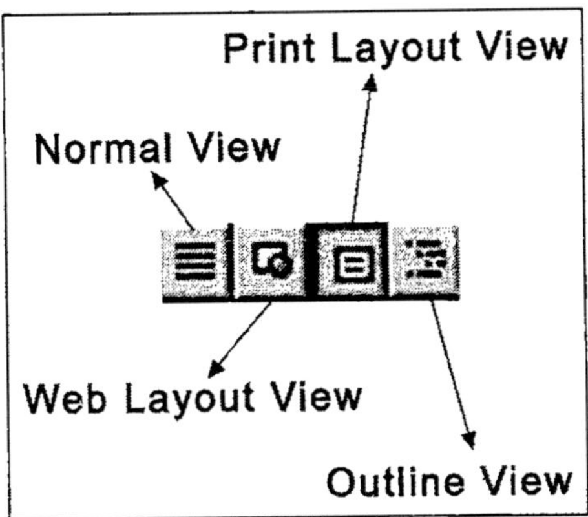

Figure 1.10: Document Views

Highlighting Text

Throughout these lessons you will be asked to highlight text. You can use either of the following methods:

Highlighting by Using the F8 and Arrow Keys

1. Place the cursor before or after the text you wish to highlight and click the left mouse button.
2. Press the F8 key, which will serve as an "anchor" showing where text you wish to highlight begins or ends.
3. Press the appropriate arrow key (left arrow to move to the left, or right arrow to move to the right) until the text is highlighted. You can use the up or down arrow key to highlight one line at a time. Press Esc to remove the anchor.

Highlighting by Using the Mouse

1. Place the cursor before or after the text you wish to highlight.
2. Hold down the left mouse button.
3. Move the mouse left, right, up, or down until the text is highlighted.

Highlighting Menu Items

To select a Menu bar item:

1. Click on the Menu bar item. A drop-down menu will appear.
2. To change the Menu bar option selected, move the mouse pointer across the Menu bar while holding down the left mouse button.

☞ *Note: After you highlight an item on the Menu bar, you can also use the left and right arrow keys to move across the Menu bar.*

Drop-Down Menu Items

When you click on any option on the Menu bar, a drop-down menu will appear. To highlight a drop-down menu item:

1. Move up or down the drop-down menu while holding down the left mouse button.
2. Press Enter to select a drop-down menu item.

☞ *Note: You can also use the arrow keys to move up and down the drop-down menu.*

Using the Mouse

- Many Word features can be carried out using the keyboard alone, but the mouse is designed to “point and click” at the screen, thus making the software easier to use.
- Some features can only be carried out using the mouse, such as drawing pictures.

Mouse Actions

There are four mouse actions.

Mouse Action	How to do it	What it's for
Click	Point and click the left mouse button	This is the "normal" way of using the mouse
Double-click	Press the left mouse button twice quickly	For shortcuts or for doing something with a bit more power than a single click
Click and drag	Click with the left mouse button and keep your finger down, then drag to a new part of the screen	For moving things around the screen
Right-click	Point and click with the right mouse button	For shortcuts

Table 1.2: Mouse Actions

Why Does the Mouse Change Shape?

The shape of the mouse signifies the action it is about to carry out. The main ones are as follows...

	Pointer For clicking on icons and menus, and selecting text.
	I-Bar For inserting text
	Double-headed arrow For re-sizing
	Cross-Arrow For moving pictures and toolbars
	Egg-timer Word is busy at the moment. This will disappear if you wait a second
	Unavailable Word cannot carry out the task you are trying to complete with the mouse

Table 1.3: Mouse Shapes

Placing the Cursor

In the following chapters, you will often be asked to place the cursor at a specific location on the screen. You place the cursor by pointing to the location specified and pressing the left mouse button or by using the arrow keys to move to the specified location.

Choosing Menu Commands by Using the Alt Key

There are many methods to accomplish tasks using Microsoft Word. Generally, when selecting items from the menu, we will ask you to click on or highlight the menu item. However, you can also select a menu option by:

1. Pressing the Alt key while typing the underlined letter on the Menu bar.

2. Typing the letter underlined on a drop-down menu. If a dialog box appears, you can move around the dialog box by pressing the Alt key and any underlined option.

Shortcut Key Demonstration

1. Hold down the Alt key and press "o" to select Format from the menu.

2. Press "p" to select Paragraph from the drop-down menu.

3. Hold down the Alt key and press "i" to select the Indents and Spacing tab.

4. Hold down the Alt key and press "b" to select Before from the Spacing frame.

5. Press Enter to close the dialog box.

Shortcut Notations

A key name followed by a dash and a letter means to hold down the key while pressing the letter. For example, Alt+o means you should hold down the Alt key while pressing "o". A shorthand notation of the above demonstration would read as follows:

1. Press Alt+o, p.
2. Press Alt+i.
3. Press Alt+b.
4. Press Enter.

To Create a New Line

1. Make sure your cursor is flashing where you would like a new line
2. Press the enter or hard return key (found on the right of the keyboard)

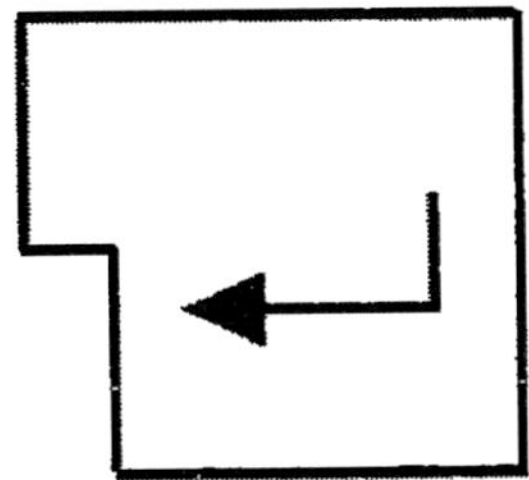

Figure 1.11: Enter Key

To Create Capital Letters

1. Hold down the shift key while you type the letters.

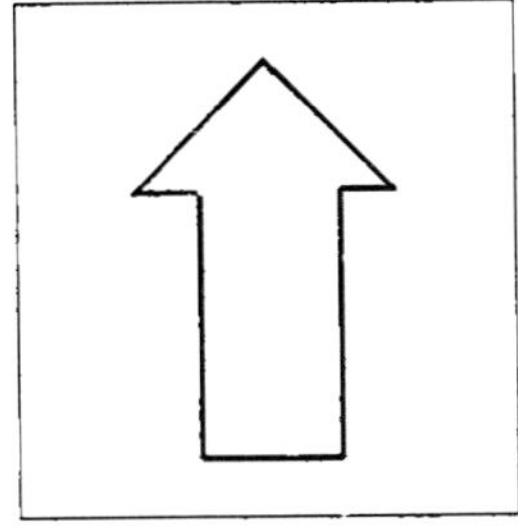

Figure 1.12: Shift Key

There are two shift keys on the keyboard, one at the bottom left and one at the bottom right

To Capitalise All the Text you are Typing

1. Press the Caps Lock key on the left of the keyboard. A light will appear above Caps Lock on the right hand side of the keyboard.
2. To turn off, press Caps Lock again

Moving the Cursor Around with the Keyboard

1. Use the cursor keys at the bottom right of the keyboard

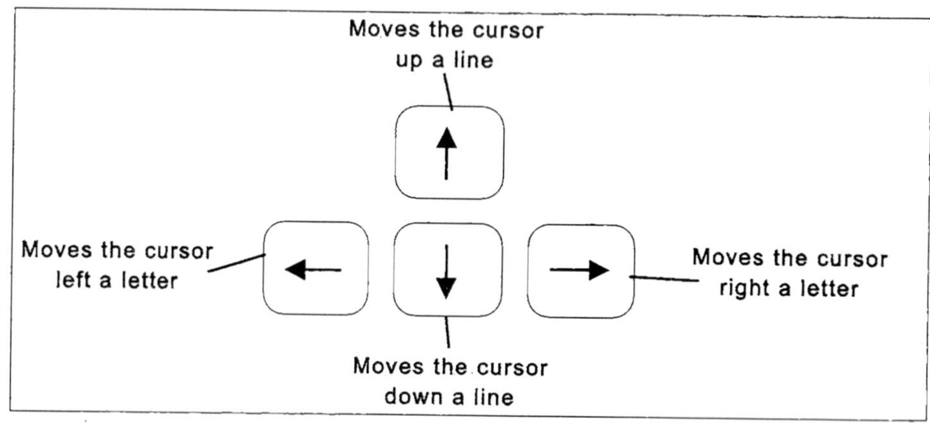

Figure 1.13: Getting familiar with cursor keys

Starting a New Paragraph

When you type in Microsoft Word, you do not need to press a key to move to a new line. To start a new paragraph, press the Enter key.

Typing and Using the Backspace Key

The exercises that follow will teach you how to enter and delete text. To enter text, simply type just as you would if you were using a typewriter. To capitalize, hold down the Shift key while typing the letter. Use the Backspace key to delete text. You do not need to press Enter to start a new line, Microsoft Word automatically wraps at the end of the line. Press Enter to start a new paragraph.

Example 1:

1. Type the following sentence: **Joe has a very large house.**
2. Now delete the word "house". Using either the arrow keys or the mouse, place the cursor between the period and the "e" in the word "house".
3. Press the Backspace key until the word "house" is deleted.
4. Type **boat**. The sentence should now read: **Joe has a very large boat.**

The Delete Key

You can also delete text by using the Delete key. First, highlight the text you wish to delete; then press the Delete key.

Example 2:

Delete the word "very" from the sentence you just typed.

1. Highlight the word "very".
2. Place the cursor before the "v" in the word "very" and press the F8 key. Then press the right arrow key until the word "very" is highlighted.
3. Press the Delete key. The sentence should now read: **Joe has a large boat.**

Inserting Text

- Normally when you type you will be in insert mode. This means that if your cursor is in the middle of an existing sentence and you start typing, nothing will be deleted. The text that is already there will shuffle along to make way for the new text.
- If you are in overtype mode, then any text you type will go over the top of existing text. Look at the right side of the Status bar. If the letters "OVR" are gray, you are in the Insert mode. If the letters "OVR" are black, you are in the Overtype mode.

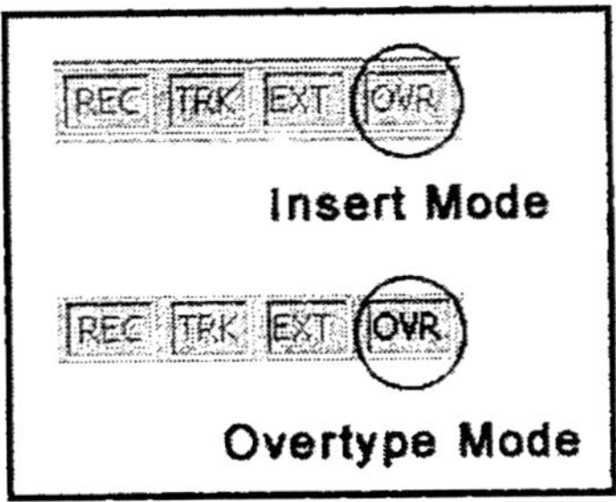

Figure 1.14: Insertion Mode

To change to the Insert mode

1. Double click on the letters "OVR".
2. The letters "OVR" should now be gray.

Alternate Method: Setting Options by Using the Menu

1. Go to the Menu bar. Click on Tools.
2. Highlight Options at the bottom of on the drop-down menu. Press Enter.
3. Click on the Edit tab.
4. The Overtype Mode box should be blank. If the box is blank, click on OK.
5. If the Overtype Mode box is not blank, click on the box to remove the checkmark. Then click on OK.

Alternate Method: Setting Options by Using Keys

1. Press Alt+t, o.
2. Click on Edit.
3. Press Alt+o (toggles between overtype and insert).
4. Press Enter.

Example 3:

Make sure the letters "OVR" are gray before proceeding. You are going to insert the word "blue" between the words "large" and "boat".

1. Place the cursor between the words "large" and "boat".
2. Type the word **blue**.
3. The sentence should now read: **Joe has a large blue boat.**

Overtype

You can type over the current text (replace the current text with new text). However, you must be in the Overtype mode. Do the following to change to the Overtype mode.

1. Double-click on "OVR" on the Status bar.
2. The letters "OVR" should now be black.

Make sure the letters "OVR" are black before proceeding to the following exercise.

Example 4:

Change the word "blue" to "gray".

3. Place the cursor before the letter "b" in "blue".

4. Type the word **gray**.

5. The sentence should now read: **Joe has a large gray boat.**

Bold, Underline and Italicize

You can bold, underline, or italicize when using Word. You also can combine these features, in other words you can bold, underline and italicize a single piece of text.

1. Select the text to change

2. Click on the icon you require as shown below:

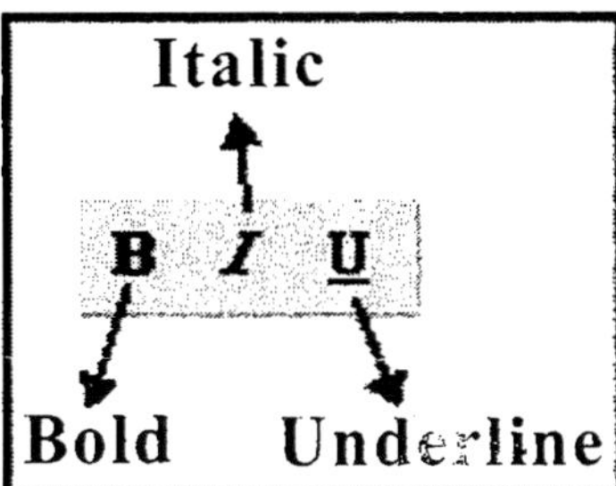

Figure 1.15: Bold, Italic and Underline Icons

Example 5:

Type the following exactly as shown. Remember, pressing the Enter key starts a new paragraph. Press the Enter key at the end of the following lines to start a new paragraph.

- Menu Bold Italicize Underline these words All three Regular
- Icon Bold Italicize Underline these words All three Regular
- Keys Bold Italicize Underline these words All three Regular

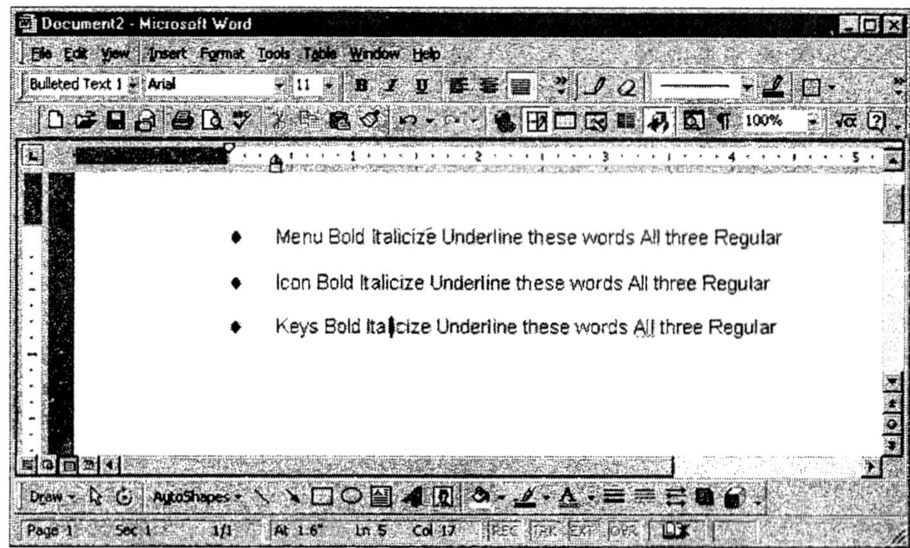

Figure 1.16: Sample Text

Bold - Using the Menu

1. On the line that begins with Menu, first highlight the word Bold. To do so, place the cursor before the letter "B" in "Bold". Press the F8 key; then press the right arrow key until the entire word is highlighted.

2. Click on Format.

3. Highlight Font. Press Enter.

4. Click on Bold in the Font Style box.

5. Click on OK to close the dialog box.

☞ *Note: You can see the effect of your selection in the Preview window. To turn off the bold, click on Regular.*

6. Click anywhere in the text area to remove the highlighting.

Alternate Method: Bold by Using an Icon

1. On the line that begins with "Icon", first highlight the word "Bold". To do so, place the cursor before the letter "B" in "Bold". Press the F8 key; then press the right arrow key until the entire word is highlighted.

2. Click on the Bold icon **B** on the toolbar.

☞ *Note: To turn off bold, highlight the text and press the Bold icon.*

3. Click anywhere in the Text area to remove the highlighting.

Alternate Method: Bold by Using the Keys

1. On the line that begins with "Keys", first highlight the word "Bold". To do so, place the cursor before the letter "B" in "Bold". Press the F8 key; then, press the right arrow key until the entire word is highlighted.

2. Press Ctrl+b (hold down the Ctrl key while pressing b).

☞ *Note: To turn off Bold, press Ctrl+b again. You can also remove formatting by pressing Ctrl+spacebar.*

3. Click anywhere in the Text area to remove the highlighting.

Italicize - Using the Menu

1. On the line that begins with "Menu", first highlight the word "Italicize". To do so, place the cursor before the letter "I" in "Italicize". Press the F8 key; then press the right arrow key until the entire word is highlighted.

2. Click on Format.

3. Highlight Font. Press Enter.

4. Click on Italic in the Font Style box.

☞ *Note: You can see the effect of your selection in the Preview window. To turn off the italics, click on Regular.*

5. Click on OK to close the dialog box.

6. Click anywhere in the Text area to remove the highlighting.

Alternate Method: Italicize by Using an Icon

1. On the line that begins with "Icon", first highlight the word "Italicize". To do so, place the cursor before the letter "I" in "Italicize". Press the F8 key; then press the right arrow key until the entire word is highlighted.

2. Click on the Italic icon *I* on the toolbar.

☞ *Note: To turn off italics, highlight the text and press the Italic icon.*

3. Click anywhere in the Text area to remove the highlighting.

Alternate Method: Italicize Using Keys

1. On the line that begins with "Keys", highlight the word "Italicize". Place the cursor before the letter "I" in "Italicize". Press the F8 key; then, press the right arrow key until the entire word is highlighted.

2. Press Ctrl+i (hold down the Ctrl key while pressing i).

☞ *Note: To toggle Italic off, press Ctrl+i again. You can also remove formatting by pressing Ctrl+spacebar.*

3. Click anywhere in the Text area to remove the highlighting.

Underline - Using the Menu

You can underline when using Word. The following types of underlines are available if you use the menu **Format → Font → Underline Style**.

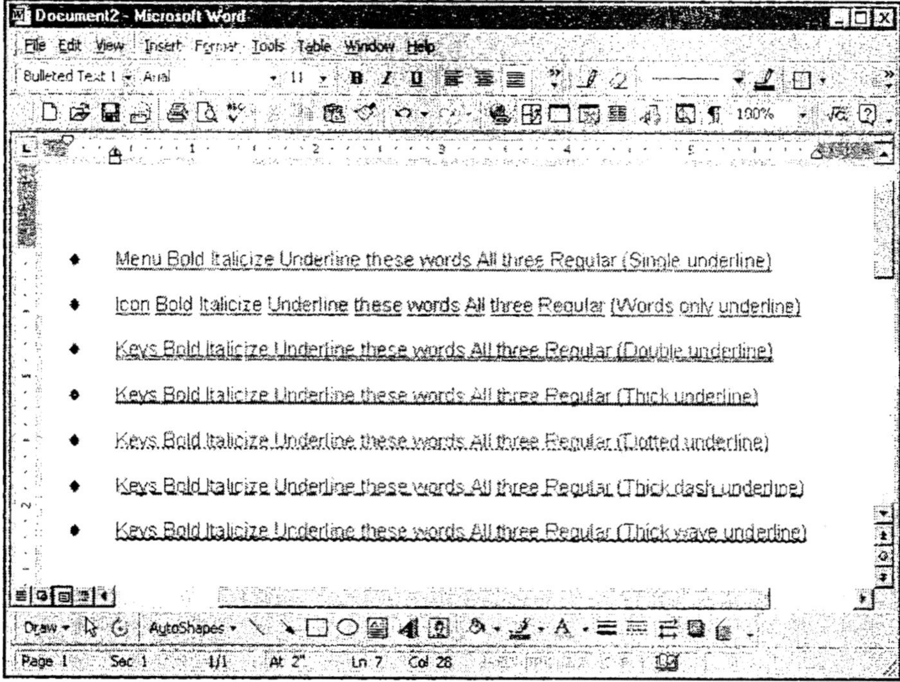

Figure 1.17: Various types of underlines

The following illustrates underlining using the menu:

1. On the line that begins with "Menu", first highlight the words "Underline these words". To do so, place the cursor before the letter "U" in "Underline". Press the F8 key; then press the right arrow key until all the words are highlighted.

2. Click on Format.

3. Highlight Font.

4. Press Enter.

5. In the Underline box, click to open the pull-down menu. Click on the type of underline you wish to use.

☞ *Note: To remove an underline, select None from the pull-down menu.*

6. Click on OK to close the dialog box.

7. Click anywhere in the Text area to remove the highlighting.

Alternate Method: Underline by Using the Icon

1. On the line that begins with "Icon", first highlight the words "Underline these words". To do so, place the cursor before the letter "U" in "Underline". Press the F8 key; then press the right arrow key until all the words are highlighted.

2. Click on the Underline icon U on the toolbar. You will get a single underline.

☞ *Note: To turn off underlining, press the Underline icon again.*

3. Click anywhere in the Text area to remove the highlighting.

Alternate Method: Underline by Using the Keys

1. On the line that begins with "Keys", first highlight the words "Underline these words". To do so, place the cursor before the letter "U" in "Underline". Press the F8 key; then, press the right arrow key until all the words are highlighted.

2. Press Ctrl+u (hold down the Ctrl key while pressing u). You will get a single underline.

☞ *Note: To turn off underlining, press Ctrl+u again.*

3. Click anywhere in the Text area to remove the highlighting.

All Three - Using the Menu

1. On the line that begins with word "Menu", first highlight the words "All three". To do so, place the cursor before the letter "A" in "All". Press the F8 key; then press the right arrow key until all the words are highlighted.

2. Click on Format.

3. Highlight Font. Press Enter.

4. In the Font Style box, click on Bold Italic.

☞ *Note: You can see the effect of your selection in the preview window. To turn off the Bold Italic, click on Regular. In the Underline box, click to open the pull-down menu. Click on the type of underline you want to use.*

To remove an underline, select None from the pull-down menu.

5. Click on OK to close the dialog box.

6. Click anywhere in the Text area to remove the highlighting.

Alternate Method: All Three by Using Icons

1. On the line that begins with "Icon", first highlight the words "All three". To do so, place the cursor before the letter "A" in "All". Press the F8 key; then press the right arrow key until all the words are highlighted.

2. Click on the Bold icon on the toolbar.

3. Click on the Italic icon on the toolbar.

4. Click on the Underline icon on the toolbar.

5. Click anywhere in the Text area to remove the highlighting.

Alternate Method: All Three by Using the Keys

1. On the line that begins with "Keys", first highlight the words "All three". To do so, place the cursor before the letter "A" in "All". Press the F8 key; then, press the right arrow key until all the words are highlighted.

2. Press Ctrl+b (bold).

3. Press Ctrl+i (italicize).

4. Press Ctrl+u (underline).

☞ *Note: You can remove formatting by highlighting the text and pressing Ctrl+spacebar.*

5. Click anywhere in the Text area to remove the highlighting.

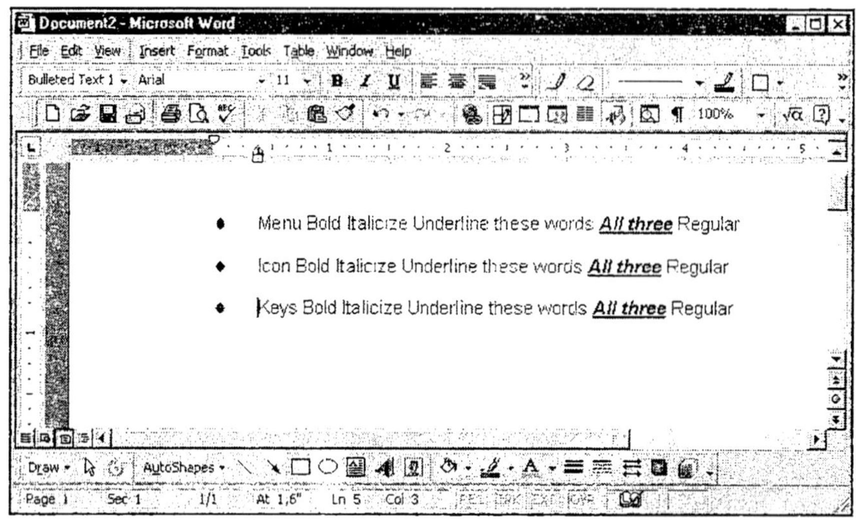

Figure 1.18: Using all three keys together

Cut and Paste

In Microsoft Word, you can cut (delete) text from one area of the document and save that text so it can be pasted elsewhere in the document. When you cut text, it is stored on the Clipboard. Information stored on the Clipboard stays there until new information is either cut or copied. Each time you execute Cut or Copy, you replace the old information on the Clipboard with whatever you just cut or copied. You can paste Clipboard information as often as you like.

Cut - Using the Menu

1. Type the following: I want to move. I am content where I am.
2. Highlight "I want to move".
3. Click on Edit.
4. Highlight Cut. Press Enter.
5. Your text should now read: "I am content where I am".

Paste - Using the Menu

1. Place the cursor after the period in the sentence "I am content where I am".
2. Press the Spacebar to leave a space.
3. Click on Edit.
4. Highlight Paste. Press Enter.
5. Your text should now read. "I am content where I am. I want to move".

Alternate Method: Cut by Using the Icon

1. Type the following: I want to move. I am content where I am.
2. Highlight "I want to move".
3. Click on the Cut icon
4. Your text should now read.
5. "I am content where I am".

Alternate Method: Paste by Using the Icon

1. Place the cursor after the period in the sentence "I am content where I am".
2. Press the Spacebar to leave a space.
3. Click on the Paste icon
4. Your text should now read.
5. "I am content where I am. I want to move".

Alternate Method: Cut by Using Keys

1. Type the following: I want to move. I am content where I am.
2. Highlight "I want to move".
3. Press Ctrl+x.

4. Your text should now read.

5. "I am content where I am".

Alternate Method: Paste by Using Keys

1. Place the cursor after the period in the sentence: "I am content where I am".

2. Press the Spacebar to leave a space.

3. Press Ctrl+v.

4. Your text should now read.

5. "I am content where I am. I want to move".

Copy and Paste

In Microsoft Word, you can copy text from one area of the document and place that text elsewhere in the document. As with cut data, copied data is stored on the Clipboard.

Copy - Using the Menu

1. Type the following: You will want to copy me. One of me is all you need.

2. Highlight "You will want to copy me".

3. Click on Edit.

4. Highlight Copy. Press Enter.

Paste - Using the Menu

1. Place the cursor after the period in the sentence: "One of me is all you need".

2. Press the Spacebar to leave a space.

3. Click on Edit.

4. Highlight Paste. Press Enter.

5. Your text should now read: "You will want to copy me. One of me is all you need. You will want to copy me".

Alternate Method: Copy by Using the Icon

1. Type the following: You will want to copy me. One of me is all you need.
2. Highlight "You will want to copy me".
3. Click on the Copy icon 

Alternate Method: Paste by Using the Icon

1. Place the cursor after the period in the sentence: "One of me is all you need".
2. Press the Spacebar to leave a space.
3. Click on the Paste icon 
4. Your text should now read:
5. "You will want to copy me. One of me is all you need. You will want to copy me".

Alternate Method: Copy by Using Keys

1. Type the following: You will want to copy me. One of me is all you need.
2. Highlight "You will want to copy me".
3. Press Ctrl+c.

Alternate Method: Paste by Using Keys

1. Place the cursor after the period in the sentence "One of me is all you need".
2. Press the Spacebar to leave a space.
3. Press Ctrl+v.
4. Your text should now read:
5. "You will want to copy me. One of me is all you need. You will want to copy me".

What is Paste Special?

Paste Special allows you to change the format of information copied from the Windows clipboard.

For example, if you need to include a bit of a spreadsheet from Excel, pasting it straight from the clipboard will add it as a Word table. Using Paste Special you can choose to paste it as a Microsoft Excel Worksheet Object instead, allowing you to edit the information using Excel menus and icons.

Undo and Redo

Word 2000 provides 500 levels of undo and redo. This means that not only can you undo the last thing you did, but the one before that and the one before that and so on up to 500 actions. Not only that, if you undo something that you did not mean to, you can redo up to 500 times as well!

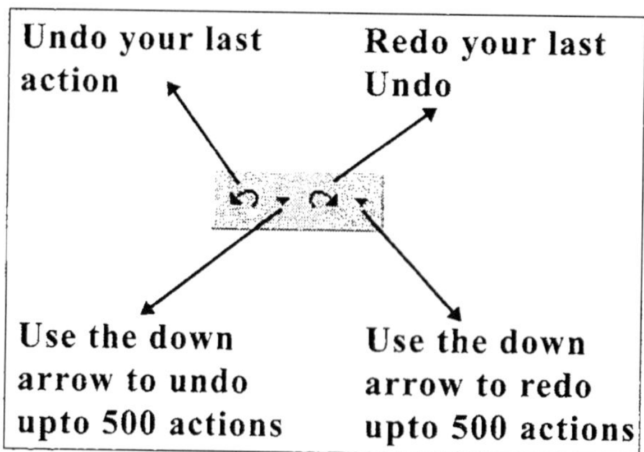

Figure 1.19: Undo and Redo Icon

Undoing the Last Thing you Did

1. Click the undo button

   Or

   Press CTRL + Z

Redoing the Last Thing you Undid!

1. Click the redo button

   Or

   Press CTRL + Y

Undoing up to 500 Actions

1. Click on the down arrow next to the undo button
2. Use the scroll-bar to scroll to the last action you wish to undo
3. Click on the action. The last x number of actions will be undone.

Repeating an Action

Imagine that you have to type the same piece of text several times. Rather than typing it out again and again, you can just use the repeat command!

1. Carry out the action you wish to repeat, e.g. typing
2. Click on Edit
3. Click on Repeat Typing

   Or

1. Carry out the action you wish to repeat

   Press CTRL & Y

Difference between Redo and Repeat

- Redo is used to cancel the effects of an undo. So if you make a mistake, and undo your action, you can redo it again!
- Repeat is for repeating your last action - it has nothing to do with the Undo command

Opening, Creating and Saving Documents

Opening an Existing Document

You can open documents from different locations from the Open dialog box. You can open a document from your computer hard disk or from your network. You can open a document located at an HTTP (Hypertext Transfer Protocol) site on the World Wide Web or at an FTP (File Transfer Protocol) site.

1. Click **Open** or **CTRL+O**.

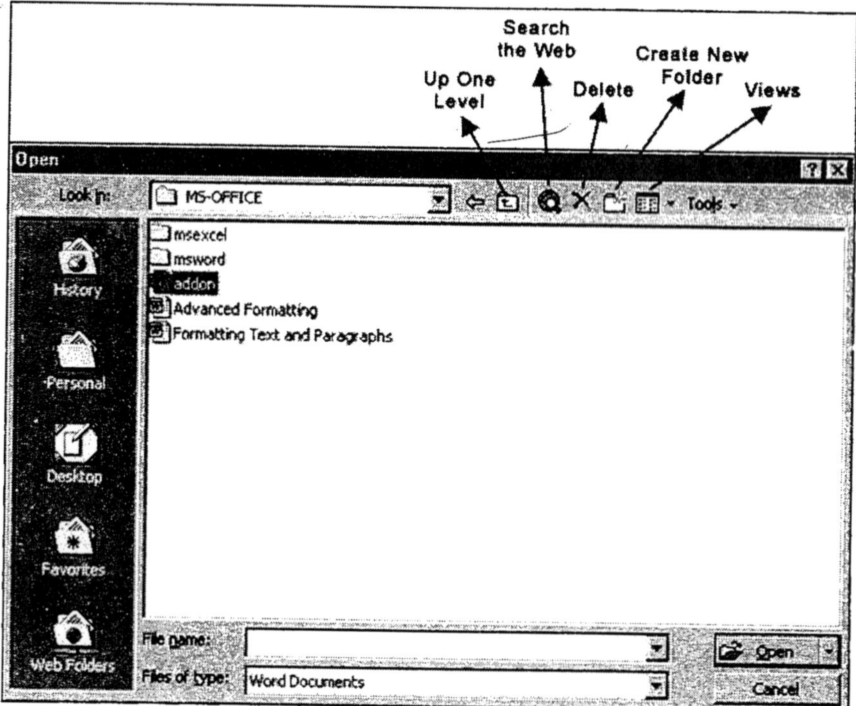

Figure 1.20: File Open dialog box

2. In the Look in box, click the drive or folder location that contains the document.
3. In the folder list, double-click folders until you open the folder that contains the document you want.
4. Double-click the document you want to open or click **Open**.

Open a Copy of the Document

1. Click **Open**.
2. In the **Look-In** box, click the drive, folder, or Internet location that contains the document.
3. In the folder list, double-click folders until you open the folder that contains the document you want. If you can't find the document in the folder list, you can search for it.

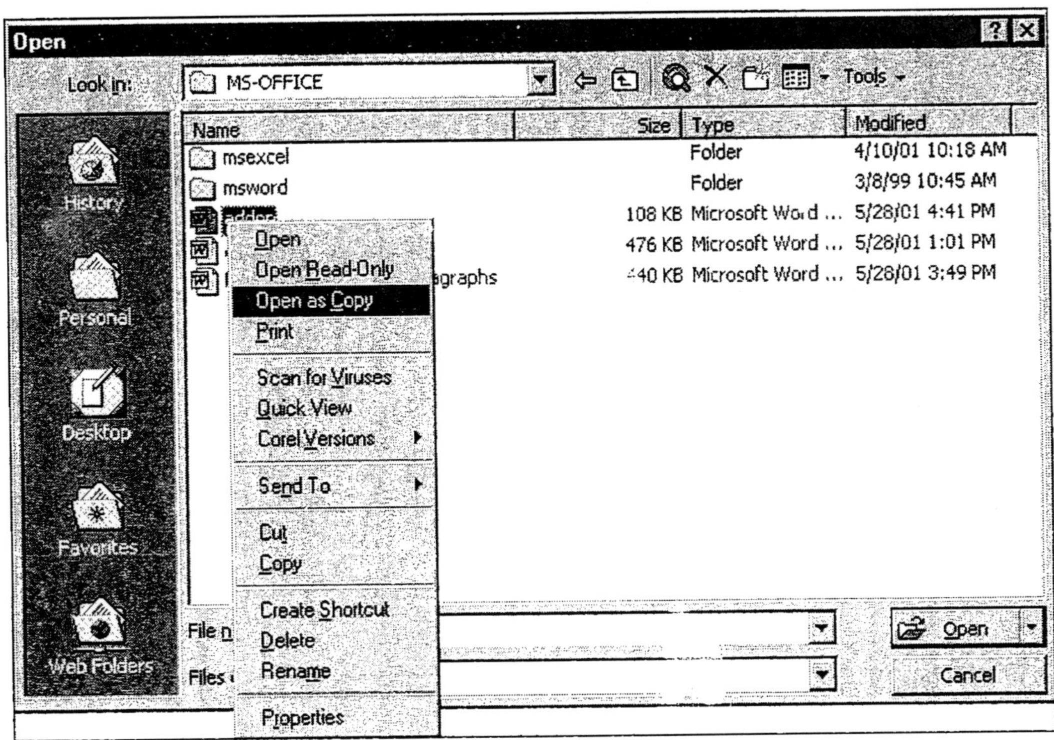

Figure 1.21: Open as a copy of a document

4. Click the document you want to open a **copy of.**
5. Select the file to Open and right click. A pop up menu is displayed, select the Option **Open as Copy**.

☞ *Notes: When you open a document as a copy, a new copy of the document is created in the folder that contains the original document.*

Open a Document as Read-Only

1. Click **Open**.
2. In the **Look-in** box, click the drive, folder, or Internet location that contains the document.
3. In the folder list, double-click folders until you open the folder that contains the document you want.
4. Click the document you want to open as **Read-only**.
5. Select the file to Open and right click. A pop up menu is displayed, select the Option **Open Read-Only**.

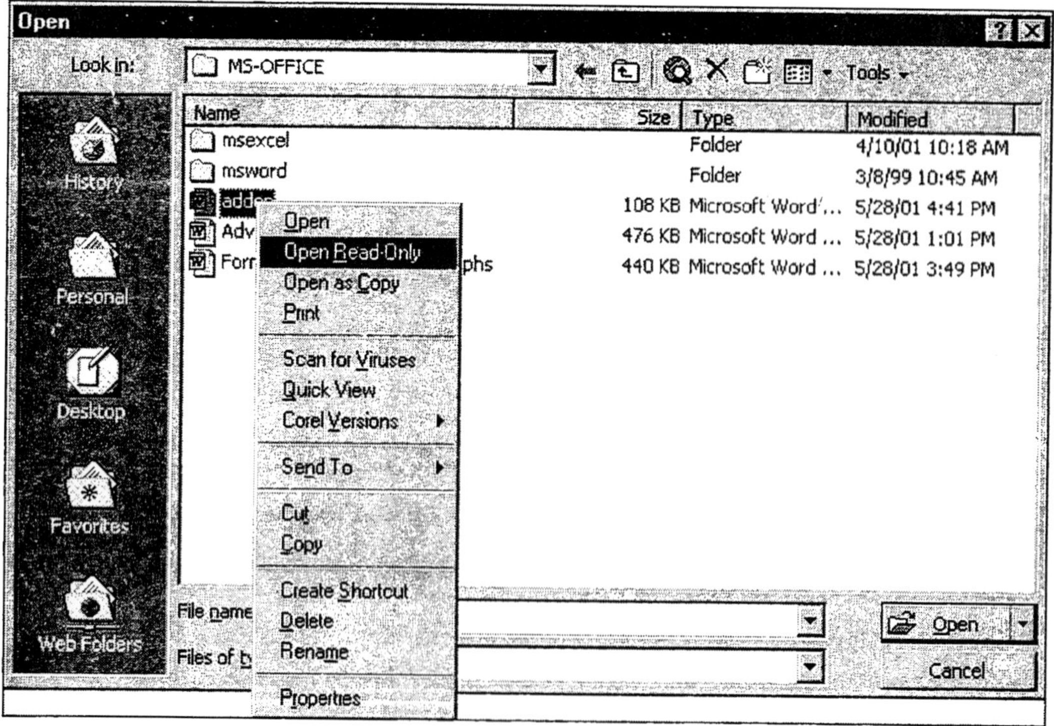

Figure 1.22: Opening File as Read-Only

Tips: To save changes to a read-only file, use the Save As command (File menu) to save it with a new name.

Open an Earlier version of a Document

1. On the **File** menu, click **Versions.**

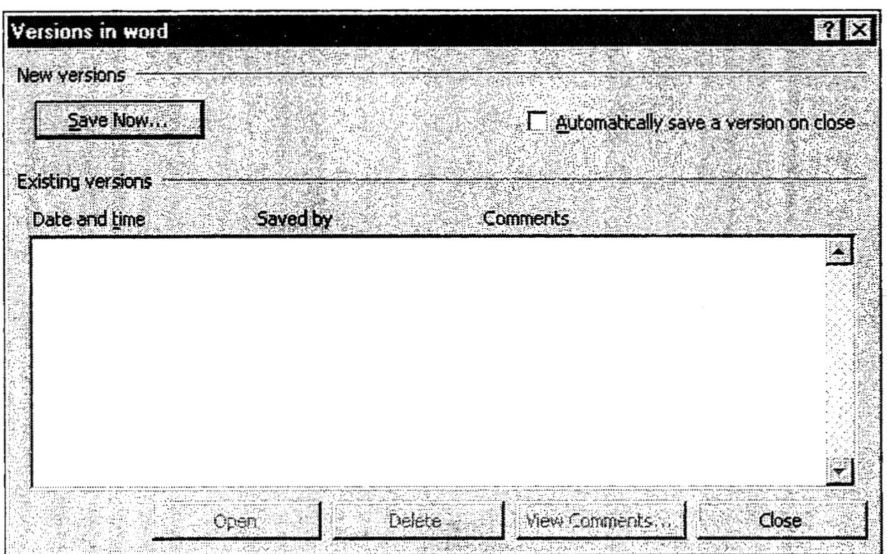

Figure 1.23: Versions of Word

2. Click the version of the document you want to open.

3. Click **Open.**

   This version contains all the previously saved versions.

Change default working folder for Microsoft Word

1. On the **Tools** menu, click **Options → File Locations**.

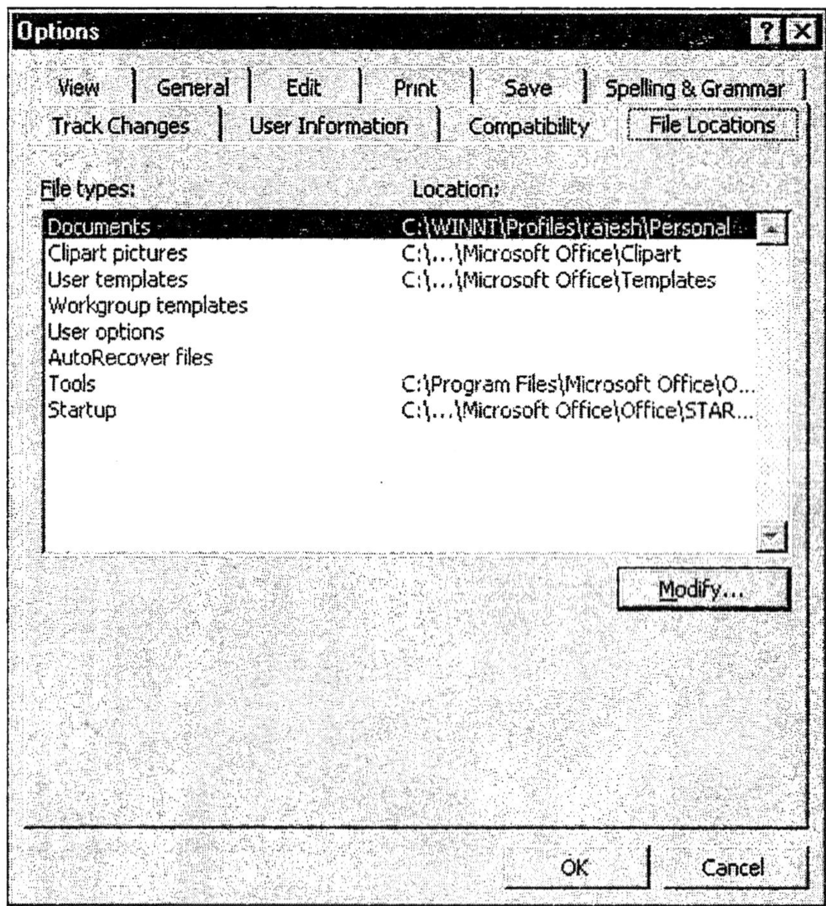

Figure 1.24: File Locations tab in the Options dialog box

2. In the File types list, click **Documents**.

3. Then click **Modify**.

4. To select an existing folder to display as the default working folder, locate and click the folder or directory you want in the folder list.

Show or hide recently used documents on the File menu

1. On the **Tools** menu, click **Options → General**.

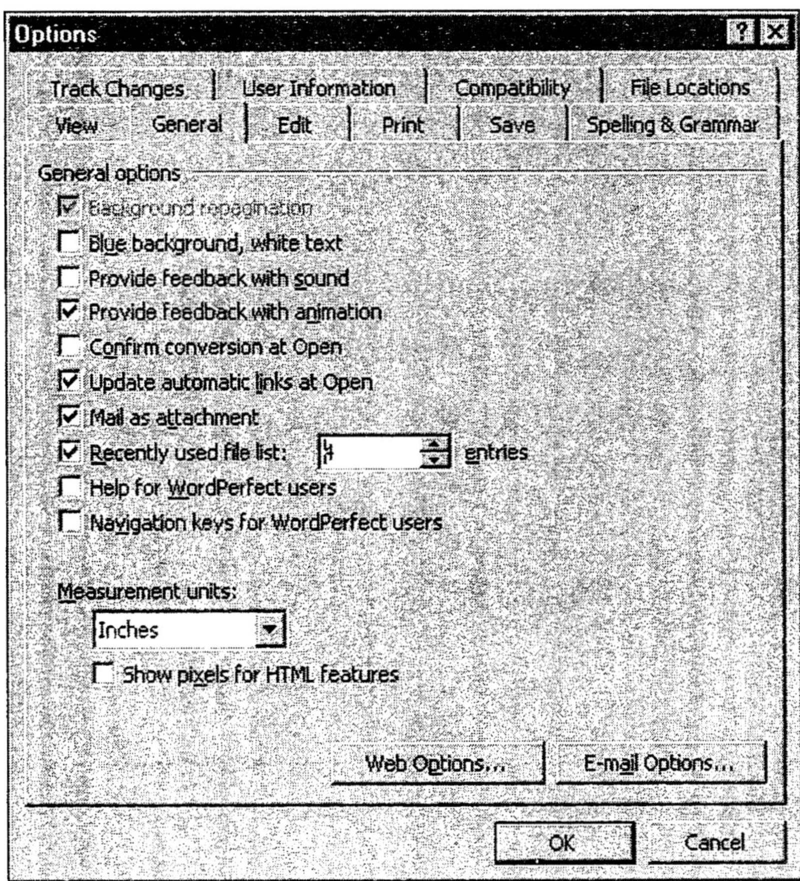

Figure 1.25: General tab in the Options dialog box

2. Select or clear the Recently used file list check box to show or hide the recently used files.

Select Multiple Files

- To select non-adjacent files in the Open dialog box, click the name of one file and hold down the CTRL key and select additional file.

- To select adjacent files in the Open dialog box, click the name of the first file and hold down the SHIFT key and click the name of the last file.

Tips: If you want to deselect a file, hold down CTRL and click the file name again.

When you save a Microsoft Word 2000 document in previous versions such as Word 6.0/95/97 format, the document is actually saved in Rich Text Format (RTF) format. You will notice this difference if Confirm Conversion at Open check box is selected. If you have selected this option you will see RTF in the **Convert File** dialog box when you open the document. Click OK to continue.

Create a New Document

1. On the **File** menu, click **New**.

2. To create a **new** blank document, click the **General** tab and then double-click the **Blank Document icon**.

3. To create a document based on a **template** or **wizard**, click the tab for the type of document you want to create, and then double-click the name of the **template** or **wizard** you want.

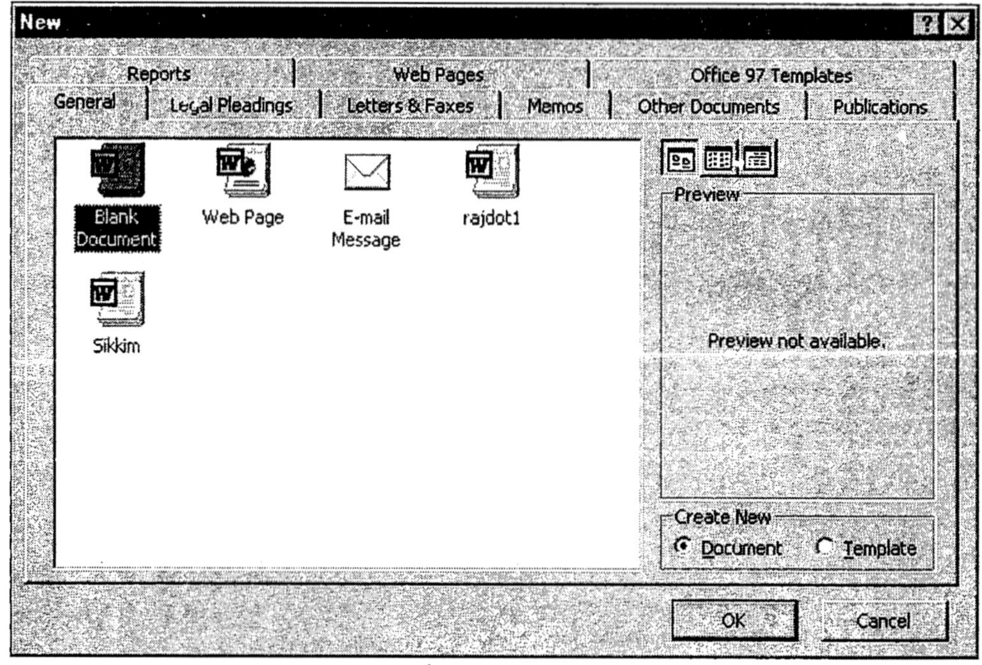

Figure 1.26: New File dialog box

Create a Letter

The Letter Wizard in Microsoft Word can help you write a letter quickly and easily. The wizard provides generally used letters such as salutations and closings that you select from lists. The wizard also helps you to structure letters from the letter styles. You can start the Letter Wizard by clicking New on the **File** menu → **Letters & Faxes** and then double-click **Letter Wizard** on the **Tools** menu.

1. Type a salutation that starts with the word "Dear" or "To", followed by a name and a colon or comma such as Dear Rupesh, or To All Board Members and then press ENTER to go to the next line.

2. In the Office Assistant, click Get help with writing the letter.

3. Follow the instructions in the Letter Wizard. If you want to skip a step or go to a specific panel, click one of the tabs.

Create a Memo

The Memo Wizard helps you quickly create memos by helping you create distribution lists, formatting your memos, and inserting headings and other used items such as the date, the subject. The wizard also helps you send the memo by e-mail or fax if your computer supports these services.

1. On the **File** menu, click **New**.

2. Click the **Memos** tab.

3. Double-click **Memo Wizard**.

4. Follow the instructions in the wizard.

Insert another Document text into an Open Document

1. Click where you want to insert the second document.

2. On the **Insert** menu, click **File**.

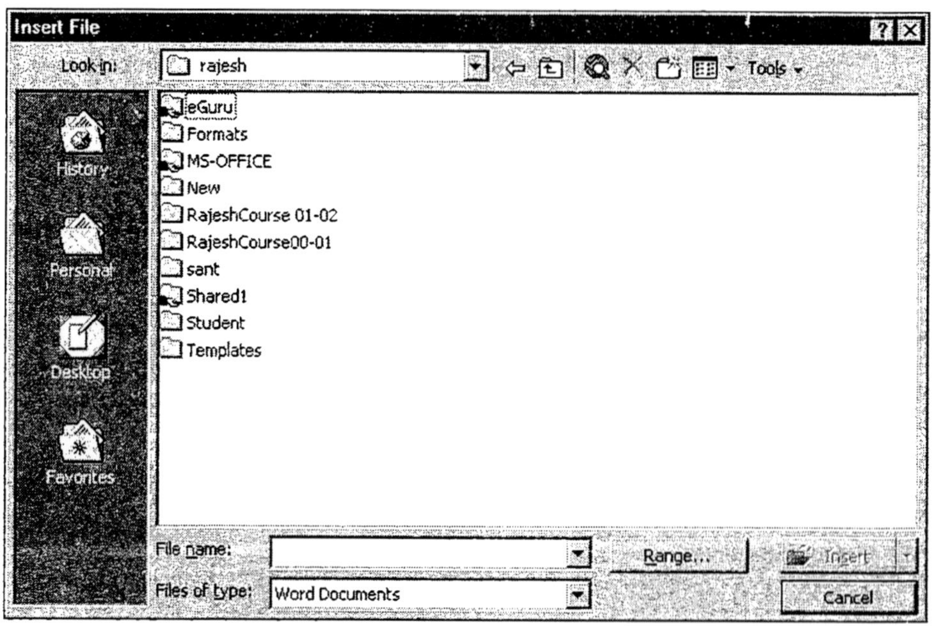

Figure 1.27: Insert File dialog box

3. In the File name box, enter the name of the file you want to insert.

Saving Documents

You can save the active document you are working on, whether it is new or existing. You can save all open documents at the same time. And you can save a copy of the active document with a different name or in a different location.

You can save a document in another file format for use in another program. For example, you can save a Word document in a file format that can be read by earlier versions of Word, Microsoft Word, or WordPerfect. You can also open a document created in a different file format in a different program, work on it in Word, and then save it in its original format. For example, you can open a WordPerfect document, make changes to it in Word, and then save it in either Word format or WordPerfect format. You can save a document with a different file extension without changing the file format. For example, you can save a Word document with the file extension *.abc*.

☞ *Note: AutoRecover is not a replacement for saving your documents, recovery file is deleted when the document is saved or closed.*

Word is default set to save documents automatically for recovery in case the program stops responding or power failure or similar problem. When the AutoRecover feature is turned on, the changes you make to a document are saved in a recovery file based on the AutoRecover save interval. For example, if you set AutoRecover to save every 5 minutes, you will recover more information than if you set it to save every 10 minutes. With AutoRecover turned on in the Options Menu, if Word stops responding while your documents are open and you have to reboot, Word automatically opens the recovery file when you Start Word again.

You can set Word to automatically save a backup copy each time you save a document. You can save multiple versions of a document within the same document. After you've saved several versions of the document, you can go back and review, open, print, and delete earlier versions.

Save Multiple Versions of a Document in a file

In earlier releases of Word, when you want to save the current version of a document, you used the Save As command to create a copy of the file and then renamed it *Filename1*. The next time you wanted a record of the changes to date, you created another copy of the document and renamed it *Filename2*. With the new versioning feature in Word, you can record "snapshots" of the changes made to a document by saving multiple versions in the same document. You save disk space because Word saves only the differences between versions, not an entire copy of each version. After you've saved versions of a document, you can go back and review, open, print, and delete earlier versions.

Options for Saving a Version

- You can save a version anytime you want. For example, you save the version you've sent to review, and after you've incorporated review changes, you save another version.
- You can set up the document so that Word saves a version automatically each time the document is closed.

After you have saved multiple versions of a document in one file, you may want to save a specific version as a separate file in two instances: If the document you are sending to review contains several versions, make sure that you're sending only the most recent version or the specific version you want.

Otherwise, reviewers will be able to open earlier versions of the document. If you want to compare an earlier version of the document with the current version of the document, you must first save the earlier version of the document as a separate file. You can only use the **Compare Documents** subcommand (Tools menu, Track Changes command) to compare separate files.

Save a New Document

1. Click **Save**.

2. To save the document in a different folder, click a different drive in the Save in box, or double-click a different folder in the folder list.

   To save the document in a new folder, click **Create New Folder**.

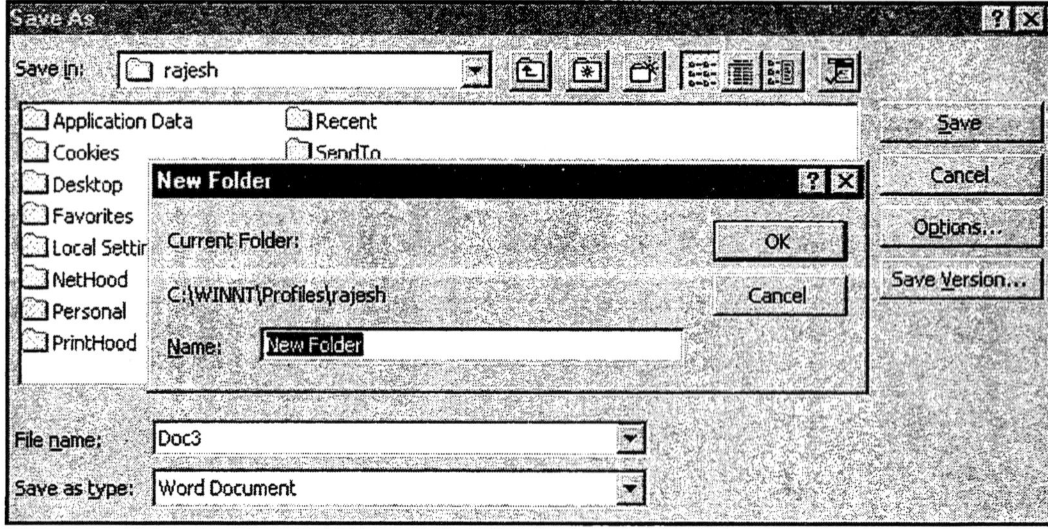

Figure 1.28: Save As and New Folder dialog box

3. In the File name box, type a name for the document.

   You can use long, descriptive file names if you want.

4. Click **Save**.

Close a Document

To remove a document from the document window, choose **File → Close**. If you close a document that has been changed since it was last saved, you will be prompted to save your changes. To close all open documents without exiting the program, hold down **SHIFT** and click **Close All** on the **File** menu.

Print

You can print the active document by clicking **Print**. To display each page as it will look when printed, click **Print Preview**. You can print specific pages, one or more sections, or a range of pages in more than one section. In the Number of copies box, enter the number of copies you want to print.

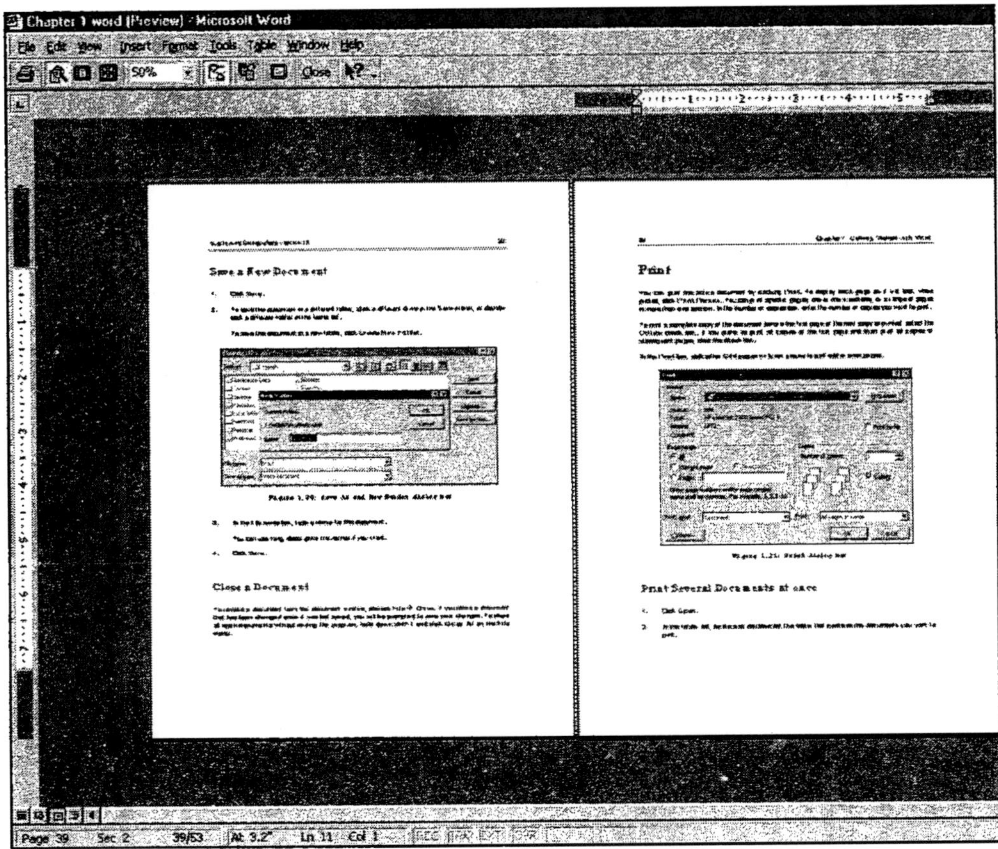

Figure 1.29: Print Preveiw

To print a complete copy of the document before the first page of the next copy is printed, select the **Collate** check box. If you prefer to print all copies of the first page and then print all copies of subsequent pages, clear the check box.

In the **Print** box, click either **Odd pages or Even pages** to print odd or even pages.

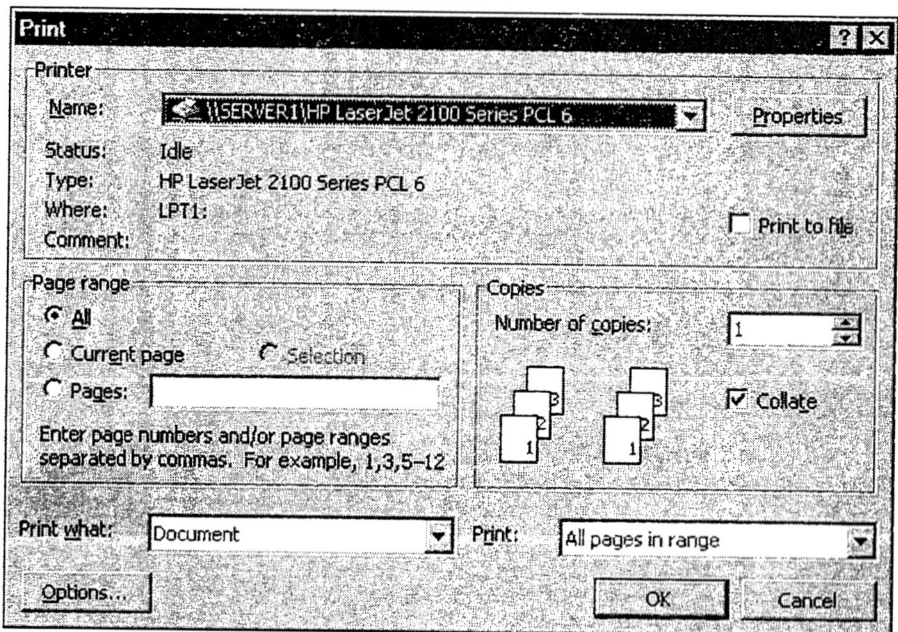

Figure 1.30: Print dialog box

Print Several Documents at once

1. Click **Open**.
2. In the folder list, locate and double-click the folder that contains the documents you want to print.
3. Select the documents you want to print.
4. Select the file or files to Print and right click. A pop up menu is displayed, select the Option **Print**.

Set a Default File Format for Saving Documents

When you save a document, Word automatically saves it in Word 2000 format. If you want to save documents in different format that can be read by earlier versions of Word you can select that file format when you save the document.

1. On the **Tools** menu, click **Options**, and then click the **Save** tab.
2. In the **Save Word files as** box, click the file format you want.

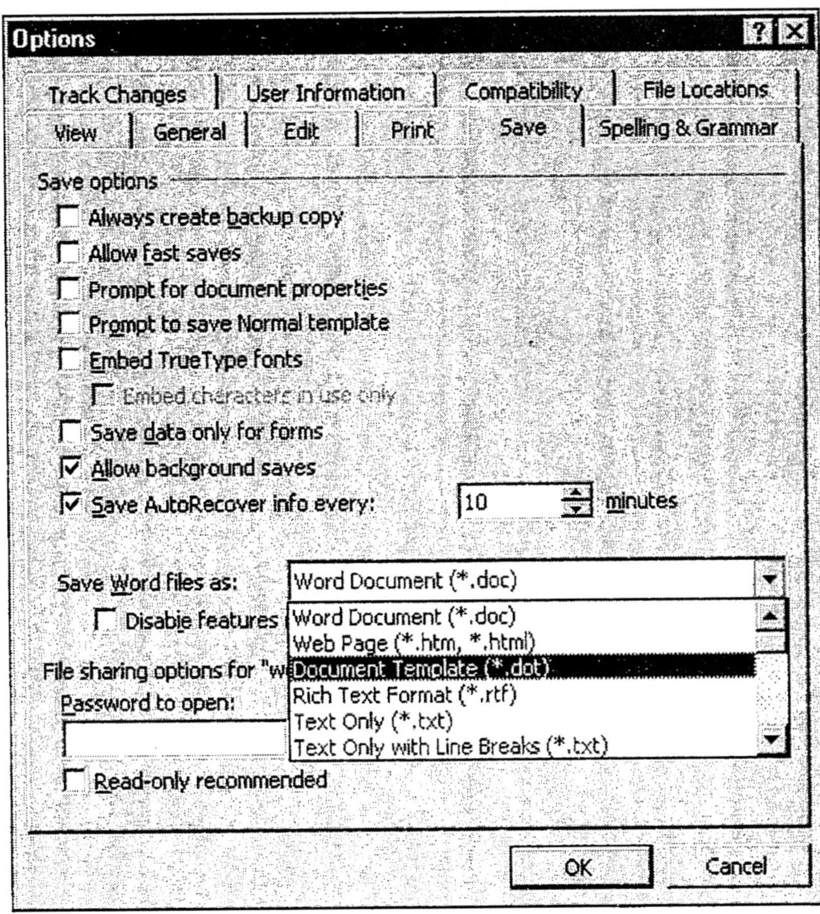

Figure 1.31: Save tab in the Options dialog box

3. The next time you save a document, a message asks if you want to save the document in the file format you selected or in another format.

Fast Save and Full Save

If you select the **Allow fast saves** check box on the **Save** tab in the **Tools → Options** dialog box, Word saves only the changes to a document. This takes less time than a full save, in which Word saves the complete, revised document. Select the Allow fast saves check box when you are working on a very large document. However, a full save requires less disk space than a fast save. If you are working on a document over a network, clear the Allow fast saves check box. Fast saves cannot be performed over a network.

You should do a full save in the following situations:

- Before you share a document with other people
- When you finish working on a document and save it for the last time
- Before you begin a task that uses a lot of memory, such as searching for text or compiling an index
- Before you transfer the document text to another program
- Before you convert the document to a different file format

Prevent loss of work and recover lost documents

You can protect your work by using AutoRecover to save a temporary copy of a document as you work, or by saving a backup copy of the document each time you save it. To recover work after a power failure or similar problem, you must have the Save AutoRecover info every check box or the Always create backup copy check box or both selected on the **Save tab** in **Tools → Options** dialog box.

Preview file contents and properties

1. Click **Open**.
2. In the **Look-in** box, click the drive that contains the file you want to view.
3. In the folder list, double-click folders until you open the folder that contains the file you want. If you can't find the file in the folder list, you can search for it.

Search for files

1. Click **Open**.

2. In the **Look-in** box, click the drive you want to search.

3. In the folder list, double-click the name of the folder you want to search.

   In the File name box in the **Open** dialog box, you can do any of the following to locate your file:

Type	Example
Partial file names	Type 'zone' to find all files with names that include "zone".
File name extensions	Type *.txt to find all files whose extension is .txt.
Wildcard characters	Use an asterisk (*) to match any number of characters, or use a question mark (?) to match single character. To find the files that end with "zone", type *zone. To find instances of both "hood" and "hold" in file names, type ho?d.
The full path	Type C:\Property Dealer\My Works in 2000. When you include a drive letter or folder, the program updates automatically the location in the Look-in box and displays the name of the file in the File name box and opens the file.
Multiple paths	Type C:\Property Dealer;C:\My Works documents. Separate each path with a semicolon. Find files that match these criteria, enter any additional search criteria you want. To search all subfolders of the selected folders and display the folders that contain the files that are found, click Commands and Settings → Search Subfolders. To search for files by specific or nontext file properties, click Advanced. Click Find Now. To cancel the search, click Stop.

Table 1.4: Find Files Options

4. Click the file you want.

5. To preview the contents of the file before opening it, click Preview. To view file properties such as file size and the date created or last modified, click **Details**. To view file properties such as **subject and statistics**, click **Properties**.

Use file Properties to Locate Files

File properties are the details of a file that helps identify it, such as title, author, subject, manager, company, category, comments and keywords. You can set file properties for the file you're working on. You can also create custom file properties with the option to link them to specific items in your active file. To set file properties for files, turn on the option to automatically display the Properties dialog box when you save files the first time.

The following are the types of file properties:

- **Preset file properties:** These are properties such as author, title and subject that already exist for you to enter a value for. For example, in Word, you can add the keyword "technical" to all your technical files and then search for all technical files with that keyword.
- **Custom file properties:** You can create custom file properties that include any value you assign, such as a named cell in Microsoft Excel, a selected item in PowerPoint, or a bookmark in Word.
- **Automatically updated file properties:** Statistics such as file size and the dates files are created and last modified are file properties that are automatically maintained for you. These file properties help you search for all files created after, say, March 31st, 2001 or last modified.

Change the Author Name for Documents

The author name is used for such features as file properties, sharing documents, and tracked changes.

1. On the **Tools** menu, click **Options → User Information.**

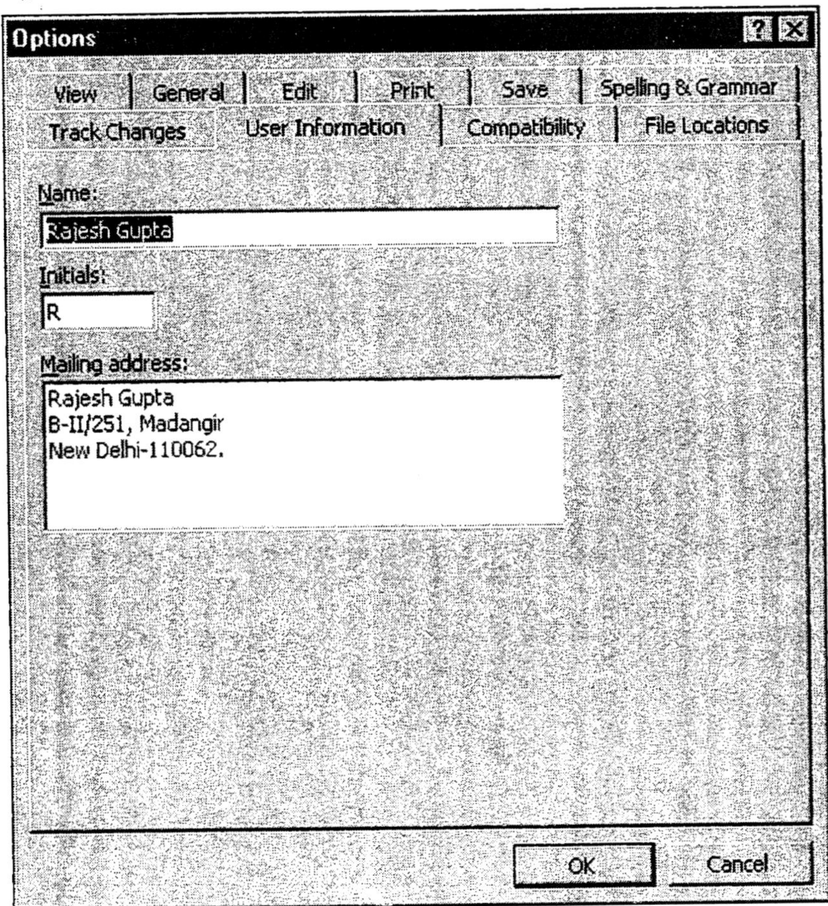

Figure 1.32: User Information tab in the Options dialog box

2. In the **Name** box, type a name.

   The name you type will appear in the **Author** box on the **Summary** tab each time you create a new file.

 Hands on Exercise

Exercise 1:

1. Type the following as shown below and include all errors.

   Open thr door for Mayrala. She is a teacher from the town of Ridgemont.

2. Highlight: "Open thr door for Mayrala. She is a teacher from the town of Ridgemont".

3. Press F7 or click on the Spelling icon on the Standard toolbar.

4. "The" is misspelled so it is highlighted on the screen and noted in the Not in Dictionary box.

5. Word suggests correct spellings. These suggestions are found in the Suggestions box.

6. To change the word to the correct spelling, make sure "the" is highlighted in the Suggestions box. Click on Change.

Note: If the word is misspelled in several places in the document, click on Change All to correct all misspellings.

7. The name "Mayrala" is not in the dictionary, but it is correct. Press Ignore to leave "Mayrala" in the document with its current spelling.

Note: If a word appears in several places in the document, click on Ignore All so you are not prompted to correct the spelling for each occurrence.

8. "Ridgemont" is not found in the dictionary. If you frequently use a word not found in the dictionary, you should add that word to the dictionary by pressing the Add button. Word will then recognize the word the next time it encounters it. Click on Add.

9. The following should appear on your screen: "Word finished checking the selection. Do you want to continue checking the remainder of the document?"

10. Click on No. If you wanted Word to spell-check the entire document, you would have clicked on Yes.

Exercise 2:

Find - Using the Menu

1. Type the following: `Monica is from Easton. She lives on the east side of town. Her daughter attends Eastern High School.`
2. Highlight: "`Monica is from Easton. She lives on the east side of town. Her daughter attends Eastern High School`".
3. Click on Edit.
4. Highlight Find. Press Enter.
5. Type `east` in the Find What field.
6. Click on Find Next. Note that the "`East`" in `Easton` is highlighted.
7. Click on Find Next. Note that "`east`" is highlighted.
8. Click on Find Next. Note that the "`East`" in `Eastern` is highlighted.
9. Click on Find Next. The following message should appear: "Word has finished searching the selection. Do you want to search the remainder of the document?"
10. Click on No.
11. Click on Cancel.

Alternate Method: Find by Using Keys

1. Highlight: "`Monica is from Easton. She lives on the east side of town. Her daughter attends Eastern High School`".
2. Press Ctrl+f.
3. Follow steps 5 through 11 in the preceding section.

Replace: Using the Menu

1. Highlight "`Monica is from Easton. She lives on the east side of town. Her daughter attends Eastern High School`".
2. Click on Edit.
3. Highlight Replace. Press Enter.

4. Type `"east"` in the Find What box.

5. Click on Find Next. Do not replace the `"East"` in `"Easton"`.

6. Click on Find Next.

7. In the Replace With box, type `west`.

8. Click on Replace.

9. The `"East"` in Eastern is highlighted.

10. Click on Replace.

11. The following message will appear: "Word has finished searching the selection. Do you want to search the remainder of the document?"

12. Click on No.

13. Click on Close.

14. Your text should now read: `"Monica is from Easton. She lives on the west side of town. Her daughter attends Western High School"`.

Alternate Method: Replace by Using Keys

1. Highlight `"Monica is from Easton. She lives on the west side of town. Her daughter attends Western High School"`.

2. Press Ctrl+h.

3. Follow steps 4 through 13 in the preceding section, but type `East` in the Replace With box.

Test Your Knowledge

Students must solve the following assignment.

Multiple Choice Questions:

1. The Print Preview toolbar icon

   a. reduces the display size to show how the document will appear when printed.
   b. prints the document without page breaks
   c. saves the document in a Print format
   d. displays statistics about the document - number of pages, number of words, etc.

2. What is displayed in the Ruler bar?

   a. tab locations
   b. paragraph indent marker
   c. type of tab which will be used for the next tab set.
   d. all of the above

3. The increase toolbar icon

   a. moves an entire paragraph over one space.
   b. moves an entire paragraph over one tab stop.
   c. moves the right margin 1 position to the right
   d. moves the left margin 1 position to the left and the right margin 1 position to the right.

4. To save a document under a new name, choose the File option

   a. Save
   b. Insert
   c. Save As
   d. Either a or b

5. To MOVE text from one area to another in a document, use

   a. Delete and Paste commands.
   b. Copy and Paste commands.
   c. Cut and Paste commands.
   d. Cut and Copy commands.

6. The end of a paragraph is defined by a hidden code called a(n)

   a. paragraph mark.
   b. insertion point.
   c. a paragraph return.
   d. end of line mark.

7. By dragging symbols in the Ruler bar, you can

   a. set page margins
   b. set paragraph margins
   c. set individual line margins
   d. all of the above.

8. What is the function of the Show/Hide button?

   a. shows or hides the footnotes and page numbers
   b. displays hidden code in the document (like tabs)
   c. displays or conceals the Ruler bar.
   d. toggles between Normal and Page Layout views.

9. What is the name of the toolbar that contains buttons for frequently used text appearance commands?

   a. the Formatting Tool Bar
   b. the Menu bar.
   c. the View bar.
   d. the Appearance bar.

10. Tab settings in a document can be seen in the

   a. Menu bar
   b. Tool bar
   c. Scroll bar
   d. Ruler bar

11. What is the selection bar used for?

   a. to select text.
   b. to set tabs.
   c. to select the active document when 2 or more windows have been opened.
   d. to set alignment.

12. Print orientation can be

   a. portrait.
   b. parallel.
   c. landscape.
   d. only a. or c.
   e. all of the above

13. The end of the document is defined by

    a. a single line consisting of asterisks.
    b. an end-of-file marker.
    c. a vertical bar.
    d. a single line consisting of dashes.

14. To display the document on the screen at a reduced size, as it will appear when printed, use

    a. Page Layout view
    b. Normal view
    c. outline view
    d. Open view

15. Undo

    a. restores to disk the last file deleted.
    b. restores the last editing change to the document.
    c. clears the contents of the clipboard.
    d. clears the document window.

16. The Ruler Bar can be used to

    a. make changes to paragraph indents.
    b. set tabs in a paragraph.
    c. both a and b.
    d. none of the above.

17. Which type of justification aligns text on both the right and left margins of a document?

    a. Justify
    b. Center
    c. Right
    d. Balanced

18. A print out of a document that has had a date inserted using the Date/Time feature

    a. always gives the date the document was created.
    b. always gives the date of the day it was printed.
    c. displays the created date or the date printed depending upon the Update Automatically option specified when the date/time was inserted.
    d. does not print the date; it is a hidden code in the document.

19. If two files have been opened, how do you select the one you wish to be active?

    a. Select the Windows menu, and select (click on) the one desired.
    b. In the Status bar, click on the file desired.
    c. Select the View menu, and select the file desired.
    d. click in the Title bar; it will toggle to the one currently not active.

20. The shortcut key used for copying selected text into clipboard is

    a. Ctrl+X
    b. Ctrl+V
    c. Ctrl+C
    d. Ctrl+D

21. The shortcut key used for pasting text from clipboard is

    a. Ctrl+X
    b. Ctrl+V
    c. Ctrl+C
    d. Ctrl+D

22. To open a new file in MS-Word, the shortcut key is

    a. Ctrl+X
    b. Ctrl+N
    c. Ctrl+C
    d. Ctrl+V

23. Which of the following will you option for saving a file

    a. Save button on standard toolbar
    b. Save option from File menu
    c. Pressing Ctrl + S
    d. Any of the above.

24. If no text has been selected and you perform a Double space command, what happens?

    a. the entire document is double spaced.
    b. nothing is double spaced since nothing was selected.
    c. only the first paragraph is double spaced.
    d. only the paragraph in which the insertion point is located is double spaced.

State whether True or False:

1. Word processor developed by Microsoft is Word Perfect.

    a. True
    b. False

2. When a document is saved, we cannot modify it.

    a. True
    b. False

3. MS-Word offers advance facilities for Desk Top Publishing.

   a. True
   b. False

4. MS-Word is a software package.

   a. True
   b. False

5. MS-Word is used for handling accounts.

   a. True
   b. False

6. The printed copy of a document is called a hard copy?

   a. True
   b. False

7. A header is the text usually printed at the top of every page in a document?

   a. True
   b. False

8. The magnifier button helps you to reduce or enlarge views of pages displayed.

   a. True
   b. False

9. A document gets printed at the same time as we type.

   a. True
   b. False

10. Multiple files may be printed simultaneously from word.

    a. True
    b. False

11. The print icon appears on standard toolbar?

    a. True
    b. False

12. Ctrl+S shortcut is used to select text in MS-Word.

    a. True
    b. False

Fill in the Blanks:

1. The opposite of typeover mode is ____________.
2. The three-character extension used to identify word 2000's document is ______________.
3. The shortcut for copy is ________________.
4. When the user presses the ENTER key a ______________ is created.
5. What shortcut __________ can I use to move to the end of a long document?
6. When __________ a word is displayed in red, WORD 2000 is saying there is a error.
7. I have finished writing an essay and realize that it should be double-spaced. What should I do first? ________________________________
8. Cut operation places the selected text into an area in the memory called __________.
9. Cut operation can also be accomplished by using the shortcut key __________.
10. Shortcut key combination to specify the character style to bold is __________.
11. Text formatting attributes are available on the __________ toolbar.
12. Shortcut key combination to specify the character style to italics is __________.
13. Alignment buttons are available on the __________ toolbar.

Formatting Text and Paragraphs

Objectives

- Introduction
- Character Formatting
- Create a Drop Cap
- Paragraph Formatting
- Indent Paragraphs
- Borders and Shading
- Adding Shading to a table, a paragraph or selected text
- Bulleted/Numbered Lists

Introduction

Changing the look of text is known as **formatting**. Formatting makes your documents look more professional and allows you to give emphasis to the important parts. This chapter explores the various formatting features provided in Word 2000.

- **Formatting Characters**
- **Formatting Paragraphs**
- **Adding Borders and Shading to Text and Paragraphs**
- **Creating and Formatting Numbered and Bulleted Lists**

Character Formatting

To apply character formatting to a single word, select the word. To apply character formatting to several words or a few characters within a word, select the text.

Changing Font of Selected Text

The following steps describe how to change the font type, size and style of a selected area of text in a MS Word document:

1. Highlight a particular area of text. e.g. the document title.
    - Click to the left or right of the title.
    - Hold the mouse button down and move the mouse cursor across the title.
2. Release the mouse button once the title is highlighted.
3. To choose a different font type, size and style follow either set of steps below:
    - Click and hold the mouse button over the **Format** menu.
    - Select the **Font...** option.
    - On the left hand side of the Font window use the scroll bar to find the font type that you want. In this case click on **Helvetica**.
    - Under **Font Style:** Choose **Bold Italic**.
    - Below **Size:** Scroll down and select **24**.
    - In the pop-down menu on the left side under **Underline:** Choose **Single**.

- We can also choose the Color of the text. Default color is *Auto (Black).*
- Under **Effects:** Choose Strikethrough or Double strikethrough; Superscript or Subscript; Shadow, Outlined; or Embossed, Engraved; Small caps or All caps; Hidden.
- Click the **OK** button on the upper right of the window.

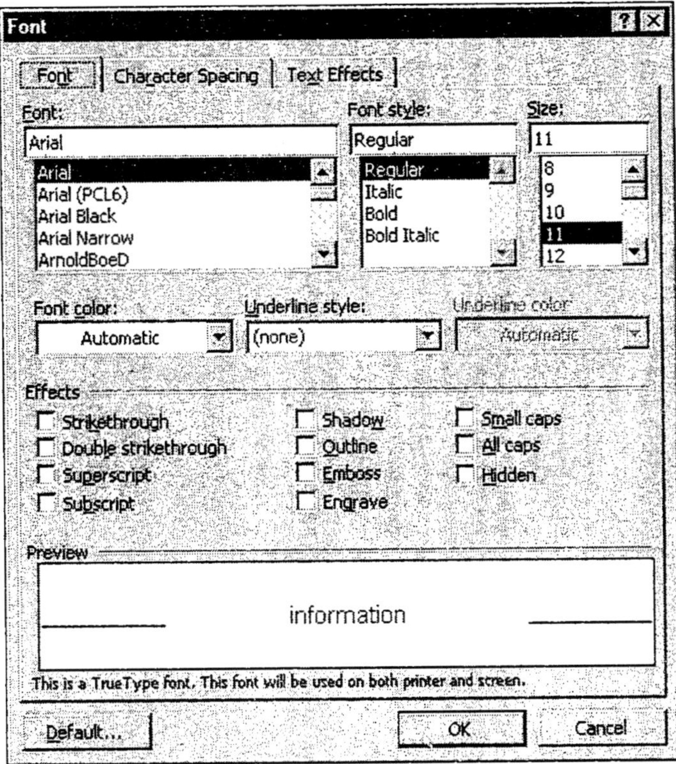

Figure 2.1: Font Style dialog box

Add a Special Text Effect

1. On the **Drawing** toolbar, click **WordArt.**
2. Click the **Special Effect** you want, and then click **OK**.
3. In the **Edit WordArt Text** dialog box, type the text you want to format select any other options you want, and then click **OK**.
4. To add or change effects to the text, use the buttons on the **WordArt** and **Drawing** toolbars.

Change the spacing between characters

1. Select the text you want to change.

2. On the **Format** menu, click **Font** → **Character Spacing** tab.

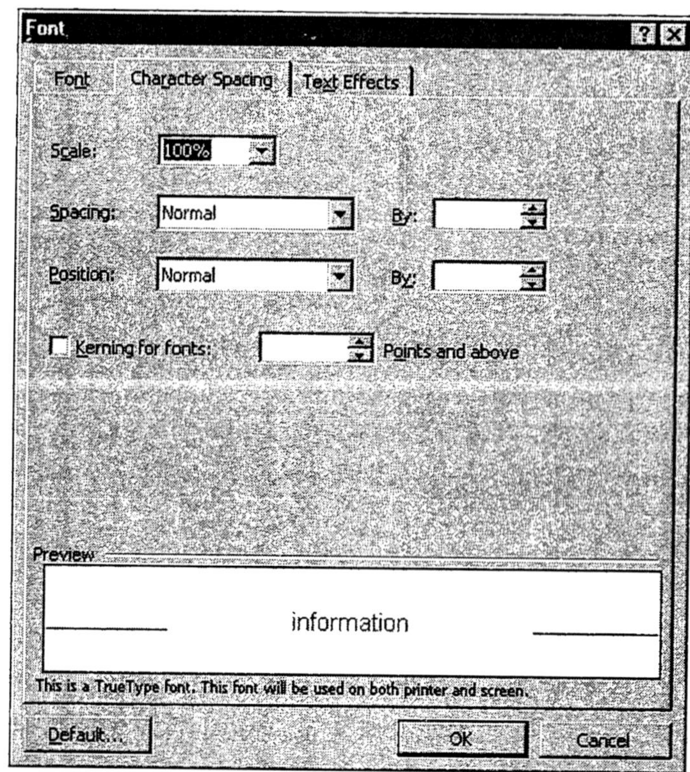

Figure 2.2: Character Spacing dialog box

3. To **expand or condense** space between characters, click **Expanded or Condensed** in the **Spacing** box, and then specify how much space you want in the **By** box. Selecting **Expanded or Condensed** alters the spacing between all letters by the same amount.

Scale text horizontally

1. Select the text you want to change.
2. On the **Format** menu, click **Font** → **Character Spacing** tab.
3. In the **Scale** box, enter the **percentage** you want and click **OK.**

Create a Drop Cap

1. Click the paragraph that you want to begin with an initial or dropped, capital letter.
2. On the Format menu, click **Drop Cap.**
3. Click **Dropped** or **In Margin.**
4. Select any other options you want.

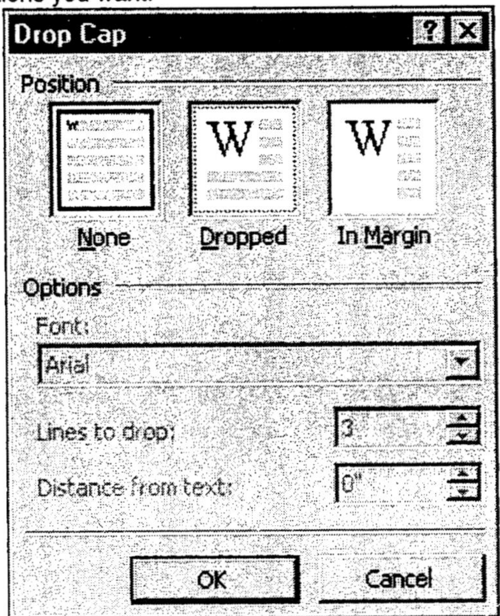

Figure 2.3: Drop Cap dialog box

Animated Text

You can create animated text effects that move or flash for documents that will be read online. The animated effects do not print.

1. Select the **text or word** you want to **animate**.

2. On the **Format** menu, click **Font → Animation** tab.

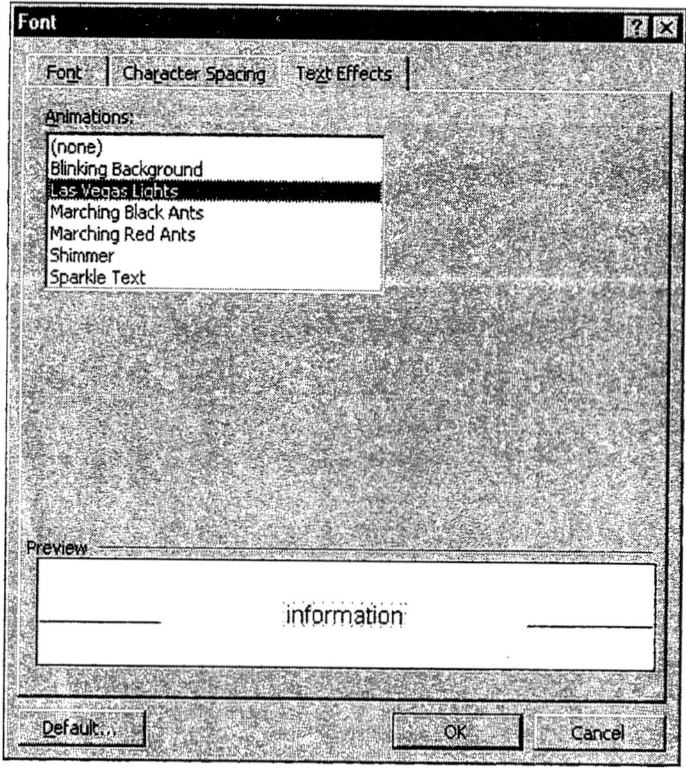

Figure 2.4: Font Animation dialog box

3. Click the effect you want in the **Animations** box.

☞ *Notes: You can apply only one animation effect at a time.*

Display or hide Animated text

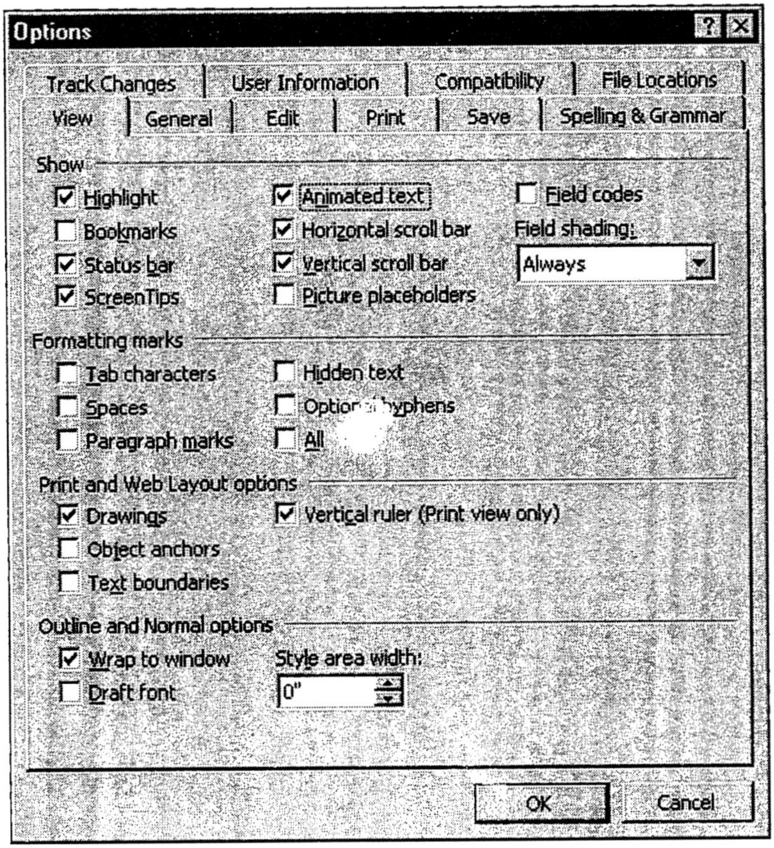

Figure 2.5: Display Animated Text Option dialog box

1. On the **Tools** menu, click **Options** → **View** tab as shown in figure 2.5.

2. **Select** or **clear** the **Animated text** check box.

Paragraph Formatting

The paragraph is the most commonly misunderstood element in Word. In order to have accurate control over paragraph formatting it is imperative that you make paragraph marks visible! Paragraph formatting information is "kept" in the paragraph mark that word invisibly appends to any word or line or lines that end with a return. Paragraph formatting governs: paragraph alignment (left, right, centered, justified) indentation (left and right) as well as spacing before and after. Tab alignment information is also kept in the paragraph mark.

The quickest way to copy complex paragraph formatting is to copy the paragraph mark of the formatted paragraph and paste it over that of the unformatted paragraph.

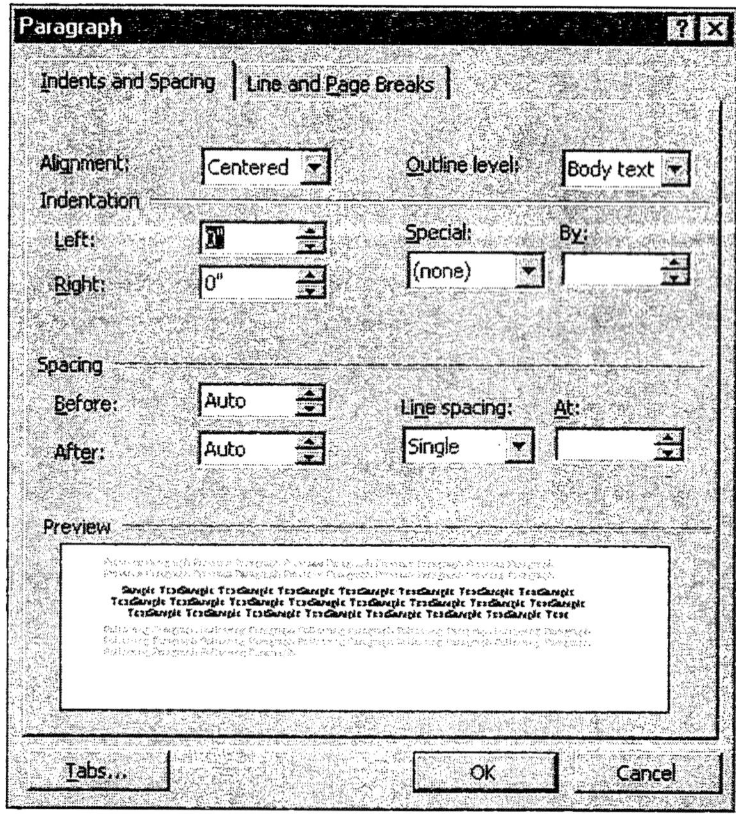

Figure 2.6: Paragraph formatting dialog box

Most of the aforementioned formatting elements are self explanatory. However, there are two items to keep in mind. First, Word will allow you to enter negative numbers for left and right indents. There are sound Desktop Publishing reasons for doing this, but in inexperienced hands negative indents create text that appears on the screen but not in the printed document. Also keep in mind that spacing before and after paragraphs is in units called *points*.

Many of our customers will want their documents spacing in inches. **There are 72 points in an inch--i.e. a 72 point font will be exactly one inch high.** Anyone can do the conversions using this information.

Tabs

Tabs are an important and often underused or misused element in Word's formatting features. Particular for those working with proportionally spaced fonts, Tabs are essential for uniform document spacing. Word allows two distinct ways for placing tabs in your text. You can double-click the mouse on the lower portion of the ruler (which will place a left aligned tab in that location for that paragraph of your document) or you can use the **Format → Tabs** dialog box displayed below:

Almost all fonts are proportionally spaced. The only monospaced font you'll likely see is Courier.

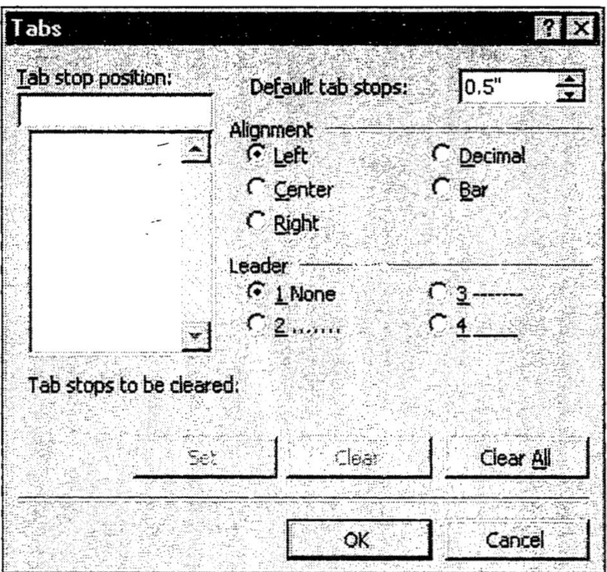

Figure 2.7: Tabs dialog box

As you can see, using the dialog box gives you more control over the exact position and alignment of the tab. (Of course you can always place the tab by double-clicking, then go back and use **Format → Tabs** to change position and alignment.) To place a tab using **Format → Tabs**, type the tab's position in inches, select the appropriate alignment and tab leader, then press the Set button.

The defintions of tab alignments are given below:

Alignment	Meaning
Left	Text typed following the tab will flow left
Right	Text typed following the tab will flow right
Center	Text typed following the tab will be centered on the tab
Decimal	Text (usually numbers) following the tab will be aligned so the the decimal point is on the tab.
Bar	A horizontal bar will appear at the tab location. Usually used as a divider.

Table 2.1: Tab Options description

Indent Paragraphs

When you increase or decrease indenting, you change the distance of the text from the margins. When you create a hanging indent, you offset an element, such as a bullet, number, or word, to the left of the first line of text.

Word does not see paragraphs in quite the same way, as you would expect. To Word **a paragraph is wherever you have pressed the hard return**, so even blank lines are paragraphs.

When do you use Indents?

- For giving emphasis to a paragraph
- For quotes
- For creating numbered or bulleted lists manually (although Word will do these for you automatically

To set Paragraph tabs

1. On the left edge of the ruler you will find the left justify tab. Click on it and the tab marker changes.
2. The following are the different tab markers:
   - Left Justify Tab
   - Center Justify Tab

- Decimal Point Tab
- Right Justify Tab

3. Keep clicking on the tab marker icon to set it back to the left alignment.

4. Click on the ruler at the half-inch location.

5. Place your cursor directly in front of the first letter of the first paragraph.

6. Press the **tab** key. The first line of the paragraph is now indented.

Set Tab Stops with Leader Characters

1. Select the paragraphs in which you want to insert leader characters before a tab stop.

2. On the **Format** menu, click **Tabs**.

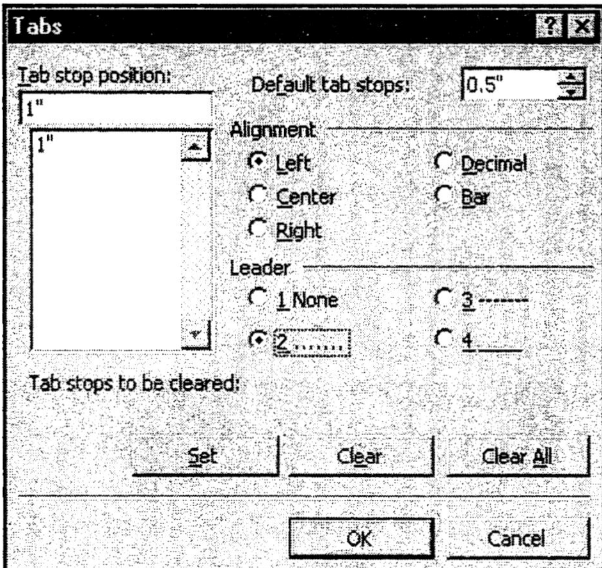

Figure 2.8: Tabs dialog box

3. In the **Tab Stop Position** box, type the position for a new tab, or select an existing tab stop to which you want to add leader characters.

4. In **Alignment**, click the alignment for text typed at the tab stop.

5. In **Leader**, click the leader option you want, click **Set** and finally click **OK**.

Make a hanging indent

To create a hanging indent by using the TAB key, first verify that the Tabs and Backspace set Left Indent check box is selected on the **Tools → Options → Edit** tab.

1. Type the text or click on the paragraph that you want to make a hanging indent. Click on **Format/Paragraph**.

2. Under **Indentation**, make the left and right indentation **.5** by clicking on the up arrow in each section.

3. Under **Line spacing**, click on **Single**. Click **OK**.

4. You may have to press Enter after the indented paragraph to assure uniformity in spacing.

Word creates a hanging indent, so that the first element hangs or is offset to the left of the lines of text that wrap below the first line.

Decrease the left indent

1. Select the paragraphs whose indents you want to change.

2. Click Decrease Indent.

Increase the left indent

1. Select the paragraphs whose indents you want to change.

2. Click Increase Indent.

Justify the last line in a paragraph

To justify a short line of text at the end of a paragraph with justified text, press **SHIFT+ENTER** to end the line.

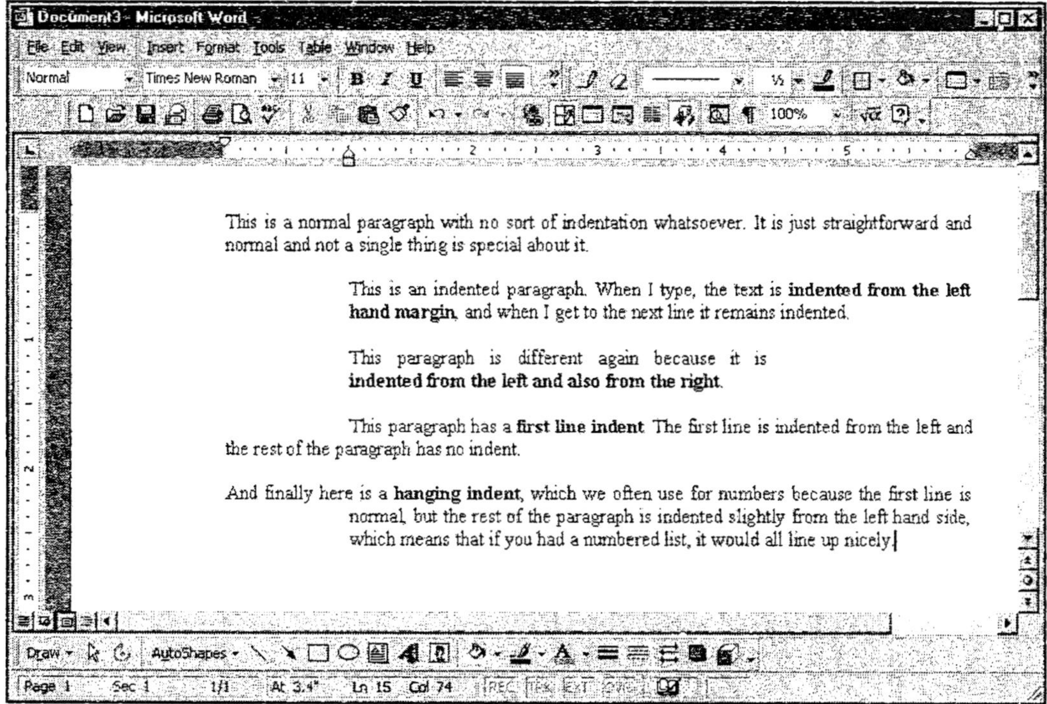

Figure 2.9: Various Indentations

Different Alignment in a single line of text

Text alignment that you set by using buttons on the Formatting toolbar, shortcut keys or the Paragraph command affects an entire paragraph. You might want to vary the alignment within a single line of text. For example, in the header of a report, you might want the report title aligned with the left margin, the date centered, and the page number aligned with the right margin. In Word, tabs can create this effect.

1. Make sure the paragraph that contains the line you want to change is left aligned.

2. Use the ruler to set tab stops corresponding to the alignment you want.

   For example, set a centered tab stop at the center and a right-aligned tab stop at the right margin.

3. Press TAB before each part of the line you want to align.

Change the Vertical Alignment of text in a Document

You can align text with the top or bottom of a page, center text, or distribute text equally between the top and bottom margins.

You can also align text in a table cell within the top and bottom edges of the table cell. This also works when you use the Text Direction command (Format menu) to orient the text vertically in Word documents.

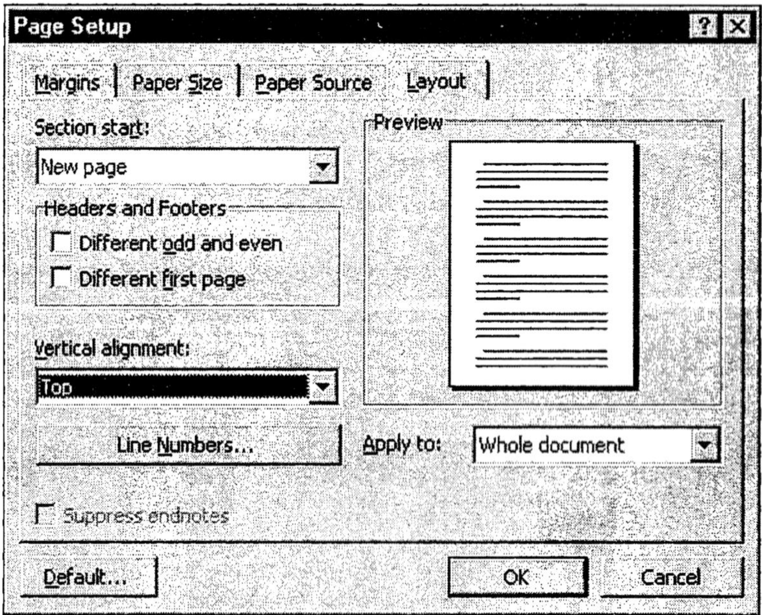

Figure 2.10: Page Setup Dialog box

1. On the **File** menu, click **Page Setup** → **Layout** tab.
2. In the **Vertical alignment** box, click the option you want.

Change the Vertical Alignment of text in a Table Cell

1. Click Tables and Borders to display the Tables and Borders toolbar.
2. Click the cell that contains text you want to align.
3. To align horizontally oriented text within the cell, use the **Align Top, Center Vertically and Align Bottom** buttons.

4. To align vertically oriented text within the cell, use the **Align Left, Center Horizontally and Align Right** buttons.

Paragraph Indenting vs. Page Margins

Be careful not to confuse between indenting paragraphs and left and right page margins, the space between the text and the edge of the page. When you indent a paragraph, you specify the distance of the text from the margins.

Borders and Shading

In a Word document, you can add a border to one or all sides of a table, a paragraph or selected text in a document. You can also add a border or line to a drawing object including a text box, an AutoShape, a picture or imported art.

You can change or modify any border you have added to a page, a table, a paragraph, or selected text in a document. You can also change a border or line on a drawing object including a text box, an AutoShape or a picture.

Use shading to fill in the background of a table, a paragraph, or selected text. Shading added to drawing objects including a text box or an AutoShape is called a fill. You can fill drawing objects with solid or gradient colors, a pattern, a texture, or a picture.

Add a border to a table, a paragraph or selected text

1. To add a border to a table, click anywhere in the table. To add borders to specific cells, select only those cells.

   To add a paragraph with a border, click anywhere in the paragraph. To add only to specific text, such as a word, select the text.

2. On the **Format** menu, click **Borders and Shading → Borders** tab.

3. Select the options you want and click **OK**.

4. To specify that only particular sides get borders, click **Custom** under **Setting**. In Preview, click the **diagram's sides**.

5. To specify the exact position of the border relative to the text, click **Options**, and then select the **distance of border from text**.

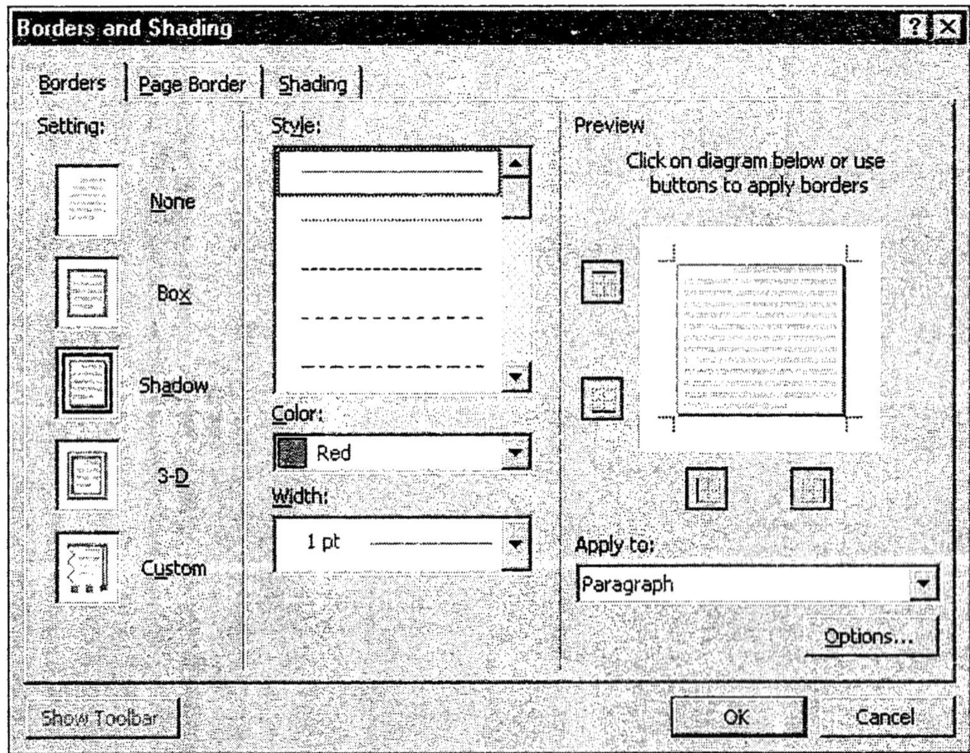

Figure 2.11: Border tab of Border and Shading dialog box

Add a border to a page

1. On the Format menu, click Borders and Shading → Page Border.
2. Select the options you want.
3. In **Setting → Custom**, specify the appearance of border on particular side of a page, as only at the top. In Preview, click where you want the border to appear.
4. To specify a particular page or section for the border to appear in, click the option you want under **Apply to**.
5. To specify the exact position of the border on the page, click **Options**, and then select the options you want.

Add a border to a drawing object

1. Select the drawing object you want to change.
2. Click **Drawing** to display the **Drawing toolbar**.
3. To add a color to the line or border, click the **arrow** next to Line Color, and then select the **color** you want. Click a color on the **Standard** tab, or to mix your own color click the **Custom** tab, and then click **OK**.
4. In order to give different style such as a thick line click **More Lines**, and then select the style you want.
5. To make a dashed line or border, click **Dash Style**, and then select the style you want.

Remove a Border from a Drawing Object

1. Select the drawing object whose border you want to remove.
2. On the **Drawing** toolbar, click the arrow next to Line Color and then click **No Line**.

Add shading to a table, a paragraph or selected text

You can use shading to fill in the background of a table, a paragraph or selected text.

1. To add shading to a table, click anywhere in the table. To add shading to specific cells, select only those cells.

   To add shading to a paragraph, click anywhere in the paragraph. To add shading to specific text, such as a word, select the text.
2. On the **Format** menu, click **Borders and Shading → Shading**.
3. Select the options you want and click **OK**.
4. In **Apply to**, click the part of the text you want to apply shading.

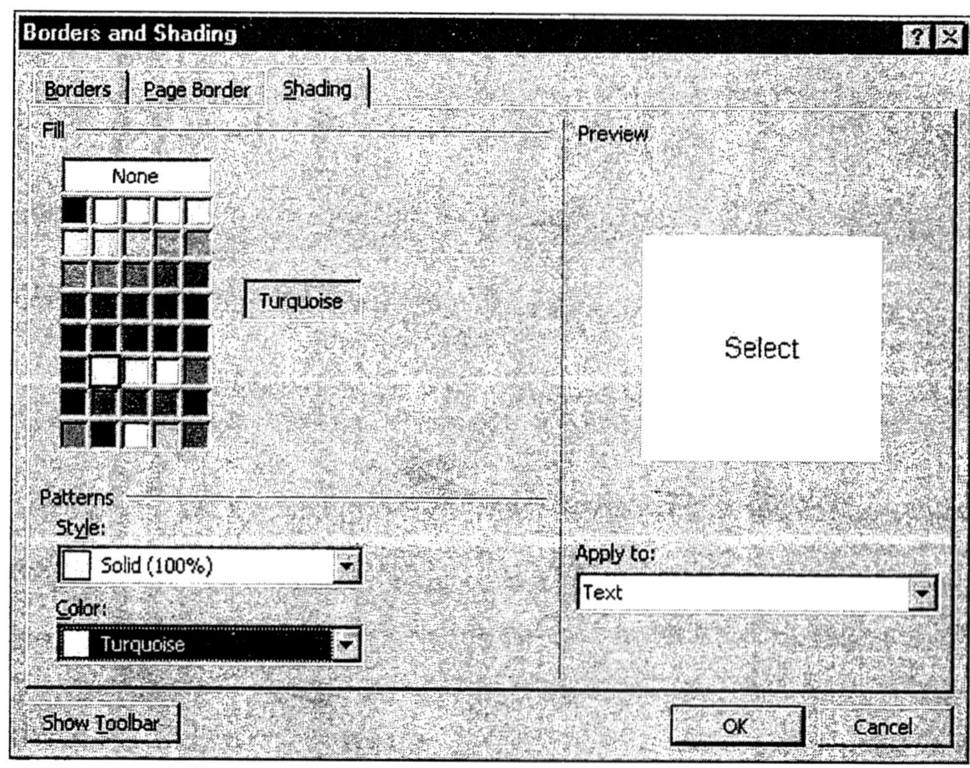

Figure 2.12: Shading tab under Border and Shading dialog box

Tips: You can use the Tables and Borders toolbar to quickly change the shading in a table, a paragraph, or selected text. In a table, select the cells, rows, or columns you want to change shading in, click the arrow next to Shading Color and then click a different color.

Add or Change gradients, patterns, textures or pictures in a Drawing Object

1. Select the drawing object you want to change.
2. On the **Drawing** toolbar, click the arrow next to **Fill Color → Fill Effects → Gradient, Texture, Pattern** or **Picture** tab.
3. Select the options you want.

4. If you don't see the color you want, click **More Fill Colors**. Click a color on the **Standard** tab, or click the **Custom** tab to mix your own color, and then click **OK**.

Add a Shadow to a Drawing Object

1. Select the drawing object you want to **add a shadow** to.
2. On the **Drawing** toolbar, click **Shadow**, and then click the option you want.

> **Tips:** To change the color or offset of a shadow, click Shadow, click Shadow Settings and then click the options you want on the Shadow Settings toolbar.

Add/Change/Remove the 3-D Effect of a Drawing Object

You can add a 3-D effect to lines, AutoShapes, and freeform objects. With 3-D options, you can change the depth of the object and its color, rotation, angle, direction of lighting, and surface texture. An object can have either a shadow or a 3-D effect, but not both if you apply a 3-D effect to an object that has a shadow, the shadow will disappear.

Move a Drawing Object or Set of Objects

1. Select the drawing object, multiple selection, or group you want to move.
2. Drag the object to its new location.

   Press **Shift** as you drag the object to constrain an object so it moves only horizontally or vertically.

Bulleted/Numbered Lists

When you manually number the items in a list, Word converts the typed numbers to automatic numbering. If you begin a paragraph with a star, Word automatically converts the paragraph to a bulleted item when you press ENTER to end the paragraph.

You can automatically add numbers to the headings in a document with the numbering format you choose by using the built-in styles. If you do not use built-in styles, you can still add numbers by linking each heading to a numbered format.

Examples: Numbering

1. Apple	1) Apple	I. Apple
2. Orange	2) Orange	II. Orange
3. Grape	3) Grape	III. Grape
4. Mango	4) Mango	IV. Mango
5. Cherry	5) Cherry	V. Cherry

A. Apple	A) Apple	(a) Apple
B. Orange	B) Orange	(b) Orange
C. Grape	C) Grape	(c) Grape
D. Mango	D) Mango	(d) Mango
E. Cherry	E) Cherry	(e) Cherry

i. Apple
ii. Orange
iii. Grape
iv. Mango
v. Cherry

Examples: Bulleting

• Apple	◆ Apple	▪ Apple
• Orange	◆ Orange	▪ Orange
• Grape	◆ Grape	▪ Grape
• Mango	◆ Mango	▪ Mango
• Cherry	◆ Cherry	▪ Cherry

❑ Apple	❖ Apple	➢ Apple
❑ Orange	❖ Orange	➢ Orange
❑ Grape	❖ Grape	➢ Grape
❑ Mango	❖ Mango	➢ Mango
❑ Cherry	❖ Cherry	➢ Cherry

✓ Apple
✓ Orange
✓ Grape
✓ Mango
✓ Cherry

To create a Bulleted and a Numbered text list

1. After the end of each sentence in the second paragraph press the **Enter** key.
2. Highlight all of these sentences.
3. Click on the **bulleted list** button, from the lower right side of tool bar. Notice how this effects your sentences.
4. Now click on the **numbered list** button, which is to the immediate left of the bulleted list button on the tool bar.

Create an Outline Numbered list

Outline numbered lists can have up to nine levels.

1. On the Format menu, click Bullets and Numbering → Outline Numbered tab.

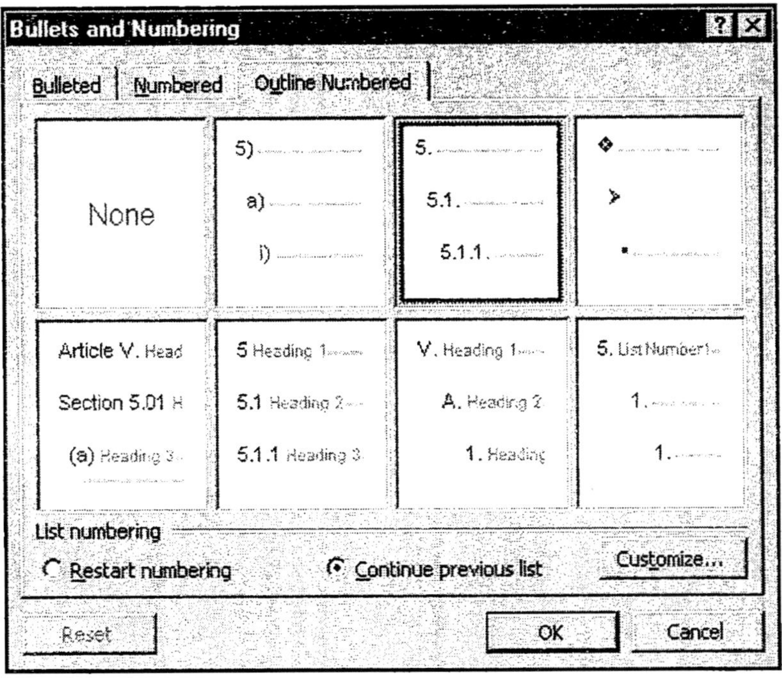

Figure 2.13: Outline Numbered tab in the Bullets and Numbering dialog box

2. Click a list format that does not contain the text "Heading 1," and then click **OK**.

   Type the list, pressing **ENTER** after each item.

3. To move an outline numbered item to the appropriate numbering level, click anywhere in the item, and then click **Increase Indent** or **Decrease Indent**.

Modify Bullet or Number Formats

1. Select the paragraphs that have the bullet or number format you want to change.
2. On the **Format** menu, click **Bullets and Numbering**, and then click the tab for the type of list you want to modify.
3. Click **Customize.**
4. Select the formatting options you want.

What is the Format Painter?

Format Painter provides a quick way of copying formatting from one piece of text to another. For example, if all the headings in your document are to be Arial, bold, italic and 16pts, you can format the first heading and then copy the format onto all the other headings.

Figure 2.14: Format Painter Icon

Using Format Painter to Copy Once

1. Select some text that is already formatted.
2. Click the format painter icon.
3. Select the text to copy onto.

Using Format Painter to Copy More than Once

1. Select some text that is already formatted.
2. Double-click the format painter icon.
3. Select the text to copy onto.
4. Select the next piece of text to copy onto etc.
5. When you have finished, click the format painter icon again to turn it off.

Using Go To

1. Press CTRL & G

   or

   Press F5 on the keyboard

   or

   Double-click on the left hand side of the status bar over the word "page".

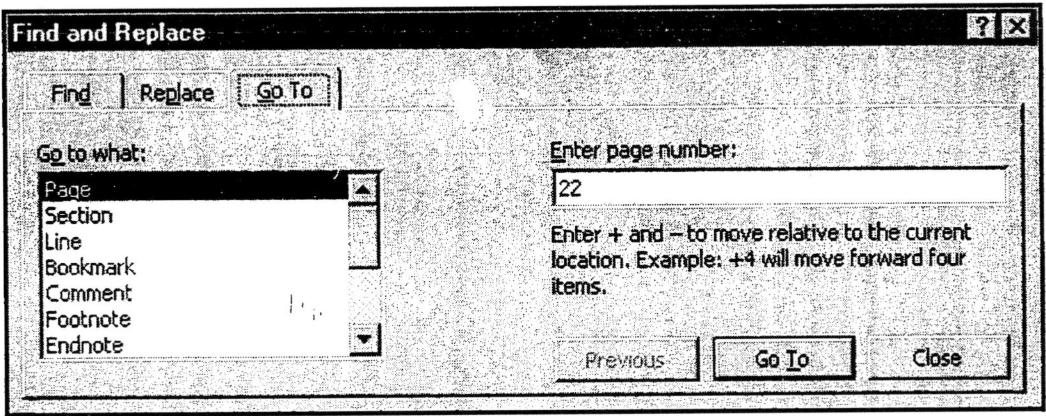

Figure 2.15: Go To tab in Find and Replace dialog box

2. Type in the page number you would like to go to.
3. Press Enter

4. Click on Close

   or

   Press Esc

Finding Text

1. Click Edit

   Click Find

   or

   Press CTRL + F

 Hands on Exercise

Exercise 1:

Font Size

The following exercise illustrates changing the font size.

Change Font Size: Using the Menu Bar

Type the following line:

I am the smallest. I am little bigger. I am the biggest.

1. Highlight "I am the smallest."
2. Click on Format.
3. Highlight Font. Press Enter.
4. Click on the Font tab, if it is not in the front.
5. Type **8** in the Size field, or click on 8 in the box below the Size field.
6. Click on OK.

7. Highlight "I am a little bigger."
8. Click on Format.
9. Highlight Font. Press Enter.
10. Click on the Font tab, if it is not in the front.
11. Type **14** in the Size field, or click on 14 in the box below the Size field.
12. Click on OK.
13. Highlight "I am a the biggest."
14. Click on Format.
15. Highlight Font. Press Enter.
16. Click on the Font tab, if it is not in the fron
17. Type **24** in the Size field, or click on 24 in the box below the Size field.
18. Click on OK.
19. Your text should now look similar to the following:

"I am the smallest. I am a little bigger. I am the biggest."

Alternate Method: Change Font Size by Using the To

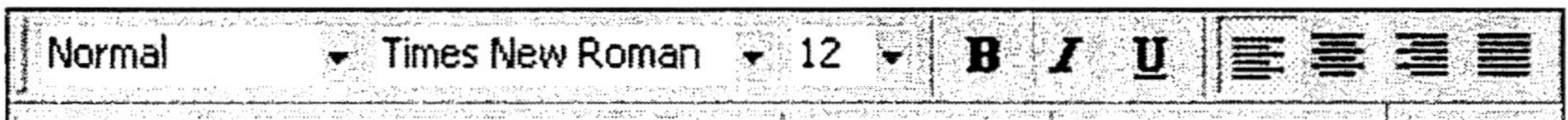

Figure 2.16: Formatting Toolb

1. Highlight:

   "I am the smallest. I am a little bigger. I am the biggest."

2. Press Ctrl-Spacebar to set the formatting back to the default.
3. Highlight "I am the smallest."

4. In the Font Size box 12 on the Tool Bar, type **8**.
5. Press Enter.
6. Highlight "I am a little bigger."
7. In the Font Size box 12 on the Tool Bar, type **14**.
8. Press Enter.
9. Highlight "I am a the biggest."
10. In the Font Size box 12 on the Tool Bar, type **24**.
11. Press Enter.

Fonts

This exercise illustrates, changing font family in Microsoft Word.

Change the Font: Using the Menu

Type the following:

1. Arial Courier Times New Roman
2. Highlight "Arial."
3. Click on Format.
4. Highlight Font. Press Enter.
5. Click on the Font tab, if it is not in the front.
6. In the box below the Font field, click on "Arial."
7. Click on OK.
8. Highlight "Courier."
9. Click on Format.
10. Highlight Font. Press Enter.

11. Click on the Font tab, if it is not in the front.
12. In the box below the Font field, click on "Courier."
13. Click on OK.
14. Highlight "Times New Roman."
15. Click on Format.
16. Highlight Font. Press Enter.
17. Click on the Font tab, if it is not in the front.
18. In the box below the Font field, click on "Times New Roman."
19. Click on OK.
20. Your text should now look similar to the following:

    "Arial `Courier` Times New Roman"

Alternate Method: Change the Font by Using the Formatting Toolbar

Figure 2.17: Formatting Toolbar

1. Highlight "Arial Courier Times New Roman."
2. Press Ctrl-Spacebar. Ctrl-Spacebar sets the formatting back to the default.
3. Highlight "Arial."
4. Click to open the Font pull-down menu on the Formatting toolbar.
5. Click on "Arial."
6. Next, highlight "Courier."
7. Click to open the Font pull-down menu on the Formatting toolbar.
8. Click on "Courier."
9. Next, highlight "Times New Roman."

10. Click to open the Font pull-down menu Times New Roman on the Formatting toolbar.

11. Click on "Times New Roman."

12. Your text should now look similar to the following:

    "Arial `Courier` Times New Roman"

Exercise 2:

In this exercise, we will look at various paragraph formatting options. When executing paragraph formatting, you do not need to highlight the entire paragraph. Placing the cursor anywhere in the paragraph will enable you to format it. After you set a paragraph format, subsequent paragraphs will have the same format unless you change their format.

Type the following sentences exactly as shown. End paragraphs where you see the end-of-paragraph marker (¶). Press Enter once to end the paragraph, **but do not leave spaces between paragraphs.** You will set the space between paragraphs during the exercise. Do not press Enter to move to a new line -- Microsoft Word automatically wraps at the end of a line.
Sample Paragraphs ¶ We will use this paragraph to illustrate several Microsoft Word features. It will be used to illustrate Space Before, Space After, and line spacing. Space Before tells Microsoft Word how much space to leave before the paragraph. Space After tells Microsoft Word how much space to leave after the paragraph. Line Spacing sets the space between lines within a paragraph. ¶

We will use this paragraph to illustrate some additional Microsoft Word features. It will be used to illustrate first-line indent. With first-line indent, you can indent the first line of your paragraph. We will also look at indentation. Indentation enables you to indent from the left or right margin of your document. ¶

Space Before and Space After

Space Before sets the amount of space before the paragraph. Space After sets the amount of space after the paragraph. Following are the sample paragraphs with Space After set to 12 pt. The exercises give you a chance to see how this works.

Example: Space After

Sample Paragraphs ¶

We will use this paragraph to illustrate several Microsoft Word features. It will be used to illustrate Space Before, Space After, and line spacing. Space Before tells Microsoft Word how much space to leave before the paragraph. Space After tells Microsoft Word how much space to leave after the paragraph. Line Spacing sets the space between lines within a paragraph.¶

We will use this paragraph to illustrate some additional Word features. It will be used to illustrate first-line indent. With first-line indent, you can indent the first line of your paragraph. We will also look at indentation. Indentation enables you to indent from the left and/or right margins of your document. ¶

Exercise:

Space Before

1. Highlight the title of the sample text: "Sample Paragraphs."
2. Click on Format.
3. Highlight Paragraph. Press Enter.
4. Click on the Indents and Spacing tab, if that tab is not in the front.
5. Enter **18 pt** in the Before field.
6. Click on OK.
7. You should now have 18 points **before** "Sample Paragraph."

Space After

1. Highlight all of the text you typed (the title and both paragraphs):
2. Click on Format.
3. Highlight Paragraph. Press Enter.
4. Click on the Indents and Spacing tab, if that tab is not in the front.
5. Enter **12 pt** in the After field.
6. Click on OK.
7. You should now have 12 points after each paragraph.

Line Spacing

Line Spacing sets the amount of space between lines within a paragraph. Single spacing is the default. The spacing for each line is set to accommodate the largest font on that line. If there are smaller fonts on the line, there will appear to be extra space between lines where the smaller fonts are located. At 1.5 lines, the Line Spacing is set to one-and-a-half times the single-space amount. For double-spaced lines, the line spacing is set to two times the single-space amount.

Exercise:

1. Highlight the first paragraph you typed, starting with "We will use" and ending with "within a paragraph."
2. Click on Format.
3. Highlight Paragraph. Press Enter.
4. Click on the Indents and Spacing tab, if that tab is not in the front.
5. Click to open the drop-down menu on the Line Spacing field.
6. Click on 1.5 Lines.
7. Click on OK.
8. Your line spacing for the paragraph should now be 1.5.

First-Line Indent

This exercise will demonstrate how you can indent the left side of the first line of your paragraph, as in the following example.

Example: First-line Indent

The first-line indent feature indents the first line of the paragraph. The amount of the indent is specified in the By field. The remainder of the paragraph is indented by the amount specified in the Indentation field.

Exercise:

1. Highlight the second paragraph you typed, beginning with "We will use" and ending with "of your document."
2. Click on Format.
3. Highlight Paragraph. Press Enter.
4. Click on the Indents and Spacing tab, if that tab is not in the front.
5. Click to open the drop-down menu on the Special field.
6. Click on First Line.
7. Enter **0.25"** in the By field.

8. Click on OK.

9. The first line of your paragraph should now be indented .25 inches.

☞ ***Special Note:*** *To remove tho first line indent:*

10. Place the cursor anywhere in the paragraph.

11. Click on Format.

12. Highlight Paragraph. Press Enter.

13. Click on the Indents and Spacing tab, if that tab is not in the front.

14. Click in the Special pull-down menu; then click on None.

15. Click on OK.

Indentation

Indentation allows you to indent your paragraph from the left or right margin. The following examples show different types of indentation.

Example: Indentation

We will use this paragraph to illustrate several Word features. It will be used to illustrate Space Before, Space After, and Line Spacing. Space Before tells Word how much space to leave before the paragraph. Space After tells Word how much space to leave after the paragraph. Line Spacing sets the space between each line within a paragraph.

We will use this paragraph to illustrate some additional Word features. It will be used to illustrate first-line indent. With first-line indent, you can indent the first line of your paragraph. We will also look at Indentation. Indentation enables you to indent from the left or right margins of your document.

Exercise:

Highlight the second paragraph, beginning with "We will use" and ending with "of your document."

1. Click on Format.

2. Highlight Paragraph. Press Enter.

3. Type **1"** in the Left field.

4. Type **1"** in the Right field.

5. Click on OK.

Your paragraph should now be indented one inch from both the left and right margins, as in the example.

Alignment

Microsoft Word gives you a choice of several types of alignment. Left-justified text is aligned on the left side. It is the default setting.

Example: Left-Justified

Sample Paragraph

This is a sample paragraph. It is used to illustrate alignment. Left-justified text is aligned on the left. Right-justified text is aligned on the right. Centered text is centered between the left and right margins. You can use Center to center your titles. Justified text is flush on both sides.

Right-justified text is aligned on the right side.

Example: Right-Justified

Sample Paragraph

This is a sample paragraph. It is used to illustrate alignment. Left-justified text is aligned on the left. Right-justified text is aligned with on the right. Centered text is centered between the left and right margins. You can use Center to center your titles. Justified text is flush on both sides.

Centered text is centered between the left and right margins.

Example: Centered

Sample Paragraph

This is a sample paragraph. It is used to illustrate alignment. Left-justified text is aligned on the left. Right-justified text is aligned with on the right. Centered text is centered between the left and right margins. You can use Center to center your titles. Justified text is flush on both sides.

Justified text is flush on both sides.

Example: Justified

Sample Paragraph

This is a sample paragraph. It is used to illustrate alignment. Left-justified text is aligned on the left. Right-justified text is aligned with on the right. Centered text is centered between the left and right margins. You can use Center to center your titles. Justified text is flush on both sides.

The following exercises demonstrate how to justify text.

Exercise: Right Justify

Return to the first paragraph you typed, beginning with "We will use" and ending with "within a paragraph." Highlight the paragraph.

1. Click on Format.
2. Highlight Paragraph. Press Enter.
3. Click on the Indents and Spacing tab, if that tab is not in the front.
4. Click to open the Alignment pull-down menu.
5. Click on Right.
6. Click on OK.
7. The paragraph should now be right-aligned.

Left Justify

1. Highlight the first paragraph you typed, beginning with "We will use" and ending with "within a paragraph."
2. Click on Format.
3. Highlight Paragraph. Press Enter.
4. Click on the Indents and Spacing tab, if that tab is not in the front.
5. Click to open the Alignment pull-down menu.
6. Click on Left.
7. Click on OK.
8. The paragraph should now be left-aligned.

Alternate Method: Right Justify by Using Keys

1. Highlight the text.
2. Press Ctrl-r.
3. The paragraph should now be right-aligned.

Alternate Method: Left Justify by Using Keys

1. Highlight the text.
2. Press Ctrl-l.
3. The paragraph should now be left-aligned.

Alternate Method: Right Justify by Using the Icon

1. Highlight the text.
2. Click on the Align Right icon
3. The paragraph should now be right-aligned.

Alternate Method: Left Justify by Using the Icon

1. Highlight the text.
2. Click on the Align Left icon
3. The paragraph should now be left-aligned.

Center: Using the Menu

1. Highlight the first paragraph you typed, beginning with "We will use" and ending with "within a paragraph."
2. Click on Format.
3. Highlight Paragraph. Press Enter.
4. Click on the Indents and Spacing tab, if that tab is not in the front.
5. Click to open the Alignment pull-down menu.
6. Click on Centered.
7. Click on OK.

Justify: Using the Menu

1. Highlight the first paragraph you typed, beginning with "We will use" and ending with "within a paragraph."
2. Click on Format.
3. Highlight Paragraph. Press Enter.
4. Click on the Indents and Spacing tab, if that tab is not in the front.
5. Click to open the Alignment pull-down menu.
6. Click on Justified.
7. Click on OK.

Alternate Method: Justify and Center by Using Keys

1. Highlight the text.
2. Press Ctrl-e. The text should now be centered.
3. Press Ctrl-j. The text should now be justified.

Alternate Method: Justify and Center by Using the Icon

1. Highlight the text.
2. Click on the Center icon . The text should now be centered.
3. Click on the Justify icon . The text should now be justified.
4. Hanging Indent

The hanging indent feature indents each line except the first line by the amount specified in the By field, as shown in the example.

Example: Hanging Indent

The hanging indent feature indents the first line of the paragraph from the margin by the amount specified in the Left field. The amount in the Left field plus the amount specified in the By field indent all subsequent lines.

Exercise:

When you begin typing the following paragraph, you might find that your paragraph is indented one inch on both sides. When you start a new paragraph in Microsoft Word, the setting from the previous paragraph carries over. If you wish, you can reset the indentation. If you choose not to reset the indentation, it will not affect your ability to perform the exercise.

Type the following:

Hanging Indent: The hanging indent feature indents the first line by the amount specified in the Left field. The amount in the Left field plus the amount specified in the By field indent all subsequent lines.

1. Highlight the paragraph you just typed.

2. Click on Format.

3. Highlight Paragraph. Press Enter.

4. Click on the Indents and Spacing tab, if that tab is not in the front.

5. In the Special field, click to open the pull-down menu. Click on Hanging.

6. In the By box, type **2.0"**.

7. Click on OK.

8. Place the cursor after the colon following "Hanging Indent."

9. Press the Tab key.

10. Notice how the indentation changes.

Exercise 3:

Type the following as shown.

Apple
Orange
Grape
Mango
Cherry

1. Highlight the words you just typed.

2. Click on Format.

3. Highlight Bullets and Numbering. Press Enter.

4. Click on the Numbered tab, if it is not in the front.
5. Several styles are available to you. Click on the style you want to use.
6. Click on OK.
7. Your list should now be numbered.

To remove the numbering:

1. Highlight the list again.
2. Click on Format.
3. Highlight Bullets and Numbering. Press Enter.
4. Click on None.
5. Click on OK.

Alternate Method: Numbering using the Icon.

1. Highlight the list you typed.
2. Click on the Numbering icon on the Formatting toolbar.
3. Your list should now be numbered.

To remove the numbering:

1. Highlight the list again.
2. Click again on the Numbering icon .

Bulleting

1. Highlight the list you typed.
2. Click on Format.
3. Highlight Bullets and Numbering. Press Enter.
4. Click on the Bulleted tab, if it is not in the front.

5. Several styles are available to you. Click on the style you want to use.
6. Click on OK.
7. Your list should now be bulleted.

To remove bulleting:

1. Highlight the list again.
2. Click on Format.
3. Highlight Bullets and Numbering. Press Enter.
4. Click on None.
5. Click on OK.

Alternate Method: Bulleting Using the Icon

1. Highlight the list you typed.
2. Click on the Bullets icon on the Formatting toolbar.
3. Your list should now be bulleted.

To remove the bulleting:

1. Highlight the list again.
2. Click on the Bullets icon again.

Test Your Knowledge

Students must solve the following assignment.

Multiple Choice Questions:

3. Paragraph markers are inserted when you

   a. press the Return key
   b. reach the end of a line
   c. use Wordwrap
   d. select the paragraph button in the toolbar

4. The insertion point marks

   e. the end of a document
   f. the start of a document
   g. where text will be entered
   h. the location of a page break

5. To select a single paragraph

   a. triple click anywhere in the paragraph
   b. click in the selection bar next to the paragraph
   c. right click in the paragraph
   d. double click anywhere in the paragraph

6. A decimal tab

   a. causes text under it to be aligned such that the period in the text is located directly under the tab.
   b. causes a period to be automatically inserted in the text that is entered under it.
   c. causes a period to be automatically inserted in the text that is entered under it only if the entered text is a number
   d. is not a valid type of tab.

7. Which of these is considered paragraph level formatting?

   a. indenting
   b. tab settings
   c. line spacing
   d. all of the above

8. By default,

   a. there are no tab stops set.
   b. tabs are placed every 1/2".
   c. tabs are placed relative to the top margin of the page.
   d. tabs are of type right align.

9. When you choose the Paragraph Hanging Indent, Word

   a. indents all but the first line of a paragraph
   b. indents only the first line of a paragraph
   c. indents all lines of a paragraph.
   d. indents all lines of a document.

10. A font type in a document

   a. must be set prior to entering the text.
   b. must be set for a minimum of 1 line.
   c. can not specify special appearance characteristics (bold, etc.).
   d. can be set any time - before or after entering text.

11. The Keep Lines Together feature

   a. can prevent Widows and Orphans in your document.
   b. can prevent page breaks between paragraphs
   c. can prevent page breaks within a paragraph
   d. all of the above
   e. only b and c

12. Default paragraph alignment is

   a. Justify
   b. Right
   c. Left
   d. Center

13. By default, the leader option of the tab command is

   a. dots
   b. dashes
   c. solid line
   d. nothing (no characters)

14. The Bullets and Numbering feature

   a. automatically inserts a bullet or number at the start of each new line.
   b. automatically inserts a bullet or number at the start of each paragraph.
   c. automatically inserts a bullet or number at the start of each sentence.
   d. inserts a bullet or number at the start of the unit of text that you select

15. Which extention is given to Word document by default ?

    a. EXT
    b. COM
    c. DOC
    d. None

16. Which of the following gives the status of your document like page numbers, number of pages.

    a. Status Bar
    b. Standard toolbar
    c. Formatting toolbar
    d. None of these

17. Alignment buttons are available on the ________ toolbar.

    a. Status Bar
    b. Standard toolbar
    c. Formatting toolbar
    d. None of these

State whether True or False:

1. Formatting of text is an example of text processing.

    a. True
    b. False

2. Insertion point shows where the typed text will appear.

    a. True
    b. False

3. A word processor automatically wraps any text extending beyond the right margin, to the next line.

    a. True
    b. False

4. END key marks the end of a paragraph.

    a. True
    b. False

5. Editing and formatting means one and the same thing.

   a. True
   b. False

6. Making modifications and corrections in a document is known as editing

   a. True
   b. False

7. Margins are the distances between the text and the edges of the paper.

   a. True
   b. False

8. Character formatting decides how a block of text appears.

   a. True
   b. False

9. A footer is printed at the bottom of every page.

   a. True
   b. False

10. Documents cannot be edited in print preview mode.

   a. True
   b. False

Fill in the Blanks:

1. The process where word 2000 will automatically move test to the next line if there is not enough space on the current line is called ____________________.

2. The ____________ alignment makes sure that none of the edges of text appear ragged.

3. Total height of a line of text including extra spacing is known as ____________.

4. Preset column position of text is called ____________.

5. The text to be searched is searched from ____________ menu.

6. The ____________ text-effect adds a line through text.

7. To remove character formatting, press ____________.

Tables

Objectives

- Introduction
- Creating a Table
- Add Rows or Columns to a Table
- Convert Table to Text

Introduction

Before you create a table, you must determine which Office program is best suited to your task. To create a table, you can use Microsoft Word, Microsoft Excel or Microsoft Access. Microsoft Excel and Microsoft Word can automatically format the table for you. In Microsoft Access, you can format an entire datasheet.

♦ For a table that includes graphics formatting such as bulleted lists, numbering, hanging indents, individual cell formatting, use Word.

♦ For a table that includes complex calculations, statistical analysis, or charts, use Microsoft Excel.

♦ For sorting and searching capabilities, use Microsoft Access or Microsoft Excel.

♦ If you need full relational database capabilities, create your tables in Microsoft Access.

♦ For a table that you can easily include in a PowerPoint presentation, use Word.

Why Use Tables?

A table can be used to position text or graphics in a document. You can use them to organise information, create forms or add interest to the information presented.

The Parts of a Table

A table has three parts: cells, columns and rows.

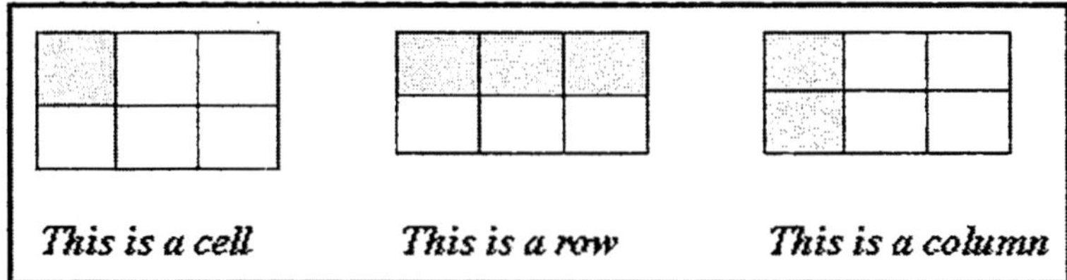

Figure 3.1: Parts of a Table

Creating a Table

Use tables to organize information and create interesting page layouts with side-by-side columns of text and graphics. The quickest way to create a simple table for example, one that has the same number of rows and columns is with the **Insert Table** button.

With the **Draw Table** feature, you can easily create a more complex and custom tables. Cells of different heights or a varying number of columns per row similar to the way you use a pen or pencil to draw a table.

You can create a new blank table and fill in the empty cells, or you can convert existing paragraphs of text to a table. You can also create a table from an existing data source, such as a database or spreadsheet.

1. Position your cursor where you require a table
2. Click on Table
3. Click on Insert Table

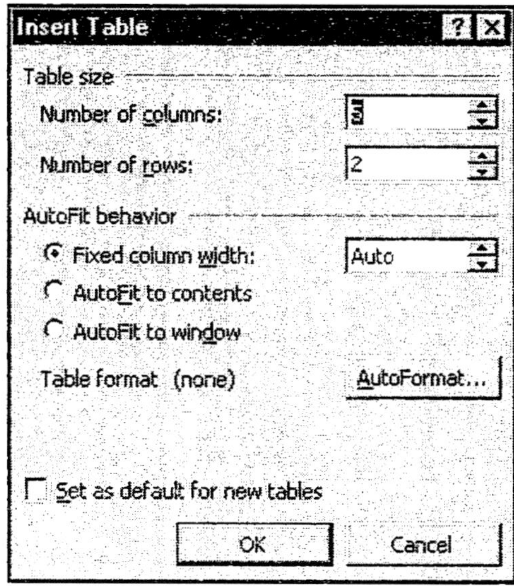

Figure 3.2: Insert Table dialog box

4. Type in the number of columns you require (or use the up and down arrows)
5. Type in the number of rows you require (or use the up and down arrows)
6. Click OK.

Add Rows or Columns to a Table

1. Select the row where you want to insert new rows, or select the column to the right of where you want to insert new columns.

2. To add a column to the right of the last column in a table, click just outside the rightmost column.

3. Click **Insert Rows** or **Insert Columns**.

Change the Column Width in a Table

1. Select the columns whose width you want to adjust.

2. On the **Table** menu, click **Table Properties → Column** tab.

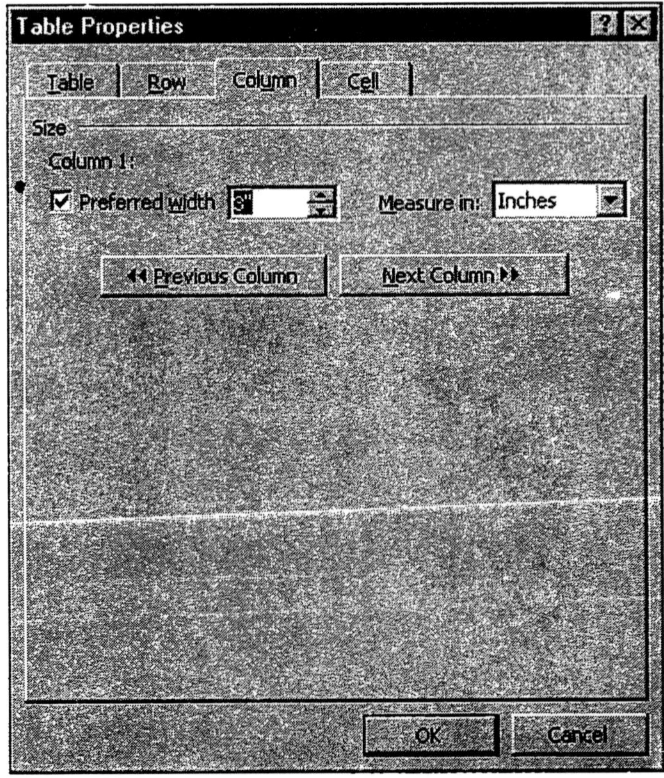

3. To specify an exact measurement, enter a number in the **Preferred Width** box.

   To make the column width fit the contents, click **AutoFit.**

4. To make multiple columns or cells the same width, select the columns or cells, and click **Distribute Columns Evenly** on the **Table** menu.

Change the Row Height in a Table

In Word documents, the height of each row in a table depends on the text written in that row and the paragraph spacing you add before or after text.

1. Select the rows you want to change.
2. On the **Table** menu, click **Table Properties → Row** tab.
3. Select the options you want.

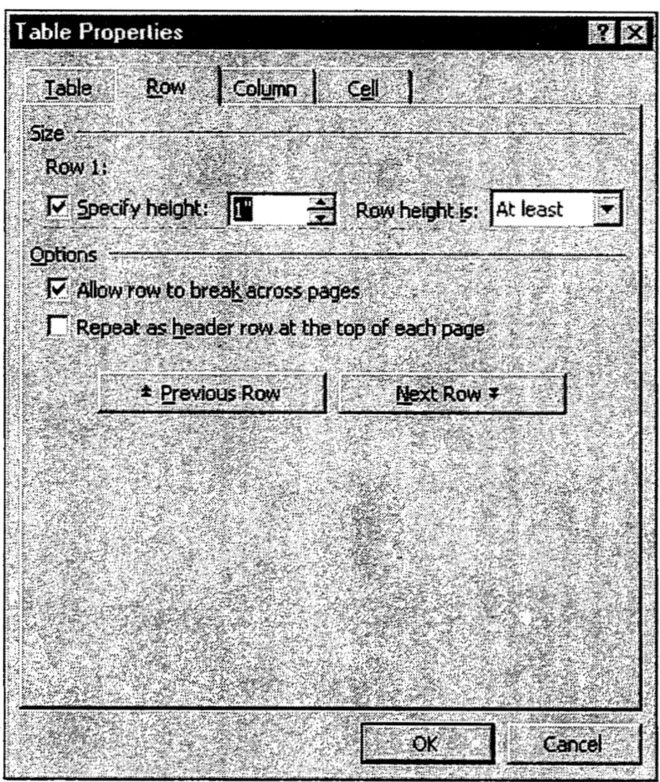

Figure 3.4: Row tab in Table Properties dialog box

Split a Table

1. To split a table in two, click the row that you want to be the first row of the second table.

2. On the Table menu, click **Split Table**.

AutoFormat a Table

1. Click the **table**.

2. On the **Table** menu, click **Table AutoFormat**.

3. In the **Formats** box, click the format you want.

4. Select the options you want.

Repeat a Table Heading on subsequent Pages

1. Select the rows of text that you want to use as a table heading. The selection must include the first row of the table.

2. On the **Table** menu, click **Heading Rows Repeat**.

Changing the orientation of text in a table

1. Click the table cell that contains the text you want to change.

2. On the **Format** menu, click **Text Direction** as shown in figure 3.3 below.

3. Click the orientation you want from bottom to top or from top to bottom.

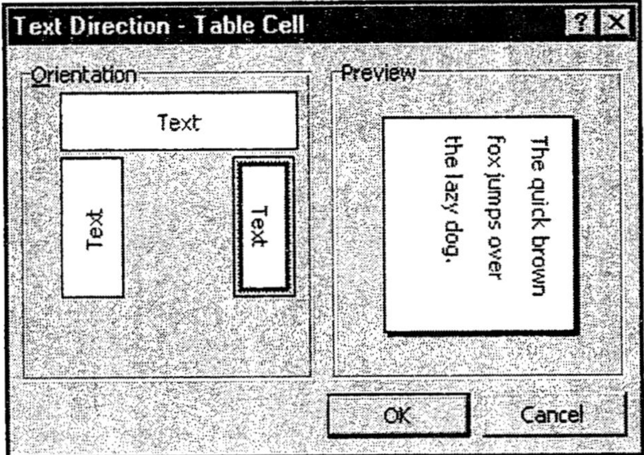

Figure 3.5: Text Direction dialog box

Changing the position of text in a table

Changing the orientation of text: By default, Microsoft Word aligns text horizontally in table cells. You can change the text orientation so that the text is displayed vertically.

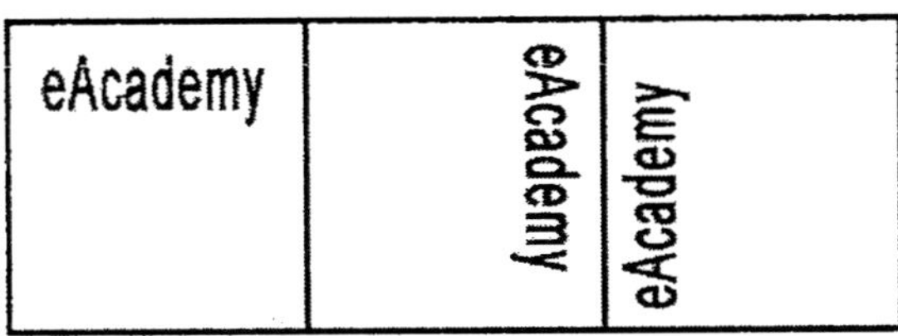

Figure 3.6: Changing the orientation of Text

Changing the alignment of text in a table cell: By default, Word aligns text in a table to the upper left of a cell. You can change the alignment of text in a cell - both the vertical alignment (top, center, or bottom) and the horizontal alignment (left, center, or right).

Horizontal Alignment

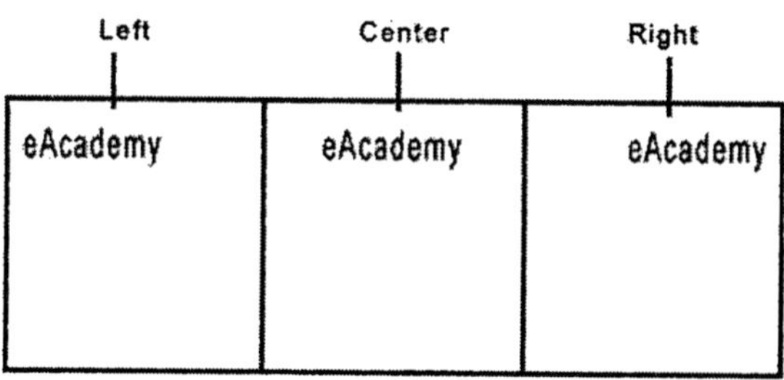

Vertical Alignment

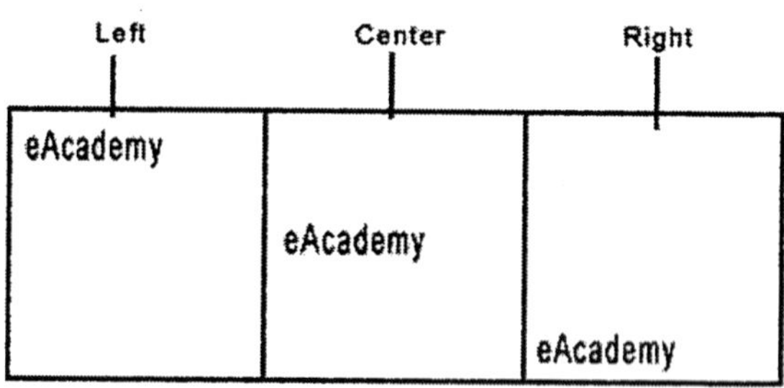

Figure 3.7: Horizontal and Vertical Alignment of Text

Convert Table to Text

When you convert a table to text, you can specify commas, tabs, paragraph marks, or another character as the separator in the converted text.

1. Select the rows or table that you want to convert to text.

2. On the **Table** menu, click **Convert Table to Text**.

3. Under **Separate text**, click the option for the character you want to use in place of the column boundaries. Rows are separated with paragraph marks.

Similarly you can convert **Text to Table**.

Sum a Row or Column of Numbers

1. Click the cell in which you want the sum to appear.
2. On the **Table** menu, click **Formula**.
3. If the cells you selected is at the bottom of a column of numbers, Word proposes the formula **=SUM(ABOVE)** and if the cell you selected is at the right end of a row of numbers, Word proposes the formula **=SUM(LEFT)**. Click **OK** if this is correct and sum of the above or to the left will be calculated.

 Hands on Exercise

Exercise 1: Creating a Table

To create a four-column, five-row table:

1. Click on Table, which is located on the Menu bar.
2. Highlight Insert Table on the drop-down menu.
3. Press Enter.
4. Type **4** in the Number of Columns field.
5. Type **5** in the Number of Rows field.
6. Select Auto in the Column Width field. Selecting Auto allows Microsoft Word to determine the size of your column widths. Alternatively, you can enter the column width you desire.
7. Click on OK. Your table should look like the one shown here, with four columns and five rows.

Table 3.1: Image of the table

Alternate Method: Creating a Table Using the Insert Table Icon

You can also create a table by clicking on the Insert Table icon on the Standard toolbar.

1. Click on the Insert Table icon.

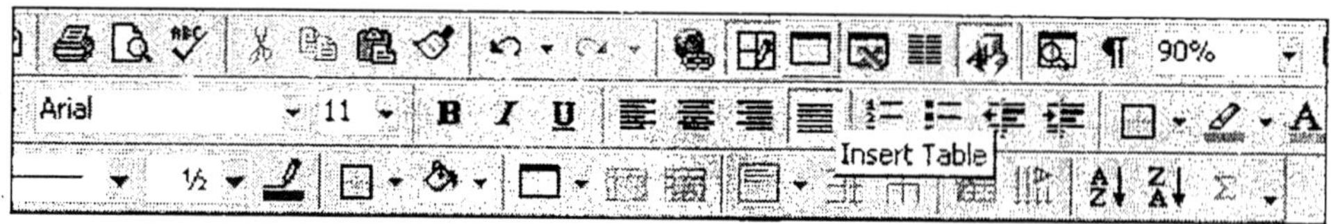

Figure 3.8: Insert Table icon in the Tables and Borders toolbar

☞ *Note: The Insert Table icon does not display on the toolbar if your cursor is located on a table. If you can not find the Insert table icon, move your cursor outside of the table.*

2. Highlight the number of rows and columns you need. The maximum table size is a four-row by five-column table.

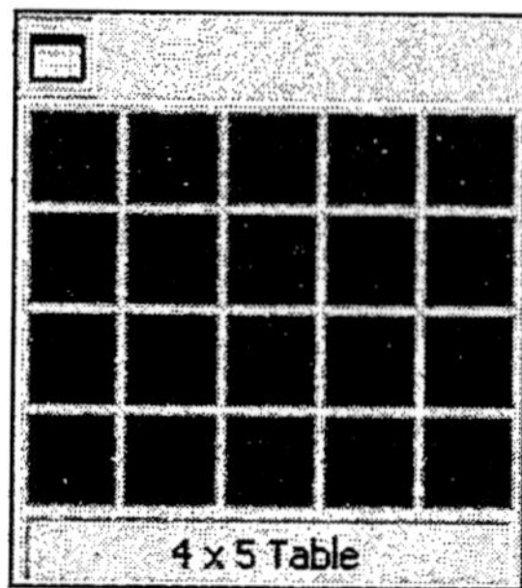

Figure 3.9: Highlight the Number of rows and columns in the dialog box

3. Press Enter (or Click) to create the table.

☞ *Note: Microsoft Word has a Tables and Borders toolbar.*

Exercise 2: Moving Around a Table

You refer to each block in a table as a cell. Use the Tab key to move between cells from left to right. Use **Shift+Tab** to move between cells from right to left. The following exercise demonstrates.

1. Click in the first cell in the first column.
2. Press the Tab key nine times. The cursor moves forward nine cells.
3. Press Shift-Tab six times. The cursor moves backward six cells.

☞ *Note: You can also move to a cell by clicking in the cell. In addition, you can move around the table by using the left, right, up, and down arrow keys.*

Exercise 3: Entering Text into a Table

To enter text into a table, simply type as you normally would. Press Tab to move to the next cell. Enter the text shown below into your table.

1. Type **Employee Name** in the first cell in the first column. Press the Tab key.
2. Type **Designation** in the first cell in the second column. Press the Tab key.
3. Type **Address** in the first cell in the third column. Press the Tab key.
4. Type **Salary** in the first cell in the fourth column. Press the Tab key.

Employee Name	Designation	Address	Salary
Aditya Chopra			
Vikram Singh			
Sunil Sikka			
Hemant Agnihotri			

Table 3.2: Enter text into the table

Exercise 4: Selecting a Row and making the Text Bold

In this exercise, you will select the first row of the table and bold all of the text on the row.

1. Click anywhere on the first row of your table.
2. Click on Table, which is located on the Menu bar.

3. Highlight Select Row, which is located on the drop-down menu.

4. Press Enter. Microsoft Word should select the first row of the table.

5. Press Ctrl+b to bold the row.

Exercise 5: Right-Aligning Text

In this exercise, you will right-align the second (Salary), third (Designation) and fourth (Address) columns of the table you created.

1. You need to highlight "Employee Name", "Designation", "Address" and "Salary". Place the cursor before the "E" in "Employee Name". Press the F8 key to anchor the cursor. Then press the right arrow key until you have highlighted "Employee Name", "Designation", "Address" and "Salary".

2. Click on Table, which is located on the Menu bar.

3. Highlight Select Column, which is located on the drop-down menu.

4. Press Enter. Microsoft Word should select the Employee Name, Designation, Address and Salary columns.

5. Press Ctrl+R to right-align the cells.

Your table should look like the one shown here. Make any needed corrections before continuing.

Employee Name	Designation	Address	Salary
Aditya Chopra	Managing Director	Greater Kailash, New Delhi	80,000
Vikram Singh	Vice President	Saket, New Delhi	50,000
Sunil Sikka	Project Leader	Pushp Vihar, New Delhi	18,000
Hemant Agnihotri	Marketing Executive	Daryaganj, New Delhi	8,000

Table 3.3: Final Output

☞ *Note: All of the formatting options you learned about in previous lessons can be applied to cells in a table.*

Exercise 6: Adding a New Row to the End of the Table

You can add additional rows to your table. The simplest way to add a new row is to move to the last column of the last row and press the Tab key. You can then type any additional text you need to add.

1. Move to the last column of the last row of your table.
2. Press the Tab key.
3. Type the text shown here.

Niraj			

Exercise 7: Adding a Row Within the Table

You can add a new row anywhere in the table. Microsoft Word adds new rows above your current row. The exercise that follows demonstrates.

To add a row just above Vikram:

1. Place the cursor anywhere in the second row.
2. Click on Table, which is located on the Menu bar.
3. Highlight Insert Rows on the drop-down menu.
4. Press Enter. Microsoft Word should create a new row above the second row.
5. Add the information shown here to the new row.

Sujit			

Exercise 8: Resizing the Columns

You can easily change the size of your column widths. In this exercise, you will first select the entire table and then you will adjust all the column widths.

1. Click anywhere in your table.
2. Click on Table, which is located on the Menu bar.
3. Highlight Select Table.
4. Press Enter.

5. Click on Table, which is located on the Menu bar.

6. Highlight Cell Height and Width.

7. Press Enter.

8. Click on the Column tab, if it is not in the front.

9. Type **1** in the Width of Columns 1-4 field. This will cause Microsoft Word to set all the columns to a width of one inch.

10. Click on OK.

Depending on your font, the first column of your table might not be wide enough and the text might be wrapping.

To widen the first column:

1. Place the cursor anywhere in the first column.

2. Click on Table, which is located on the Menu bar.

3. Highlight Select Column.

4. Press Enter.

5. Click on Table, which is located on the Menu bar.

6. Highlight Cell Height and Width.

7. Press Enter.

8. Click on the Column tab, if it is not in the front.

9. Type **1.5** in the Width of Column 1 field.

10. Click on OK.

Alternate Method: Resizing Your Column Widths by Using the Width Indicator

You can resize your column widths by placing the cursor on the line that separates two columns. This will cause the width indicator to appear. After the width indicator appears, left-click and drag with the mouse to adjust the column width.

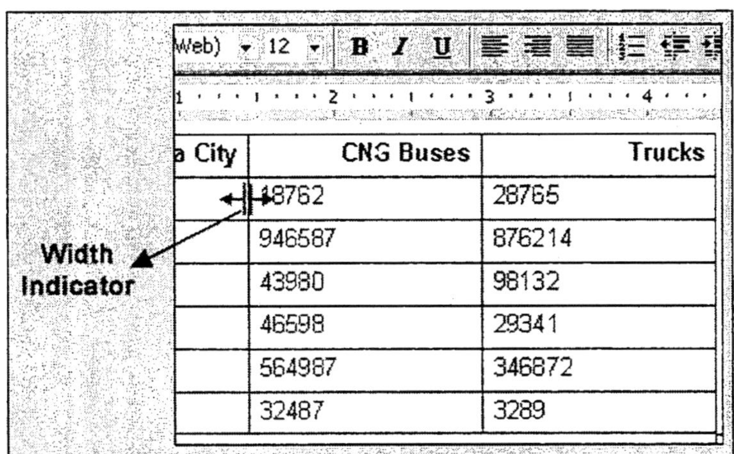

Figure 3.10: Width Indicator used for resizing of rows and columns

Exercise 9: Adding a New Column to a Table

You can add new columns to your table. Microsoft Word adds new columns to the left of your current location.

To add a new column between the Designation and Address columns:

1. Place the cursor anywhere in the Address column.
2. Click on Table, which is located on the Menu bar.
3. Highlight Select Column on the drop-down menu.
4. Press Enter. Microsoft Word should select the first column.
5. Click on Table, which is located on the Menu bar.
6. Highlight Insert Columns on the drop-down menu.
7. Press Enter. Microsoft Word should create a new column between the Designation and Address columns.
8. Label the new column **Region** and add the text shown in the table below.

Employee Name	Designation	Region	Address	Sales

Table 3.4: Insert a new column Region

Exercise 10: Sorting a Table

With Microsoft Word, it is easy to sort the data in your table. To sort your table data by Region and within Region by Employee Name in ascending order:

1. Click anywhere on your table.
2. Click on Table, which is located on the Menu bar.
3. Highlight Sort on the drop-down menu.
4. Press Enter.
5. Select Region in the Sort By field.
6. Select Text in the Type field (because you are sorting text).
7. Select Ascending.
8. Select Employee Name in the Then By field.
9. Select Text in the Type field (because you are sorting text).
10. Select Ascending.
11. Select Header Row (because your table has titles across the top of the table).
12. Click on OK.

Exercise 11: The Sum Function

You can perform a limited number of calculations on the numbers in your table. Several functions are available to you. The following exercise demonstrates the Sum function. In this exercise you will add a new row to your table, place the word **"Total Salary"** at the bottom and sum the Salary column.

1. Place your cursor in the cell located on the last row in the last column.
2. Press the Tab key to create a new row.
3. Type **Total Salary** in the cell on the bottom row in the Employee Name column.
4. Move to the Salary column.
5. Click on Table, which is located on the Menu bar.
6. Highlight Formula.
7. Press Enter.
8. Type **=SUM(ABOVE)** in the formula field, if it does not automatically appear.
9. Select #,##0 in the Number Format field. This selection will cause Microsoft Word to separate thousands with a comma.
10. Click on OK.

Exercise 12: Deleting a Column

You can delete columns from your table. To delete the Designation column:

1. Place your cursor anywhere in the Designation column.
2. Click on Table, which is located on the Menu bar.
3. Highlight Select Column.
4. Press Enter. Microsoft Word will select the entire column.
5. Click on Table, which is located on the Menu bar.
6. Highlight Delete Column.
7. Press Enter.

Exercise 13: Deleting a Row

You can delete rows from your table. To delete the Vikram row:

1. Place your cursor anywhere in the Vikram row.
2. Click on Table, which is located on the Menu bar.
3. Highlight Select Row.
4. Press Enter. Microsoft Word will select the entire row.
5. Click on Table, which is located on the Menu bar.
6. Highlight Delete Rows.
7. Press Enter.

Recalculate

Microsoft Word does **not** automatically recalculate every time you make a change to the table. To cause a function to recalculate, you must first move to the cell that contains the function and then press the F9 key. Alternatively, you can move to the cell that contains the function, right-click, and select Update Field from the context menu. Because you deleted a row in the previous exercise, your calculations are now incorrect.

To recalculate:

1. Move to the Total Salary cell.
2. Press F9.

☞ *Note: The context menu is a useful tool. When you right-click, Microsoft Word supplies you with a list of menu choices. You can execute a command by selecting an option from the menu.*

Exercise 14: Merge Cells

Using Microsoft Word, you can merge cells: turn two or more cells into one cell. In this exercise, you are going to create a new row at the top of your table, merge the cells, and add a title to the table.

1. Move to the cell located on the first row of the first column of your table.
2. Click on Table, which is located on the Menu bar.

3. Highlight Insert Rows on the drop-down menu.

4. Press Enter. Microsoft Word should create a new row above your row of headings.

5. Click on Table, which is located on the Menu bar.

6. Highlight Merge Cells.

7. Press Enter.

8. Type **Months Salary** in the new cell.

9. Press Ctrl+e to center the title.

Exercise 15: Table Headings

If Microsoft Word splits your table with a page break, the table heading will display on the first page but not on subsequent pages. To correct this problem, you can designate rows as headings. Heading rows are repeated on the top of your table at the top of each page. To designate a row as a heading:

1. Place your cursor on the row.

2. Click on Table, which is located on the Menu bar.

3. Highlight Headings on the drop-down menu.

4. Press Enter.

Exercise 16: Converting Text to a Table

You can convert text to a table; however, a delimiter such as a comma, paragraph marker, or tab must separate columns of text. In the exercise that follows, you will convert comma-delimited text into a table.

1. Type the following as shown (do not bold).

```
Color,   Style,   Item
Blue,    A980,    Van
Red,     X023,    Car
Green,   YL724,   Truck
Name,    Age,     Sex
Bob,     23,      M
Linda,   46,      F
Tom,     29,      M
```

2. Highlight the text.

3. Click on Table, which is located on the Menu bar.

4. Highlight Convert Text to Table on the drop-down menu.

5. Press Enter.

6. Type **3** in the Number of Columns field.

7. Select Auto in the Column Width field.

8. Select the Comma radio button in the Separate Text At frame.

9. Click on OK.

Microsoft Word should have converted your text to a table and your table should look like the one shown here.

Color,	Style,	Item
Blue,	A980,	Van
Red,	X023,	Car
Green,	YL724,	Truck
Name,	Age,	Sex
Bob,	23,	M
Linda,	46,	F
Tom,	29,	M

Table 3.5: Converting Text to Table

Exercise 17: Splitting a Table

With Microsoft Word, splitting a single table into two tables is easy. To separate the table you just created into two tables:

1. Place your cursor anywhere on the row that reads "Name, Age, Sex."

2. Click on Table, which is located on the Menu bar.

3. Highlight Split Table on the drop-down menu.

4. Press Enter.

You should now have two tables.

Exercise 18: Table AutoFormat

You can use AutoFormats to easily apply borders, shading, special fonts, and color to your table. Microsoft Word lists all Formats in the Table AutoFormat dialog box. While in the Table AutoFormat dialog box, click on a format to see it displayed in the Preview box. You can customize how the format is applied. Check the features you want in the Formats to Apply and the Apply Special Formats To frames. Microsoft Word comes with a long list of **AutoFormats**.

To apply an AutoFormat to your Name, Age, and Sex table:

1. Click anywhere in the table.
2. Click on Table, which is located on the Menu bar.
3. Highlight table AutoFormat.
4. Press Enter.
5. Select Colorful 1 in the Formats box.
6. Select Borders, Shading, Font, and Color in the Formats to Apply frame. Do not select AutoFit.
7. Select Heading Rows and First Column in the Apply Special Formats To frame. Do not select Last Row and Last Column.
8. Click on OK.

Test Your Knowledge

Students must solve the following assignment.

Multiple Choice Questions:

1. A blank table is inserted

    a. at the location of the insertion point
    b. at the end of the paragraph containing the insertion point
    c. at the end of the page containing the insertion point
    d. at the end of the word containing the insertion point

2. To advance to the next cell in a table

    a. press the Enter key
    b. press the Tab key
    c. press End key
    d. press the Insert key

3. Markers found in a table are

    a. end of row markers
    b. cell markers
    c. end of column markers
    d. all of the above
    e. a and b

4. Which of the following features can be used in a Word table?

    a. Sort rows according to the values in a column you specify.
    b. Set appearance characteristics of the contents of any cell.
    c. Perform a calculation in a cell using other cell values
    d. All of the above

5. Which of the following statements about tables is NOT true?

    a. Since Word can perform mathematical calculations with tables, you should save yourself some money and use Word's tables for your calculation needs instead of buying a spreadsheet program.
    b. You can split a cell into several smaller cells or merge several smaller cells into a single, larger cell.
    c. You can format the characters and paragraphs in a table.
    d. You can sort information in a table alphabetically, numerically or chronologically.

6. Which of the following procedures can you use to add borders to a table? (Select all that apply).

   a. Click the Draw Table button on the Tables and Borders toolbar and then draw the border.
   b. Select the cells where you want to apply the borders and select the desired border from the Borders button on the Tables and Borders toolbar.
   c. Select Tables > Table Border Wizard from the menu and follow the onscreen instructions.
   d. Select the cells where you want to apply the borders, select Format > Borders and Shading from the menu, and specify the borders.

7. A table you're working with has become so large that it breaks across several pages. How can you ensure the column heads always appear at the top of the table?

   a. You can't - there isn't a way to do this.
   b. Select the row that contains the column headings and select Table > Heading Rows Repeat from the menu.
   c. Press F1 to summon the Office Assistant and type "Fix this table for me, slave!" in the Office Assistant's speech ballon.
   d. Select the row that contains the column headings and click the Table Headings button on the Tables and Borders toolbar.

8. Which of the following is NOT a way to create a table?

   a. Select Insert > Table from the menu.
   b. Click the Insert Table button on the Standard toolbar.
   c. Select View > Toolbars > Tables and Borders to view the Tables and Borders toolbar. Click the Draw Table button on the Tables and Borders menu and draw the table.
   d. Select Table > Insert Table from the menu.

9. Which of the following statements is NOT true?

   a. A table's gridlines always appear when printed.
   b. You can prevent a row from breaking across pages by selecting Cell Height and Width from the menu and checking the Allow row to break across pages.
   c. You can merge several cells into a single cell and split a single cell into several smaller cells.
   d. The AutoFit feature automatically adjusts the width of a column so that it fits its longest entry.

10. How can add shading to a table?

   a. Select Tables > Shading from the menu.
   b. Click the Fill Color button on the Formatting toolbar.
   c. Click the Shading button on the Tables and Borders toolbar.
   d. Put an umbrella over the table.

State whether True or False:

1. You can use the Draw Table tool to draw doodles and pictures in a table.

   a. True
   b. False

2. You can change the text direction in a cell, so that you can read it from bottom to top or from top to bottom by selecting Format → Text Direction from the menu.

   a. True
   b. False

3. Word can sort text alphabetically in a table, but not numerical information.

   a. True
   b. False

Creating Merge Documents

Objectives

- What is Mail Merge?
- View Merged Documents before Printing
- Print a Mail Merge document

What is Mail Merge?

Mail merge is a feature in Word that allows you to merge generic information or standard that is repeated in each form letter, mailing label, envelope or catalog with variable information (such as a database of names and addresses of customers). This allows you to have virtually identical documents in which the substance of the documents is the same for every customer, yet each is customized to a particular individual in your database.

For instance, If you want to send a form letter to 5 people or 500, you can use Word to personalize each one and create mailing labels or envelopes.

Main components to a Mail Merge

1. The main document that contains the standard information information: text and graphics. The main document also determines the format of the resulting merged document; for example, form letter, envelopes, or labels.

   There are four types of main documents:

   - **Form Letters:** The letters or reports you want to personalize.
   - **Mailing Labels:** Address labels or any other kind of label, such as name tags, video tape or disk labels, and file folder labels.
   - **Envelopes:** Envelopes fed directly into your printer.
   - **Catalogs:** Lists of data, such as phone lists or membership directories.

2. A data source that contains the variable information i.e. a record of each individual item. Each record consists of fields. A person's name might consists of FirstName, MiddleName, LastName. The address probably will contain a separate field for the StreetAddress, City, State and Postal Code. A data source contains multiple records, so you can enter information about many different people.Using Word, you can access the data stored in any of the following:

   - A data source file created using Word.
   - A file created with other Microsoft Office Products such as Excel spreadsheet or Access database.
   - A database file created using software distributed by other companies.
   - A database from the Address Book.

3. The merged document that contains the combination of standard or generic text and variable information.

   In the main document, you insert special instructions, called merge fields, to indicate where you want the variable information to appear. When you merge the information in the data source with the main document, the variable information replaces the merge fields with the individualized information. The result is the merged document that contains the combination of generic text and variable information.

   The data source is set up with a header row (also called a header record) and data records. The header row is the first item in the data source. It contains the field names that identify the variable information. The data records contain the individualized information. Each data record consists of one or more fields, depending on how much variable information you have for each individual. This set of information makes up one data record.

The mail merge process has four main steps:

1. Opening or creating the main document
2. Opening or creating the data source
3. Editing the main document
4. Performing the merge

The following procedure demonstrates how to create a form letter, attach it to a data source, format it, and merge the documents. The procedure for creating merged envelopes or labels is similar.

Step 1: Opening or Creating the Main Document

1. If you have a document that contains the text that you want to use, open it. Or, if you want to create a new form letter and you don't see a blank document, click the New button on the Standard toolbar.
2. On the **Tools** menu, click **Mail Merge**.
3. In the Main Document area of the Mail Merge Helper dialog box, click the Create button.
4. Click Form Letters.

   A dialog box appears, asking whether you want to use the active window for the main document or to create a new main document. Click Active Window. The active document becomes the mail merge main document.

   Word returns to the Mail Merge Helper.
5. Proceed further with step 2 given below.

Step 2: Opening or Creating the Data Source

When you open or create a data source by using the Mail Merge Helper, you are telling Word to use a specific set of variable information for your merge. Use either of the following methods to attach the main document to the data source.

Method 1: If you are typing the Names and Addresses for the first time

To create a new database, follow these steps:

1. In the Data Source area of the Mail Merge Helper dialog box, click Get Data.
2. Click Create Data Source. The Create Data Source dialog box appears. In this dialog box, you can specify the field names to include in the data source. The Field Names in the Header Row box lists field names that are often used in form letters, mailing labels, and envelopes. You can remove the fields that you do not want by selecting them one at a time and then clicking Remove Field Name. If you want to create new field names, type the new field name in the Field Name box, and then click Add Field Name.

   When you finish creating new fields and removing fields that you do not want, click OK.
3. The Save As dialog box appears. In the File Name box, type the name that you want to give your data source, and then click Save.
4. When Word asks whether you want to edit the data source or set up the main document, click **Edit Data Source**.
5. When the Data Form dialog box appears, type your information into the form. If there is no information for a particular field, leave the box blank. By default, Word skips blank fields, so the merge is not affected if blank entries are in the data form. The set of information in each form makes up one data record.
6. After you type the information for a record, click **Add New** to move to the next record.
7. After you add all of your data, click OK to return to the main document.

   Notice the Mail Merge toolbar.
8. Save the main document.

   When you save the main document at this point, you are also saving the data source and attaching it to the main document.
9. Go to step 3.

Method 2: If you are using an Existing Data Source

To use an existing data source, follow these steps:

1. In the **Mail Merge Helper** dialog box, click **Get Data**.

2. Click Open Data Source.

3. In the Open Data Source dialog box, select the file that contains the variable information that you want to use, and then click Open.

☞ *Note: If the data source is not listed in the list of files, choose the appropriate drive and folder. If necessary, select the appropriate option in the List Files of Type box. Select the file, and then click Open.*

Word prompts you with the following message:

```
"Word found no merge fields in your main document. Choose
the Edit Main Document button to insert merge fields into
your main document".
```

4. Click the Edit Main Document button to return to the main document.

   Notice the Mail Merge toolbar.

5. Save the main document. When you save the main document at this point, you are also saving the data source and attaching it to the main document.

6. Proceed further with Step 3.

Step 3: Editing the Main Document

In step 1, you chose either to open an existing document or to create a new one. Choose either of the following methods, based on the selection that you made in step 1.

Method 1: If you are using an Existing Document

1. Click where you want to insert the information from your data source.

2. On the **Mail Merge** toolbar, click the **Insert Merge Field** button, and then click the merge field that you want to use.

☞ *Note: Make sure that you type any spaces or punctuation that you want between two merge fields or after a merge field. You can also format (apply bold or italic formatting to) the merge fields, just like regular text.*

3. Repeat steps 1 and 2 for each merge field that you want to add to your document.

4. When you finish editing the main document, click **Save** or **Save As** on **the File** menu. Name the file, and then click **Save**.

5. Go to step 4.

Method 2: If you are using a New Main Document

1. Type or add any text and graphics that you want to include in your letter.

2. Each time that you come to a place where you want to insert information from the data source, click the **Insert Merge Field** button on the **Mail Merge** toolbar, and then click the merge field that you want to use.

☞ *Note: Make sure that you type any spaces or punctuation that you want between two merge fields or after a merge field. You can also format (apply bold or italic formatting to) the merge fields, just like regular text.*

3. When you finish editing the main document, click **Save** or **Save As** on the **File** menu. Name the file, and then click **Save**.

4. Go to step 4.

Step 4: Performing the Merge

1. On the **Tools** menu, click **Mail Merge.**

2. In the Merge the Data with the Document area, click **Merge**.

3. In the **Merge** dialog box, click **Merge To**, and select **New** document to display the merged document on the screen. You can print the merged document by clicking **Print** on the **File** menu.

☞ *Note: In the **Merge To** box, select **Printer** if you want to send the merged document to the printer without first viewing it on your screen.*

4. Click **Merge**.

View Merged Documents before Printing

To check your merge results quickly, you can display merged data in the main document and view the resulting merged documents one by one. To add comments or other information to individual form letters and then print them later, you can collect all resulting merged documents in a single, new document.

Print a Mail Merge document

You can review your mail-merge results online before you send or print the form letters. You can print addresses on envelopes or mailing labels.

 Hands on Exercise

Exercise 1:

1. In Microsoft Word, from the FILE menu, select "New..." and then click on "Blank Document." Click OK.

2. From the TOOLS menu, select MAIL MERGE (**not** the "Merge Documents" command)

3. The MAIL MERGE HELPER window appears.

4. In section "1: Main Document", click and hold down the mouse button on the CREATE button. A drop down menu appears; select FORM LETTERS...

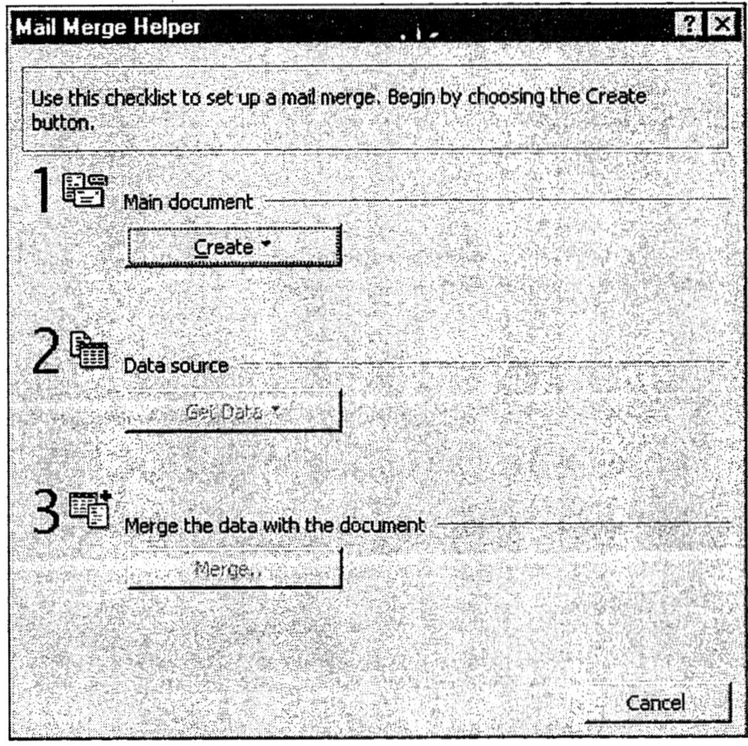

Figure 4.1: Mail Merger Helper dialog box

5. You must tell Word whether you are going to use the active document (the one you created and have open) or if you want to create a totally new document to use for your MAIN document. Click on the ACTIVE WINDOW window button to select your currently active document.

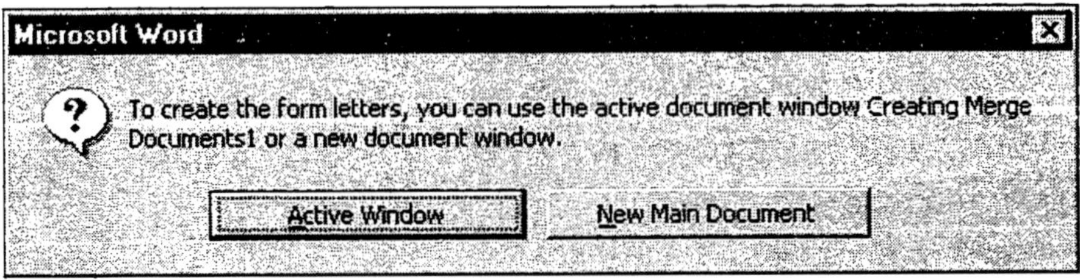

Figure 4.2: Message Box confirming to use a New Main Document or an Active Window

6. Word returns you to the MAIL MERGE HELPER. The next step is select your DATA SOURCE.

7. In section "2: Data Source", click and hold down the mouse button on GET DATA. A drops down menu appears; select CREATE DATA SOURCE...

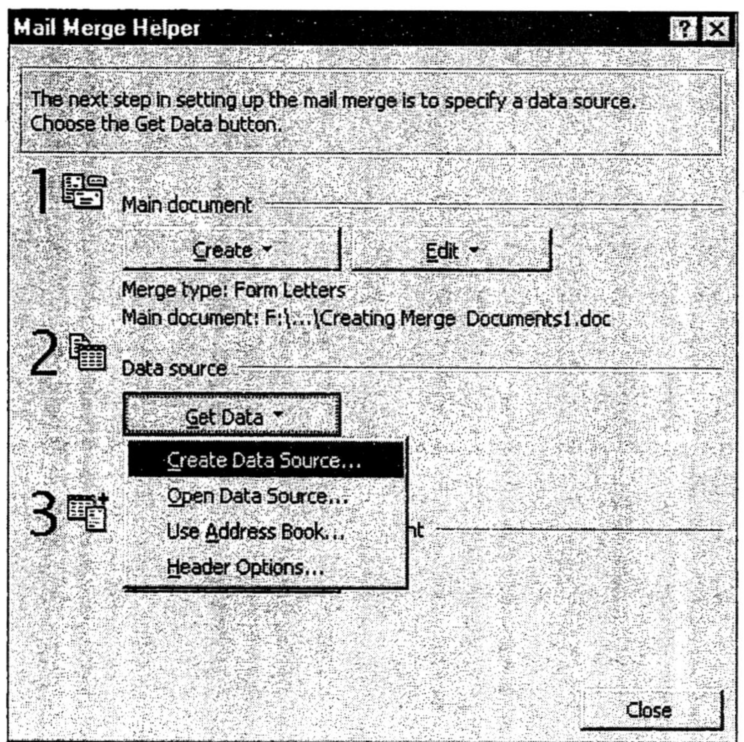

Figure 4.3: Mail Merge Helper dialog box

- In the CREATE DATA SOURCE window, you define the FIELDS that you will use for the merge process.

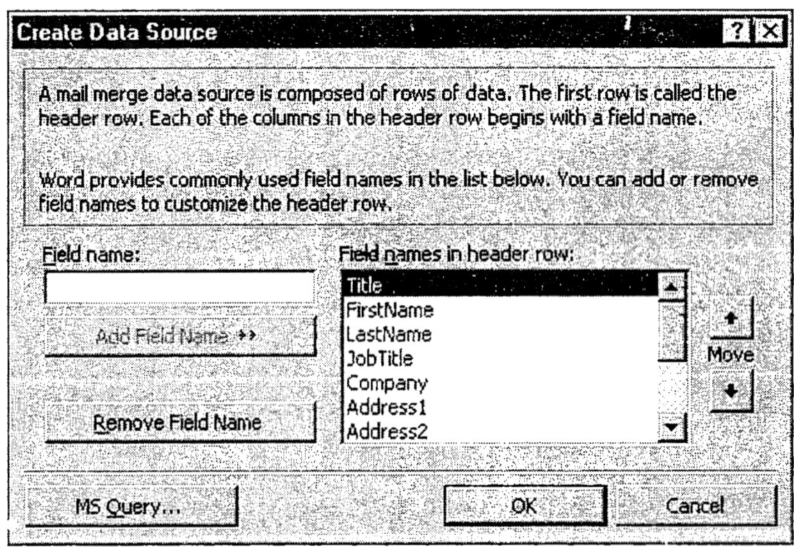

Figure 4.4: Create Data Source dialog box

- Word give you a predefined list of commonly used FIELD NAMES. These appear as options for you to use in your Form Letter.
- Scroll through the list on the right to see all the FIELD NAMES.
- If these are suitable to you and none need to be added or removed, click OK
- If these are not suitable, you can add or subtract FIELD NAMES.
    - To add a FIELD NAME, type in your desired FIELD NAME in the text box on the left and click once on the ADD FIELD NAME button underneath the text box.
    - To delete a FIELD NAME, select it from the list and press the REMOVE FIELD NAME button.
- Click on the OK button when you are finished adding or removing FIELD NAMES.

8. Word prompts you to save the DATA SOURCE document. Name it something appropriate like "Prize Winner Data Source" and click SAVE

9. A window pops up asking you to add data records to your newly created and saved DATA SOURCE document. Click on the EDIT DATA SOURCE button.

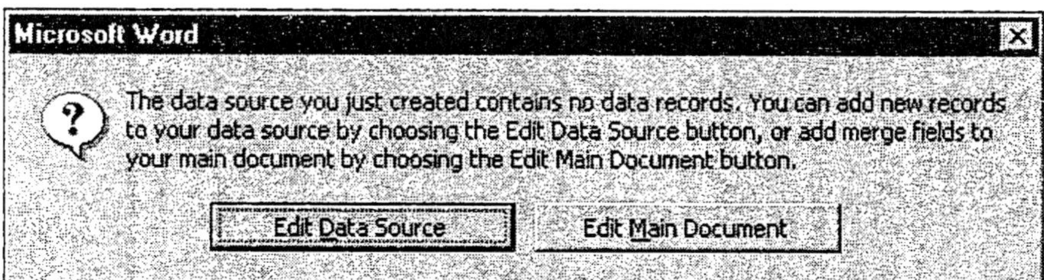

Figure 4.5: Message box confirming to Edit Data Source or Edit Main Document

10. The DATA FORM window appears. Here is where you enter the data for your records. The FIELD NAMES are listed on the left; the edit boxes for you to fill in information are in the middle.

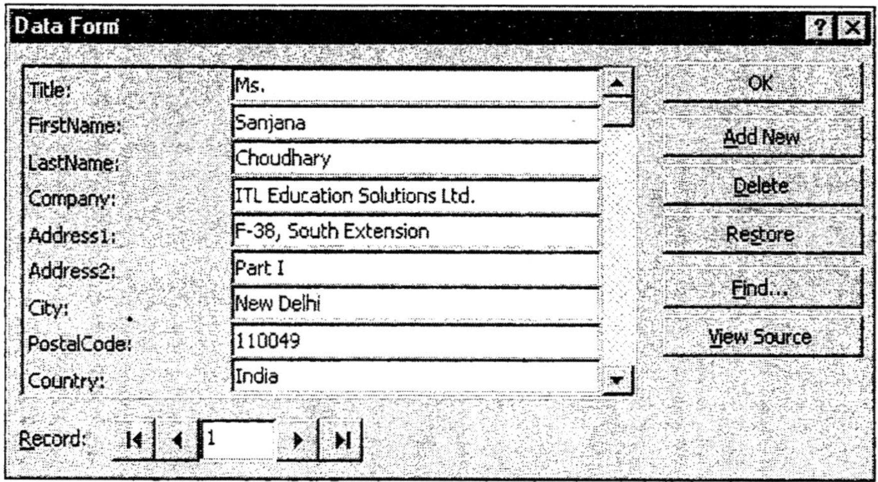

Figure 4.6: Data Form dialog box

- Type the information for your first record into the corresponding boxes. Use the TAB key to move between fields.

- When you are finished with the FIRST record, click the ADD NEW button on the right. The fields will reset and you can enter the information for the second record.

☞ *Notes:*

If you want to delete a record (or if you hit ADD NEW too many times and want to delete it) simply press the DELETE button on the right. The DELETE key removes the last record in the DATA FORM window and takes you to the new last record.

The RESTORE button restores the contents of the last deleted field.

The FIND button allows you to search the DATA FORM by FIELD NAME.

The VIEW SOURCE button shows you the specifically defined TABLE that Word uses in the Mail Merge process. NOTE: this exits you from the DATA FORM window -- only click this if you know what you are doing.

- Continue entering records and clicking ADD NEW until you are finished entering your last record.
- When you are finished adding records, click once on the OK button.

11. Word takes you back to the blank document you created back in step 1. Edit this document and create your MAIN document (the "form letter").

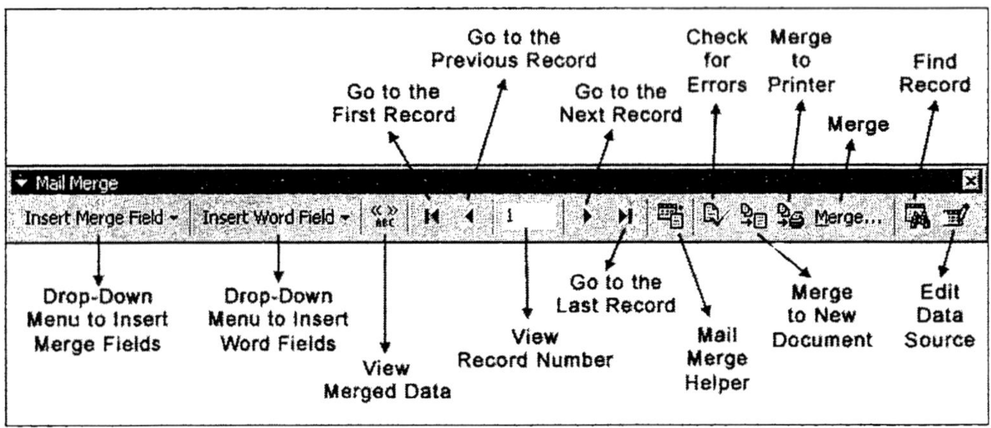

Figure 4.7: Mail Merge Toolbar

- Notice there is now another Toolbar above your window, called the MAIL MERGE TOOLBAR.
- Click on the INSERT MERGE FIELD button in the MAIL MERGE TOOLBAR. A menu drops down, revealing all your FIELD NAMES. Use these FIELD NAMES in your "form letter" as placeholders for people's names, addresses, departments, etc.

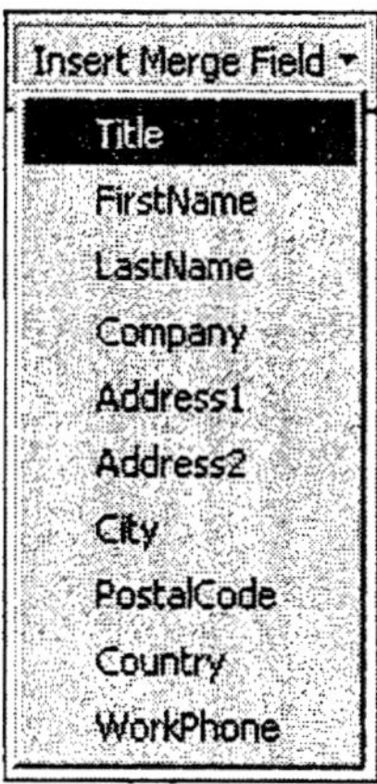

Figure 4.8: Insert Merge Field pop up displays a list of fields you have entered in your Data Source

- To insert a FIELD NAME, position your cursor on your document where you want the placeholder to appear, click on INSERT MAIL MERGE and select the FIELD NAME you want; it appears surrounded by << and >> on your document.

- Type the rest of your form letter as you would like it to appear, taking care to replace any unique names or words with your FIELD NAME placeholders

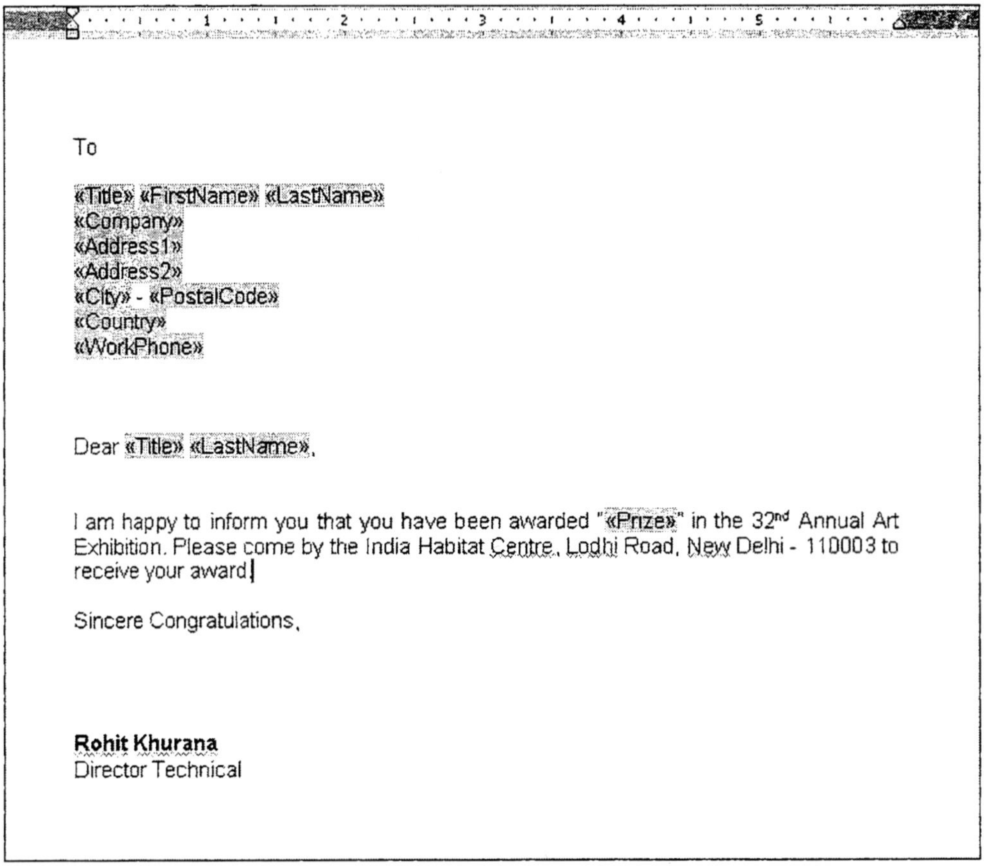

To

«Title» «FirstName» «LastName»
«Company»
«Address1»
«Address2»
«City» - «PostalCode»
«Country»
«WorkPhone»

Dear «Title» «LastName»,

I am happy to inform you that you have been awarded "«Prize»" in the 32nd Annual Art Exhibition. Please come by the India Habitat Centre, Lodhi Road, New Delhi - 110003 to receive your award.

Sincere Congratulations,

Rohit Khurana
Director Technical

Figure 4.9: The final letter with merge fields

12. Now you are ready to create the MAIL MERGE.

    - Go to the TOOLS menu and select MAIL MERGE...
    - The MAIL MERGE HELPER window appears, now with section "3: Merge the data with the document" available.
    - Click on the MERGE button.

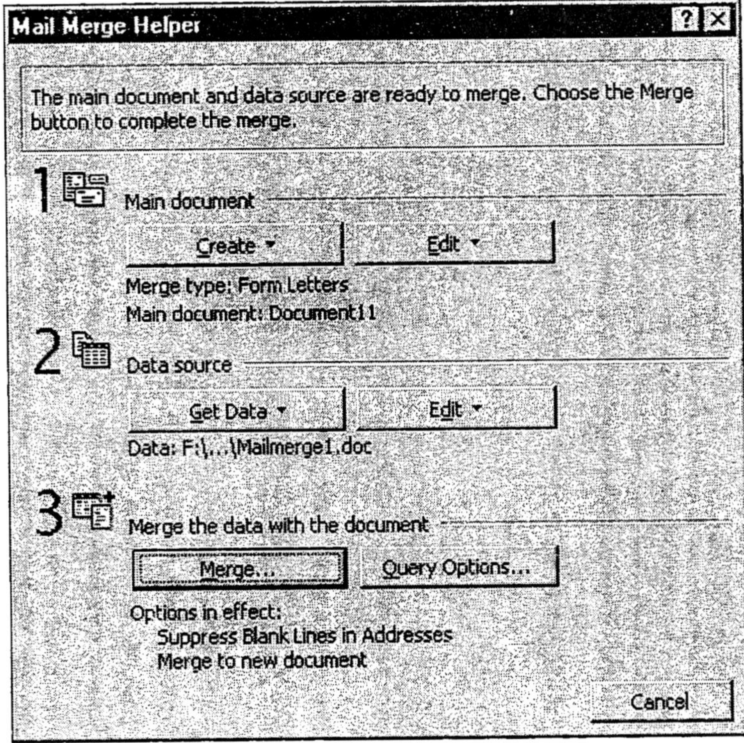

Figure 4.10: Mail Merge Helper dialog box

♦ The "Merge" window presents a few options:

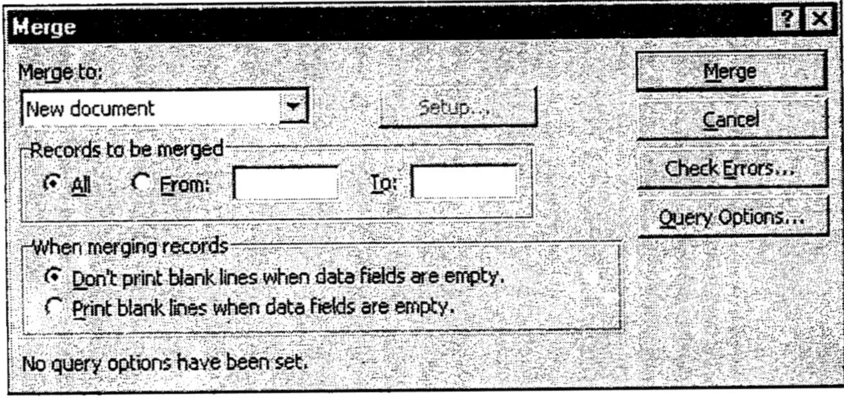

Figure 4.11: Merge dialog box

- MERGE TO:
  - "New document" - allows you to print it later, do future editing and/or save it for future use
  - "Printer" - sends the completed merge immediately to the printer
- RECORDS TO BE MERGED:
  - "All" - merges every record in your DATA SOURCE
  - "From: / To: " - allows you to specify a range of DATA SOURCE records to merge
- WHEN MERGING RECORDS: Option to print blank fields or not
- CHECK ERRORS button - either simulates or completes the merge, checking for syntax and incomplete Field Names
- QUERY OPTIONS button - allows you to filter certain fields and sort records by ascending or descending order.

- Select NEW DOCUMENT as what to merge to
- Click on the MERGE button

13. A new document is created, the MAIL MERGE. It contains one page for every record recorded in the DATA SOURCE as shown in figure 4.12.. It has also replaced the FIELD NAME placeholders with the specific records you entered in, along with the general text from your MAIN document.
14. Save the MAIL MERGE document, naming it something like "Prize Winner Merge", and close the window.
15. Notice that your MAIN document is still present and intact with the FIELD NAME placeholders.
16. Save the MAIN document, naming it something like "Prize Winner Form Letter." Close the window.
17. If Word tells you that a data source is still linked to this document and is still not saved, click YES to save it.

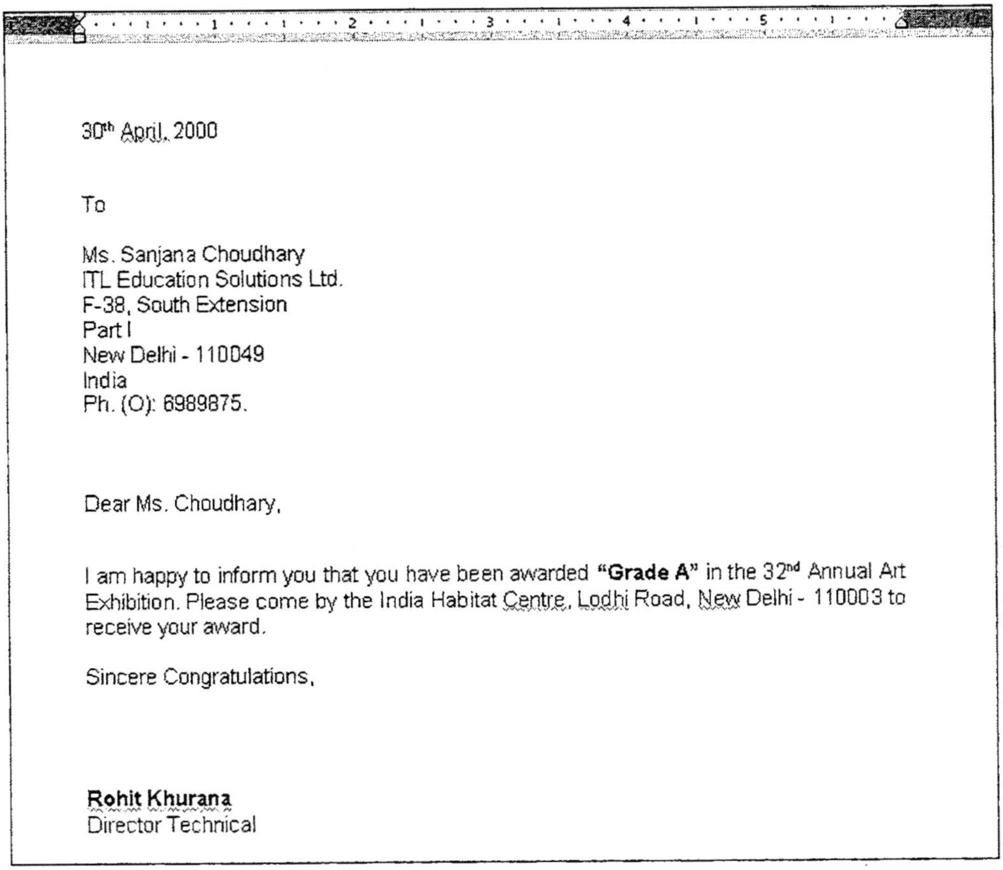

30th April, 2000

To

Ms. Sanjana Choudhary
ITL Education Solutions Ltd.
F-38, South Extension
Part I
New Delhi - 110049
India
Ph. (O): 6989875.

Dear Ms. Choudhary,

I am happy to inform you that you have been awarded **"Grade A"** in the 32nd Annual Art Exhibition. Please come by the India Habitat Centre, Lodhi Road, New Delhi - 110003 to receive your award.

Sincere Congratulations,

Rohit Khurana
Director Technical

Figure 4.12: The final document with merge fields replaced with data in data source

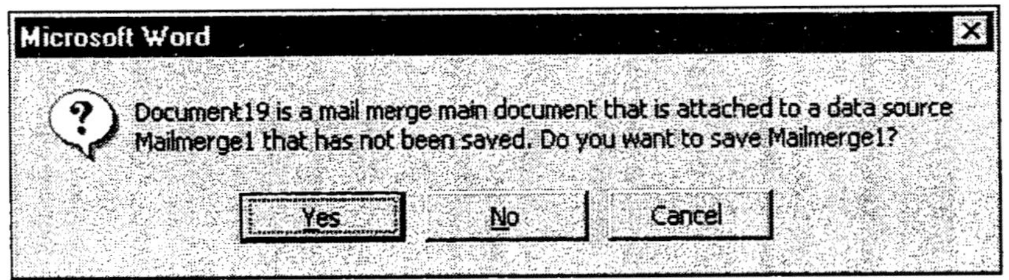

Figure 4.13: The message box prompting to save the final document

Test Your Knowledge

Students must solve the following assignment.

Multiple Choice Questions:

1. Which of the following is NOT a type of document that you can create using mail merge?

    a. Form letters
    b. Envelopes
    c. Web pages
    d. Catalogs

2. When you perform a mail merge, you can directly send the results to: (Select all that apply.)

    a. A Microsoft Excel spreadsheet.
    b. A Microsoft Access database.
    c. A new document
    d. A printer

3. Instead of confusing Merge Fields you want to see the actual records that will appear in the main document. How can you do this?

    a. You can't
    b. Select Tools > Mail Merge from the menu and click View Records.
    c. Select Tools > Mail Merge > View Records from the menu.
    d. Click the View Merged Data button on the Mail Merge toolbar.

4. Which of the following files can you use for the data source for a mail merge? (Select all that apply).

    a. A Microsoft Word document.
    b. A comma delimited text file.
    c. A Microsoft Access database.
    d. A Microsoft Excel spreadsheet.

5. To perform a mail merge you need to either create or open these two files:

    a. A mail merge form and a merge document.
    b. A data source and a merge field source.
    c. A main document and a merge document.
    d. A main document and a data source.

6. You can open the Mail Merge Helper dialog box by: (Select all that apply)

   a. Selecting Table > Mail Merge Helper from the menu.
   b. Clicking the Mail Merge Helper button on the Standard toolbar
   c. Clicking the Mail Merge Helper button on the Mail Merge toolbar.
   d. Selecting Tools > Mail Merge from the menu.

7. What file contains the information, or records, to be inserted in a mail merge?

   a. The data field
   b. The data source
   c. The merge document
   d. The main document

8. Word saves the records for a data source file in:

   a. A tab delimited text format
   b. A rich text file format
   c. A table
   d. A comma delimited text format

9. You want to add several more addresses to a data source. You can do this by: (Select all that apply).

   a. Click the Add Record button on the Mail Merge toolbar.
   b. Select Tools > Mail Merge from the menu and click Edit Data Source.
   c. Select Tools > Mail Merge > Add Records from the menu.
   d. Open the data source document and add the record.

State whether True or False:

1. It is not possible to merge print letter only for a specific record in a word processor.

   a. True
   b. Fase

2. Data source file is also known as form letters.

   a. True
   b. Fase

3. The document containing the common text for all the letters is known as the main document.

   a. True
   b. Fase

4. Merging two documents into single one is called Mail Merge.

   a. True
   b. Fase

5. You can specify which records you want to include in a mail merge by clicking the Query Options button in the Mail Merge Helper dialog box.

   a. True
   b. False

6. You can convert an existing document to a Main Document for mail merge.

   a. True
   b. False

Advanced Formatting

Objectives

- Introduction to Styles
- Templates
- Import Graphics & Create Drawing Objects
- Frames
- Working with Tables
- Master Document and Subdocuments
- Macros
- Shortcut Keys

Introduction to Styles

Styles make formatting your document easier. Styles define the appearance of various text of your document, such as headings, captions and body text. When you want to change the formatting of all the text of a particular document at one go, you just have to change the style that is applied. When you use styles, you can change all text formatted with the style just by redefining the style. If your main headings are 14 point Arial, flush left and bold and you later decide you want your headings to be 16 point Arial and centered, you don't have to reformat every instance of the heading. Just change the properties of that style.

Word creates styles automatically as you type, when the Define styles based on your formatting check box is selected. Word detects the type of formatting and the placement of text and applies styles associated with that formatting.

You can create your own styles. You can turn off automatic style definition if you want. You can also choose a style update automatically. When Word automatically updates the style, all text formatted with that style changes to match the formatting of the text you just changed.

Styles also serve as the basis for outlines and tables of contents. When you click the Table of Contents command on the Insert menu Word automatically creates a table of contents based on your headings and subheading.

Why Use Styles?

Styles make working with Word a lot easier. Once you have mastered them you can....

- Format your documents quickly and consistently
- Change the formatting in your documents quickly and consistently
- Use the styles you create in other documents and templates
- Create a Table of Contents
- Use Outline View to work with long documents

Create New Styles

The quickest way to create a new paragraph style is to format a paragraph, select it and then base the new style on the formatting and other properties applied to the selected text.

1. Apply the formatting to the paragraph until it appears the way you want.

2. Click the **Style** text box on the formatting toolbar to highlight the name of the current style.

3. Type the name of your **new style** and then press **Enter**.

Apply a different Style

1. To apply a different paragraph style, click the paragraph or select a group of paragraphs you want to change. Select the text you want to change and apply the character attributes such as bold or italic of a paragraph style.

2. On the **Format** menu, click **Style**.

3. In the **Styles** box, click the style you want to apply, and then click **Apply**. If the style you want is not listed, select another group of styles in the List box.

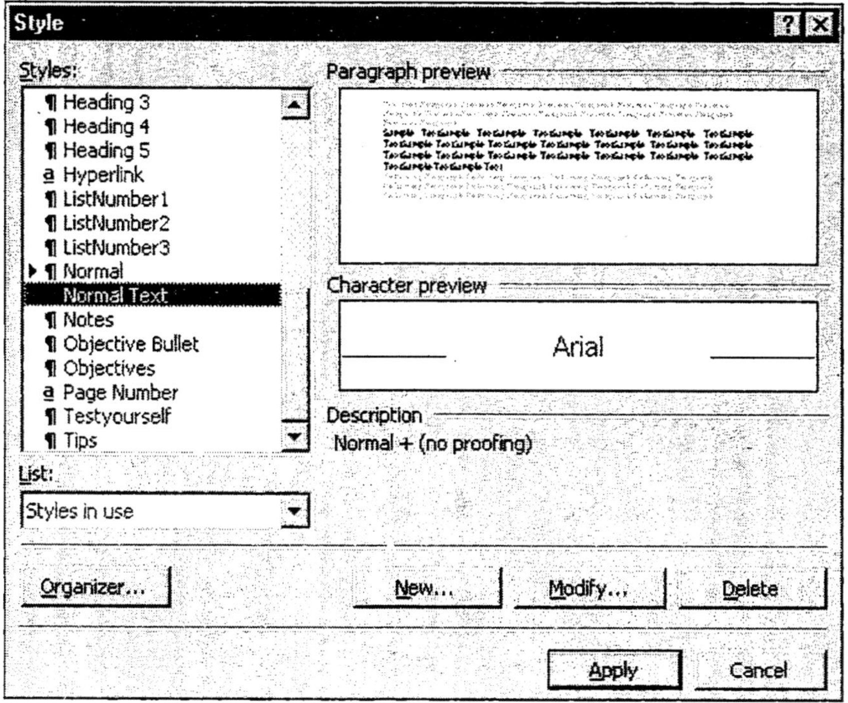

Figure 5.1: Style dialog box

☞ *Note: In the Styles box, a paragraph mark (¶) appears beside paragraph style names, and the letter "a" appears beside character style names.*

Modify a Style

1. On the **Format** menu, click **Style**.
2. In the **Styles** box, select the style you want to modify, and then click **Modify**.
3. Click **Format**, and then select the **Font or Numbering** you want to change.
4. Click **OK** after you have changed each attribute, and then repeat for any additional attributes you want to change.

☞ *Notes: To use the modified style in new documents based on the same template, select the Add to template check box. Word adds the modified style to the template that is attached to the active document. If you delete a paragraph style that you created, Word applies the Normal style to all paragraphs formatted with that style and then removes the style definition from the template. Once you apply a built-in Heading style to a paragraph in your document, you cannot remove it from the Styles list. The Normal style is always present in the Styles list, and you cannot delete it.*

Rename Styles, AutoText Entries, Macros & Toolbars

1. On the Tools menu, click Templates and Add-Ins.

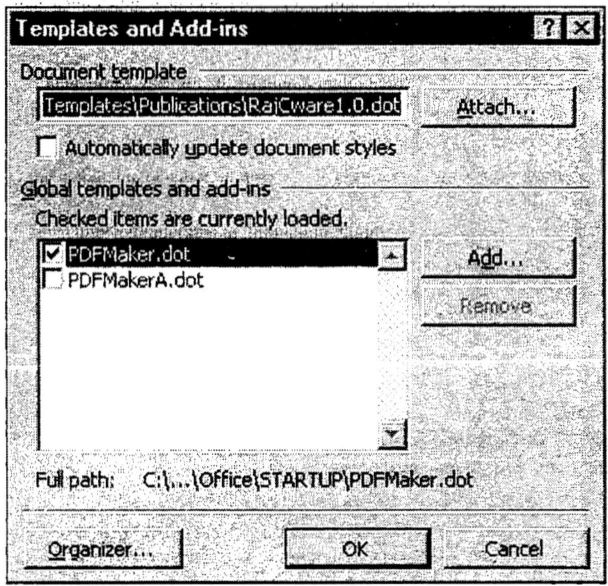

Figure 5.2: Templates and Add-Ins dialog box

2. Click **Organizer**.
3. Click the **Styles, AutoText, Toolbars or Macro Project Items** tab.
4. In the **In-box** on the left, click the entry you want to rename, and then click **Rename**.
5. In the **Rename** dialog box, type a **new** name for the entry.
6. Click **OK**, and then click **Close**.

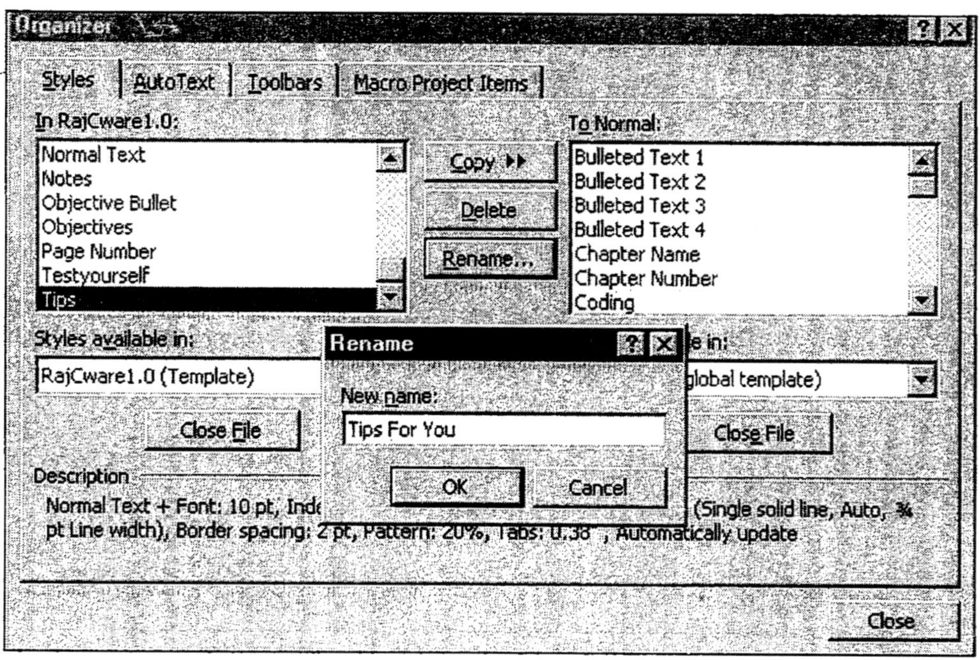

Figure 5.3: Organizer and Rename dialog box

Turn-off Automatic Style Definition

1. On the **Tools** menu, click **AutoCorrect → AutoFormat As You Type** tab.

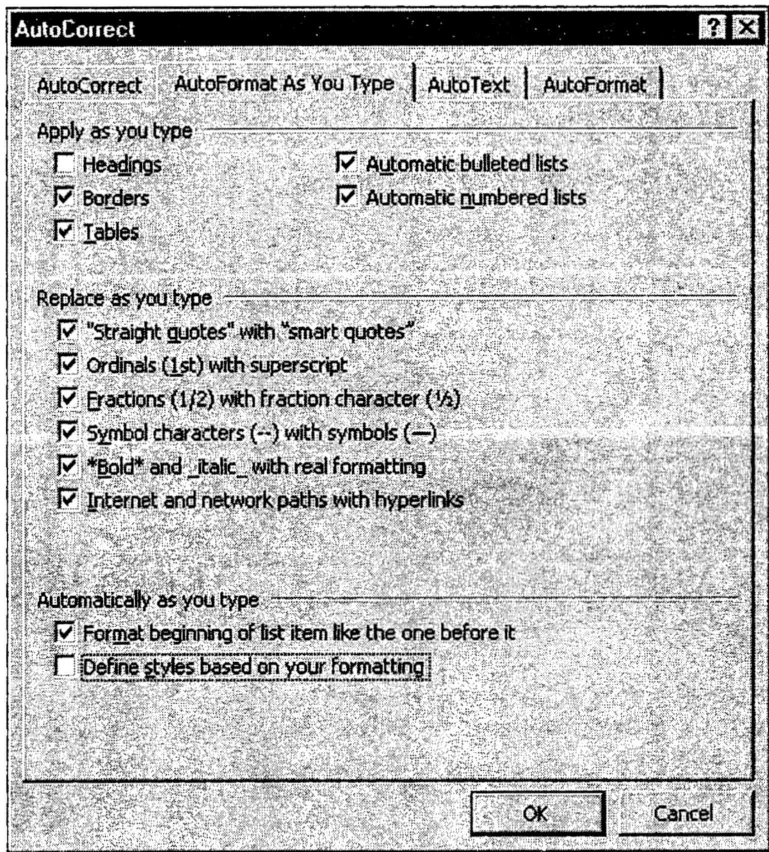

Figure 5.4: AutoCorrect dialog box

2. In **Automatically as you type**, clear the checkbox **Define styles based on your fomatting** to turn-off Automatic Style Definition.

View or Copy Styles from another template

1. On the **Format** menu, click **Style Gallery**.

2. In the **Template** box, select the **Template** whose styles you want to use.

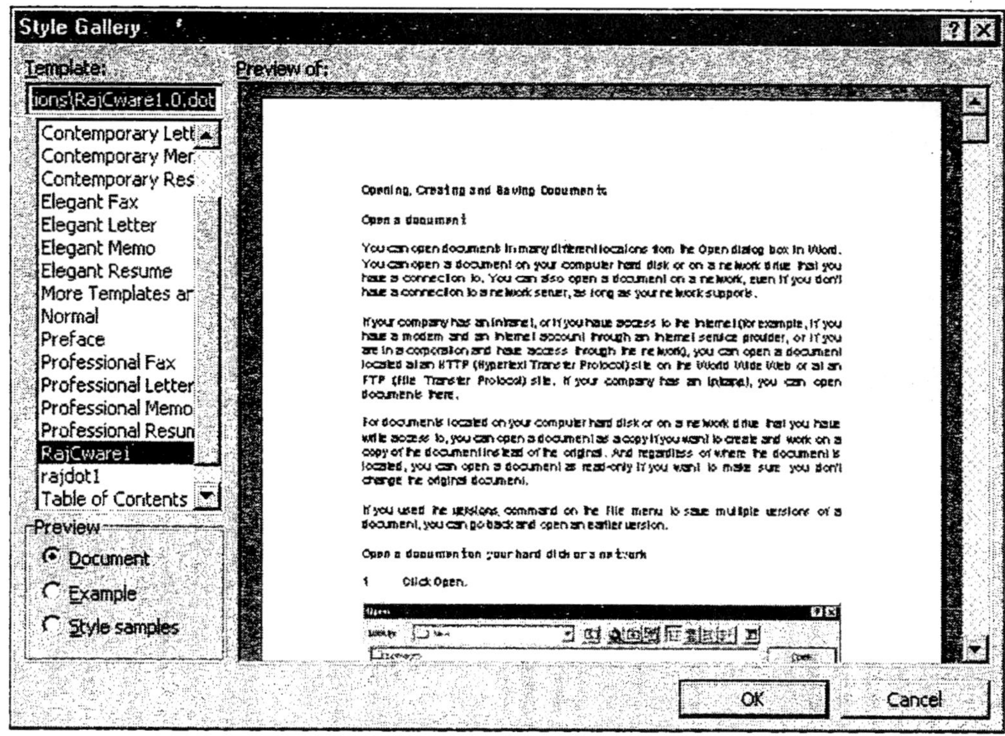

Figure 5.5: Style Gallery dialog box

3. Styles from the template you select are copied to your document.

Using AutoFormat while formatting

The AutoFormat feature in Word is used to produce an attractive, easy-to-read document while you concentrate on the content. Word analyzes each paragraph to see how it is used in the document.

AutoFormat works in these ways:

- Word automatically formats headings, bulleted lists, numbered lists, borders, symbols as you are typing your document.
- You can automatically format selected text or the entire document, such as a fax message, in one pass with the **AutoFormat** command.
- Word automatically formats headings and lists in your plain text when you open them. You can easily distinguish the current message from the previous messages.

AutoComplete command

To use **AutoComplete**, type the first few characters in an item for example, type *janu* for the current month. When Word suggests the entire item such as *"January"* press ENTER. If you then type an additional space, Word suggests the current date, such as *"January 10, 2001"*. To reject the item, just keep typing.

You can automatically complete the following items:

- The current date
- A day of the week
- A month
- Your name
- AutoText entries

Templates

A template allows you to store the layout and formatting for an entire document, along with styles, custom toolbars, macros, shortcut keys and AutoText entries. An easy way to create a template is by opening a document that contains the items you want to re-use and saving it as a template.

What are Templates?

All documents are based on a template. Every time you create a new document you are actually using a template that decides the basic format of that document, for example...

- The size of the margins
- Which font you will use
- What headers and footers you will have
- Which toolbars you will see

- Which AutoText's you have access to
- Whether any text appears before you have started typing (e.g. the headings in a fax or memo)

The template that you are probably used to using is the **normal template**. Whenever you click on the new document icon, Word brings you a copy of the normal template to start typing on. That's why the margins and the fonts, and the toolbars are already set for you.

There are other templates which come with Word for creating letters, memos and faxes etc. You can also create your own for work or personal use.

The difference between Templates and Documents

- **Templates are standard:** They contain all the things that don't change. For example, a template for a memo will usually contain headings such as "From" and "To" and they will be formatted correctly. Templates end in the extension ***.dot***

- **Documents are based on templates:** Whenever you create a new document it is based on a template. Word brings you a copy of the template to start typing on. Documents end in the extension ***.doc***

Create a New Template

If you save a template in the Templates folder, the template will appear on the General tab when you click New on the File menu. You can edit a template directory, if you save a template in a subfolder of the Templates folder, such as Publications or Reports or Memos, the template will appear on the corresponding tab when you click the New command.

Follow these steps to create a new template:

1. Choose **File → New** to display the **New** dialog box.

2. To create a template from scratch, select the **Blank Document icon** on the **General tab**. To create a template based on any other template, click on the tab of the category that contains the template, and then highlight its icon on the displayed tab.

3. Choose either of the following options and then click **OK**.

   Document: Opens a new document based on the selected template.
   Template: Opens the selected template.

4. Fill in any information that would be repeated, and enter any necessary text in the document or template.

5. Choose **File → Save As** to display the **Save As** dialog box.

6. In the **Save As** drop-down dialog box, choose **Document Template** (*.dot). The Templates folder is automatically selected as the storage location for the file in the **Save-In** drop-down list.

7. Choose one of the following options to specify where to store the template file:

   - Leave Templates as the location in the Save In drop-down list to have the new template appear on the General tab in the New dialog box.
   - To have the template file appear on a category page other than General in the New dialog box, highlight the name of the folder in that category.
   - Create a new folder in the Templates folder in which to store the file. Each subfolder in the Templates folder appears as a category tab in the New dialog box.

8. If necessary, type a different name for the new template in the File Name text box.

9. Choose **Save** to save the new template file.

☞ *Notes: To make AutoText entries and macros available only to documents based on this template, store them in this template, not in the Normal template.*

Modify a Template

1. On the **File** menu, click **Open**, and then open the template you want to modify.

   If there is no templates listed in the **Open** dialog box, click **Document Templates** (*.dot) in the **Files** of type box.

2. Change any of the template's text, graphics, styles, formatting, macros, AutoText entries, toolbars, menu settings or shortcut keys.

3. Click **Save**.

Copy Styles, AutoText Entries, Toolbars or Macros

If you create any styles, AutoText entries, custom toolbars, or macros in a document or template, you can use Organizer to copy them to another template to be used in any document to which that template is applied. You can also rename a style, or even delete a style from a template, including the Blank document based on the Normal template.

1. On the **Tools** menu, click **Templates and Add-Ins.**

2. Click **Organizer**, and then click the tab for the items you want to copy.

3. On the left is a list box displaying the styles in the current document; on the right is a list of styles in the Normal template. Highlight the style you want to save in the template, and then click the Copy button. The new style will appear in the right-hand list.

4. Choose **Close** when you have made all the necessary changes.

Add colors, texture or illustrations to Background

You can add different kinds of backgrounds, such as a texture, to Word documents and Web pages to make them look more interesting and attractive.

- You can add colors and textures to Word documents.
- You can use pictures as backgrounds in Word documents.
- You can create a watermark that appears only on the printed pages of a document.

Using Graphics

In Word there are two types of graphics available. These are drawing objects, which you can create yourself, and pictures, which have been created outside of Word. Drawing Objects could be things such as different shapes, lines or WordArt. You can create things using the drawing toolbar.

There are a number of pictures available in ClipArt that you can add to your document. You can also insert pictures from file, for example, a picture that you have scanned in.

Why Use Graphics?

Graphics can add interest to your document. You may want to use drawings to create diagrams or insert pictures to illustrate your words.

Use a picture as a background

Word displays backgrounds that you add with the Background command on the Format menu in online layout view only.

1. On the **Format** menu, click **Background → Fill Effects → Picture** tab.

2. Click Select picture, switch to the folder that contains the picture you want to use, select a picture, and then click **OK.**

Create a Watermark

To print a watermark, you must insert it into a header or footer. The watermark is printed wherever you place it on the page, it doesn't have to be confined to the area at the top or bottom of the page.

1. On the **View** menu, click **Header and Footer**.

2. On the Header and Footer toolbar, click Show/Hide Document Text to hide the text and graphics in the main document.

3. Insert a graphic (a drawing object) such as an AutoShape, clip art, WordArt, pictures, and imported art that appears on every page.

   To insert text, such as "Sample," click Text Box on the Insert menu, and then type the text 'Sample' you want to appear on every page. You can size the text box by dragging the sizing handles.

4. To format the graphic, select it, and then click **Picture** or **Object** (Format menu). On the Picture tab, under Image control, select Watermark from the Color box to format the picture with preset brightness and contrast settings that work well for watermarks, or adjust the picture's brightness and contrast manually using the Brightness and Contrast slide controls. To format the graphic so that document text flows above it instead of wrapping around it, click **Picture or Object → Wrapping** click **None**.

   To format the text in the text box, select it, click Font on the Format menu, and then select the options you want. To rotate the text, click Text Direction on the Format menu, and then select the option you want. Because the text box is a drawing object, you can use options on the Drawing toolbar to format its borders, background color, and so on.

5. On the **Header and Footer** toolbar, click **Close**.

Import Graphics & Create Drawing Objects

Pictures or graphics adds visual interest to a document. Graphics can illustrate a concept, serve as a corporate logo, or simply make your document look better. Graphics can consist of charts, line art, text, clip art, or photos. You can either use existing images stored in a file or create your own graphic objects.

Word has its own set of pictures in the Clip Art Gallery. The Clip Gallery includes a wide variety of clip arts that makes it easy for you to make your documents look attractive with professionally designed images. You can also insert pictures and scanned photographs from other programs and locations. To insert a picture from another program, click **Insert → Picture → From File**. When you select a picture, the Picture toolbar appears with options you can use to crop the picture, add a border to it, and adjust its brightness and contrast.

You can create special text effects by using the new WordArt button on the Drawing toolbar and you can use additional features, such as 3-D effects and textured fills. Word recognizes a wide variety of picture formats. Because all Office programs share the same graphics filters, if you installed a graphics filter when you installed another Office program PowerPoint or Microsoft Excel, for example you can use that same filter in Word.

☞ *Notes: By default, Word inserts imported pictures as floating pictures. Pictures that are inserted in the drawing layer so you can position them precisely on the page or in front of or behind text or other objects. To change a floating picture to an inline picture that is positioned directly in the text at the insertion point, select the picture and then click Picture on the Format menu. On the Position tab, clear the Float over text check box.*

Create Transparent areas in a Picture

You can use transparent areas to integrate a picture on your page. When you have a picture of a person and don't want the background color to be visible.

1. Select the picture you want to create transparent areas in.
2. On the **Picture** toolbar, click **Set Transparent Color**.
3. Click the color you want to make transparent and click **OK**.

Add or Edit a Special Text Effect

You can add a special effect to text by using the **WordArt** button on the **Drawing** toolbar. You can create shadowed, skewed, rotated and stretched text, as well as text that has been fitted to predefined shapes. A special text effect is a drawing object, you can also use buttons on the Drawing toolbar to change the effect i.e., to fill a text effect with a picture.

What is WordArt?

WordArt is one of the drawing tools available in Word 2000. You can use WordArt to add text in a variety of styles, colours and formats.

To create WordArt:

1. Place the insertion point where you want the graphic, and click on the Insert WordArt button on the Drawing toolbar to open the WordArt Gallery dialog box as shown in figure 56.

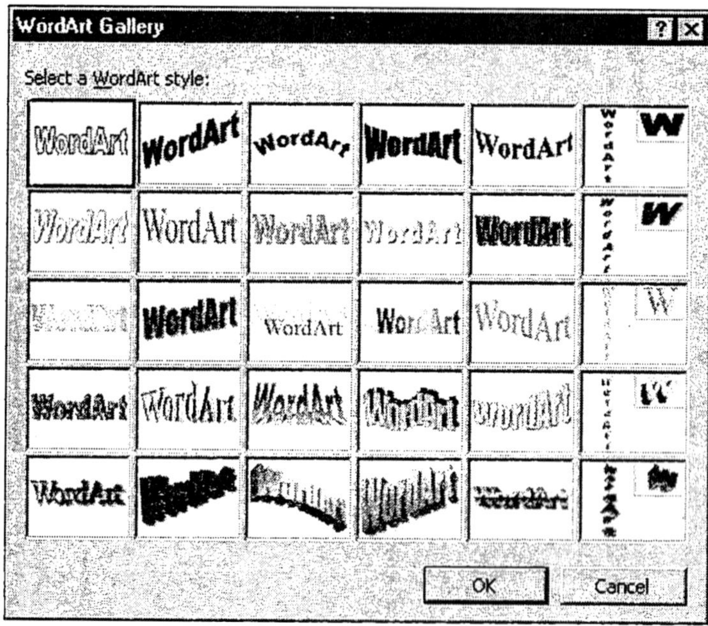

Figure 5.6: WordArt Gallery dialog box

2. Click on the style in which you want your text graphic to appear in the **Select a WordArt Style** area.

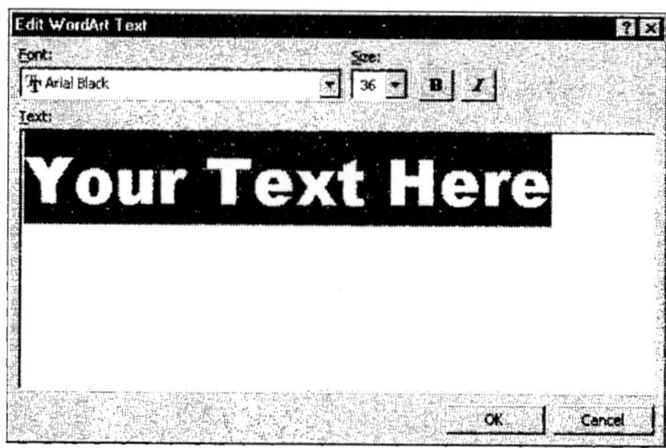

Figure 5.7: Edit WordArt Text dialog box

3. Choose **OK** to display the **Edit WordArt Text** dialog box.

4. Type the text in the **Text** area of the dialog box.

5. If required, apply the following formatting to the text in the Text area:

   - Select a different font in the Font drop-down list.
   - Select a different font size in the Size drop-down list.
   - Click on Bold and/or Italics button to apply that formatting.

6. Choose **OK** to place the WordArt object in your document.

Add Illustrations from the ClipArt Gallery

ClipArt are the pictures that come with Word. There are lots for you to choose from on a number of different themes in the ClipArt Gallery. You can insert them in your document, move and resize them and change the way that text wraps around them.

The steps are as following:

1. Position the insertion point where you want to insert the clip.

2. Click on the **Insert Clip Art** button on the **Drawing** toolbar, or choose **Insert → Picture → Clip Art** to display the **Insert ClipArt** dialog box.

3. Click on the Pictures, Sounds, or Motion Clips tab to display the categories of files available for that type of clip.

4. Scroll through the list to find the category and select the category that contains the clip you want.

5. Click on the **thumbnail** of the clip you want, and then click on the **Insert Clip** button on the clip's toolbar that appears.

6. Click on the **Insert ClipArt** dialog box. **Close** button to return to your document.

Add illustrations to the Clip Art Gallery

1. From the **Insert** menu, click **Picture → Clip Art**.

2. On the **Clip Art** tab, click **Import Clips**.

3. Find the folder that contains the image you want to add.

4. Select the image, and then click **Open**.

5. Select the categories or create a new category or add any keywords you want to store the image in, and then click **OK**.

Arrange Text and Graphics on a Page

To move drawing objects including text boxes, AutoShapes, clip art, WordArt, pictures, and imported art in most cases, you simply drag them to where you want them. However, you can also place drawing objects in a precise position, and you can "attach," or anchor, an object to a paragraph so that if you move the paragraph, the object automatically moves with it.

You can wrap text around a picture of any size and shape. You can specify particular sides of the text box or graphic you want the text to wrap to and the distance between the text box and the text that surrounds it.

You can layer text and graphics. For example, you can create a watermark that appears on the printed pages of a document.

You can align drawing objects with other drawing objects, or you can align them in relation to the entire page for example, at the top or left edge of a page. You can also arrange or distribute drawing objects so they are equidistant from each other either vertically or horizontally, or in relation to the entire page.

You can move a drawing object, a multiple selection, or a group. To move a drawing object or a set of drawing objects in small increments, you can "nudge" it.

Group, Ungroup and Re-group Drawing Objects

When you group objects, you combine them so you can work with them as they were a single object. You can flip, rotate, and resize or scale all objects in a group as a single unit. You can also change the attributes of all objects in a group at one time for example, you might change the fill color or add a shadow to all objects in the group. You can also create groups within groups to help you build complex drawings.

When your drawing is complete, you can group all the drawing objects so that they are treated as a single object. When you select any one object in the group all are selected when objects are grouped. Any formatting you apply is applied to every object in the group. To combine several objects into a group hold down the Shift key while you click on each object to select it and in the drawing toolbar choose group.

You can ungroup a group of objects at any time, and as long as the document is still active you can easily regroup them by selecting any one of the objects that was previously grouped.

Align and Arrange Drawing Objects

There are several ways to align drawing objects. You can align them with other drawing objects, such as when you align the sides, middles, or top or bottom edges of objects. You can also align objects by using the grid to align them with a corner on the grid as you draw or move the objects. You can arrange or distribute drawing objects so they are equal distances from each other either vertically or horizontally or in relation to the entire page.

Rotate or Flip a Drawing Object

You can rotate a drawing object 90 degrees to the left or right or to any other angle. You can also flip an object horizontally or vertically. You can flip or rotate one object, a set of objects, or a group of objects.

Some pictures and charts that you import can't be rotated or flipped because they weren't created in Word. If you can ungroup an imported object and then regroup its components, you might be able to flip or rotate it. Bitmaps images cannot be rotated or flipped.

Label a Graphic or Insert Text in a Shape

You can add text to your pictures or shapes in several ways:

- You can add a caption, such as *"Diagram 1"* to an item and have Word automatically add similar captions, numbered sequentially, when you insert other pictures or illustrations in your document. The Caption command on the Insert menu is the best tool for creating captions.

- You can use a text box to label a graphic. If you want the label to include a leader, use an AutoShape callout.

- You can also insert text in an AutoShape with the exception of lines and freeforms from the drawing toolbar.

Add a Callout or Label

To add a label to an item, use the following procedure. If you want the label to include a leader, see the first note after the procedure.

1. On the Drawing toolbar, click Text Box.

2. To insert a text box with a predefined size, click the document.

   To insert a different size, drag the text box to the size you want. To maintain the text box's width-to-height ratio, hold down SHIFT while you drag.

3. Position the text box by dragging it to the location you want.

Format a Callout Leader

You can change the leaders of line callouts. Leaders from nonline callouts, such as the cloud, cannot be changed.

1. Click the callout whose leader you want to format.

2. On the Format menu, click AutoShape, and then click the Text Box tab.

3. Click Format Callout.

4. Select the options you want.

You can display text in callouts, text boxes, AutoShapes, or table cells vertically instead of horizontally.

1. Click the callout, text box, AutoShape, or table cell.

2. On the Format menu click Text Direction.

3. Click the orientation you want.

Flow Text to another part of a Document

If you want to make text flow in a continuous story from one location in your document to the next, you can place the text in text boxes and then create text box links throughout your document, even if the locations aren't adjacent. Linked text boxes can be used for desktop publishing for example, you can flow an article from page 2 to page 9 in a newsletter.

When you add lines of text to a linked text box, the text flows forward into the next text box. When you delete lines of text from a text box, the text in the next text box moves backward. You can link several text boxes in a story, and you can have multiple stories in a document. The links don't have to occur in a forward direction.

1. On the **Insert** menu, click **Text Box**.
2. Click or drag in your document where you want to insert the first text box.
3. Insert additional text boxes where you want the text to flow.
4. Click the **first text box**.
5. On the **Text Box** toolbar, click **Create Text Box Link.**
6. Click in the **text box** that you want the text to flow to.
7. To **link** to additional text boxes, click the **text box** that you just created the link to, and then repeat steps 5 and 6 to create links.
8. In the first text box, type text that you want. As the text box fills, the text will flow into the other text boxes that you've linked.

Curve and Freeform Drawing Objects

When you want to draw curves with greater control and accuracy, use the Curve tool. To change the basic shape of a curve or freeform by moving, deleting, and adding vertexes, click Edit Points on the Draw menu of the Drawing toolbar.

The AutoShapes menu on the Drawing toolbar includes several categories of tools. With the Lines tool, you can draw the Curve, Scribble and Freeform lines and curves, as well as shapes that combine both lines and curves. With the Scribble tool you can draw objects so that it look like it was drawn with a pen. The resulting shape closely matches what you draw on the screen. Use the Freeform tool when you want a more refined shape. You can enhance freeforms and curves just as other AutoShapes that is you can add color, patterns, or change the line style, flip or rotate them.

Add or Change an AutoShape

Word has a set of ready-made shapes for you to use in your documents. The shapes can be resized, rotated, flipped, colored, and combined with other shapes such as circles and squares to make more complex shapes. The AutoShapes menu on the Drawing toolbar contains several categories of shapes, including lines, basic shapes, flowchart elements, stars and banners.

You can also add text to AutoShapes. Just right-click the shape, click Add Text on the shortcut menu, and then start typing. Text you add becomes part of the shape if you move the shape, the text moves with it. However, if you rotate or flip the shape, the text doesn't rotate or flip with it. You can rotate the text 90 degrees to the left or right by using the Text Direction command on the Format menu.

Word uses the following graphics file types

You can insert many popular graphics file formats into your document either directly or with the use of separate graphics filters. You don't need a separate graphics filter installed to insert Enhanced Metafile *(.emf)*, Joint Photographic Experts Group *(.jpg)*, Portable Network Graphics *(.png)*, Windows Bitmap *(.bmp, .rle, .dib)*, and Windows Metafile *(.wmf)* graphics. However, you need a graphics filter installed to insert all other graphics file formats listed below:

- AutoCAD Format 2-D *(.dxf)* file
- Computer Graphics Metafile *(.cgm)*
- CorelDRAW *(.cdr)* file
- Encapsulated PostScript *(.eps)* file
- Enhanced Metafile *(.emf)*
- Graphics Interchange Format *(.gif)* file
- JPEG File Interchange Format *(.jpg)* file
- Kodak Photo CD *(.pcd)* file
- Macintosh PICT *(.pct)* file
- Micrografx Designer/Draw *(.drw)* file
- PC Paintbrush *(.pcx)* file
- Portable Network Graphics *(.png)* file
- Tagged Image File Format *(.tif)* file
- Targa *(.tga)* file
- Windows Bitmap *(.bmp, .rle, .dib)* file
- Windows Metafile *(.wmf)*
- WordPerfect Graphics *(.wpg)* file

Footnotes and Endnotes

Footnotes and endnotes provide references for text in a document. You can include both footnotes and endnotes in one document. You can use footnotes for detailed comments and endnotes for sources. Footnotes appear at the end of each page in a document. Endnotes typically appear at the end of a document.

A footnote or an endnote consists of two linked parts: the note reference mark and the corresponding note text. When you add, delete or move notes that are automatically numbered, Word renumbers the note reference marks. You can add note text of any length and can format as other text.

Insert a Footnote or an Endnote

1. Click where you want to insert the note reference mark.
2. On the **Insert** menu, click **Footnote or Endnote**.

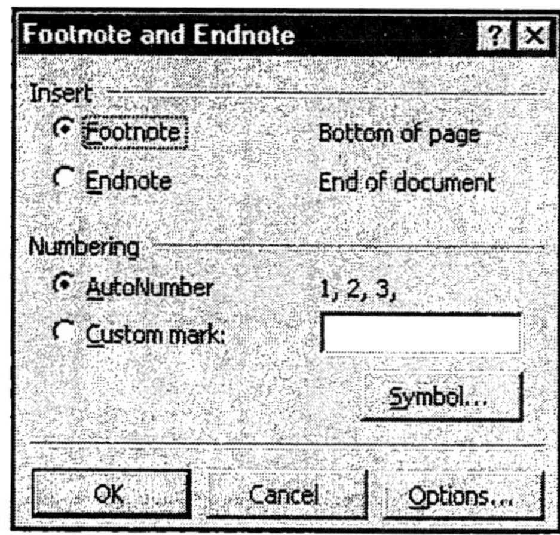

Figure 5.8: Footnote and Endnote dialog box

3. Type the note in the **footnote** pane and then click in the document to continue typing.

Word separates document text from footnotes and endnotes with a short horizontal line called a note separator. If a note overflows onto the next page, Word prints a longer line called a note continuation separator, to which you can add text. You can also customize separators by adding borders, text, or graphics.

Master Documents and Subdocuments

A master document is a "container" for a set of separate files. You can use a master document to set up and manage a multi-part document, such as a book with several chapters. For example, you can view, reorganize, format, proof, print, and create a table of contents for multiple documents.

To create a new master document from scratch, open a new document, and then display it in Outline view. To change to Outline view, choose **View → Outline**. In Word 2000, the Master Document tools appear on the Outlining toolbar. Create an outline just as you normally do, using the same heading level for each section that you want subdivided into its own document.

Click the subdocument button on the Outlining toolbar and Word will create individual subdocuments using the highest level heading text you selected as the subdocument name. The master document will show each subdocument in a box with a small subdocument icon in the upper left corner when displayed in Master Document view. Now click the **Master Document View** button on the **Outlining** toolbar to display the master document in the **Outline** view. When you do, the subdocument icon and box no longer appear, and the display shows the section break marks that Word inserted before each selected heading when you created subdocuments.

When you save the master document, each subdocument is automatically saved in a separate file in the same folder as the master document, using the first part of the heading text as the filename. Each document automatically becomes a **hyperlink** in the master document. When the master document is open, you can simply click the hyperlink of a subdocument to open it for editing.

If a user is currently working on a subdocument, the document is "locked" to other users. This means that they are read-only files which can be viewed, but no changes can be saved to them. When the user closes the subdocument, you can unlock the document and start working on it. If you want to prevent unauthorized users from viewing or working on a master document or subdocument, you can open the document and assign a password or set document protection options.

Steps to create a Master Document

1. Create and save each chapter of a book as an individual document. End each document with a carriage return. Be sure to assign a descriptive name, such as Chapter1.doc, Chapter2.doc, etc. Using sequential names sorts them within the active file folder, making each subdocument file easy to locate.

2. Open a new document after all individual chapter documents have been created and saved.

3. Click **View → Outline** to display the **Outlining and Master Document** toolbars.

4. Click the **Insert Subdocument** button, pick the first document in sequence, and click **OK**.

5. Press **<CTRL+End>** to go to the end of the first document. Backspace so that you delete the section break at the bottom of the inserted document.

6. With the cursor on a new line i.e., at the end of the first section, click **Insert Subdocument** again.

7. Pick the second document to be inserted and click **OK**. The first two subdocuments are inserted.

8. Again delete the last section break and put the cursor on a new line at the bottom of the last section. Then insert the third subdocument as above and similarly insert all the subdocuments until all are included within your master document.

9. Now set the **Layout** tab in the **File → Page Setup** menu. Be sure that every subdocument has been set up so that each of your sections starts on a new page. Also check the Different Odd and Even and Different First Page check box.

10. Click the print preview button on the Standard toolbar to ensure that every subdocument starts on a new page.

Printing Master Documents

When all the text is entered in the subdocuments and all the formatting is applied to the master document along with a table of contents and index, you are ready to print the master document depending on the heading levels and text displayed on your screen.

To print the entire master document, do the following:

1. Click the **Expand Subdocument** on the **Outlining** toolbar to expand the subdocuments.
2. Change the display to **Normal** or **Print Layout** view.
3. Print as you would any other document.

Adding Headers and Footers

1. Use the **View → Header and Footer** menu selection to enter header and footer text.
2. Use Align Left for even-numbered headers and footers and Align Right for odd-numbered headers and footers.
3. Go to the first page of the first subdocument that uses Arabic page numbers. Then move to the footer using **View → Header and Footer**.
4. Click the Page Numbers button on the **Header and Footer** toolbar to insert a page number.
5. Use the **Insert → Page Numbers** menu selection to set the first number to 1. Click **OK** twice to close both dialog boxes.
6. Set the page number font, point size, and weight (bold / italic, etc.) to your requirement.
7. Close the **Header and Footer** toolbar. Then use **Page Preview** to examine each page number and its placement.
8. Once the headers and footers are properly adjusted and examined, you are ready to create a table of contents.

Headers, Footers and Page Numbering

Word considers the Header and Footer (as defined in Page Setup) a different region of the document from the remainder of the page. The typical Word document consists of three areas (header/footer, non-printing margin, and the area available to the user for "body" of their documents. Header and Footer sizes are set in Page Setup and can be varied by the user through Section Formatting. Typically users will want to place page numbers in the headers and footers of their Word documents. To access (edit) the header and footer, use the **Header and Footer** option under the **View** menu. Word will shift into Page View and display the header as a region contained in a box defined by dashes. In addition, a toolbar of shortcuts for common header/footer activities will appear.

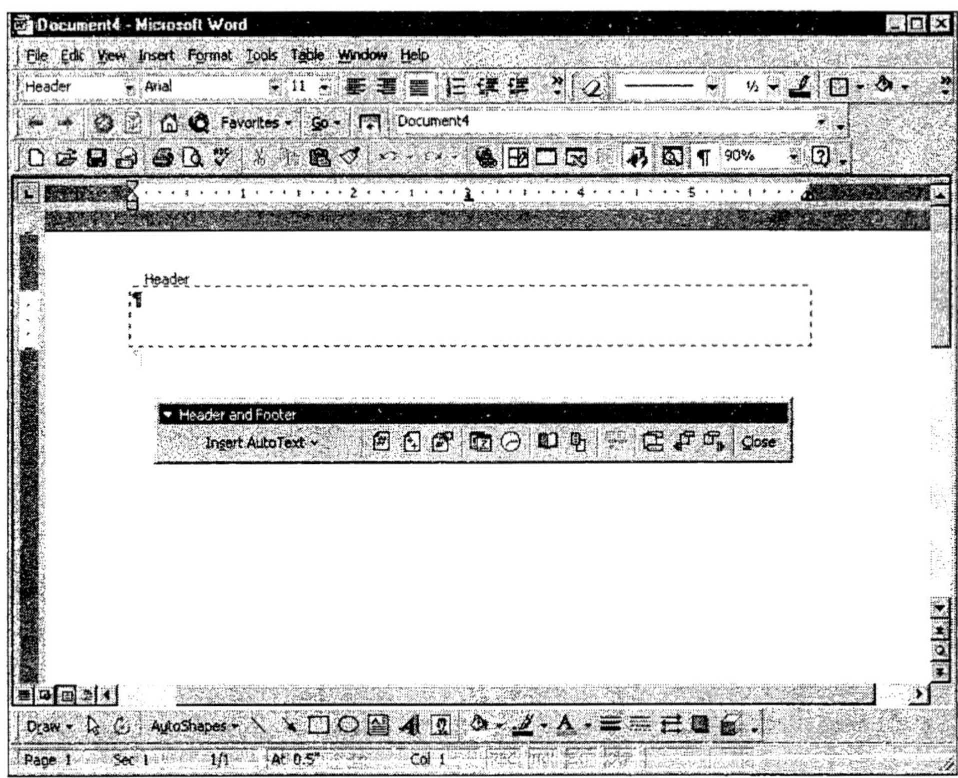

Figure 5.9: Viewing Header and Footer in Word

The icons are defined below:

Icon	Function	Description
	Toggle Header/Footer	Switch from Header to Footer
	Previous Header/Footer	Display the Previous header or footer. Useful in documents with multiple sections only.
	Next Header/Footer	Display the Next header or footer. Useful in documents with multiple sections only.
	Same as Previous	Make the current header or footer the same as the header or footer for the previous section.
	Page Number	Insert Page Number variable.
	Date	Insert Date Variable
	Time	Insert Current time variable
	Page Setup	Displays Page Setup dialog box.
	Show/Hide Text	Show or Hide document text. Word's default behavior is to "hide" (grey out) the document's body text in page view.

Table 5.1: Header and Footer Options

Most users will be interested in the third group of icons. Clicking on one of these three icons will insert the current date, current time, or page variable. If you print a page with the date variable, it will display the date the document was printed, not the date it was created, or the variable inserted, etc.

You are not inserting fixed numbers; you are inserting variables or field codes

The first and second grouping of icons is of most interest to persons with chapter oriented headers or page numbering schemes. In order to use these icons, you must have a document with multiple sections. Once section breaks are in place, these buttons will allow you to "jump" back and forth among different headers and footers. Word allows you to combine plain text with the page, date, and time variables to create complex headers, such as Chapter x pg. x. Header text and variables can be formatted with other standard character and paragraph formatting. You can even place tables, pictures called "watermarks" and frames in headers and footers.

For those wishing to apply page numbering and **avoid** headers and footers, Word also offers a separate way to insert simple page numbering: Insert/Page Numbers. A dialog box controls gives you control over page numbering and location.

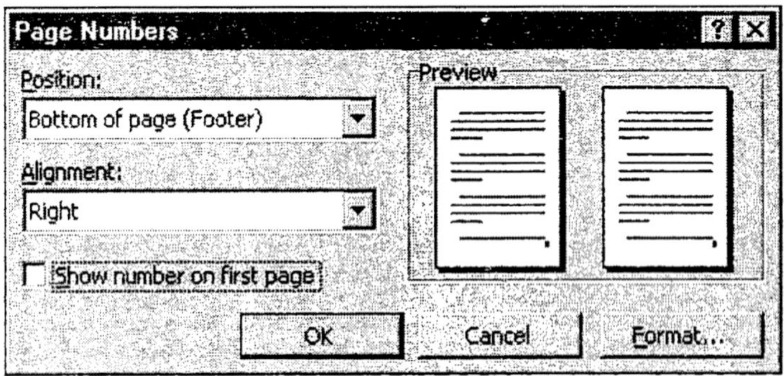

Figure 5.10: Page Number dialog box

Using the Format button, the user can control the starting number and even the type of page numbering, alphabetic, roman, Arabic, etc. While unsuited to complex headers and footers, the Insert / Page Numbers option will probably satisfy most users

Create a Table of Contents

To create a table of contents or figures among multiple documents, use the master document.

Make sure to update the table of contents from within the master document. If you update the item from an open subdocument, it won't reflect the entries in the entire master document.

To create a table of contents is similar to creating an index. Instead of marking entries into the table of contents, you first apply the built-in heading styles to the text that you want to include in the TOC. Word automatically selects the document's headings to list in the TOC.

To create the table of contents, follow these steps:

1. Position the insertion point at the beginning of the document, and then choose **Insert → Index and Tables** to display the Index and Tables dialog box.

2. Click the **Table of Contents** tab to display the page in the Index and Tables dialog box as shown in figure 5.11.

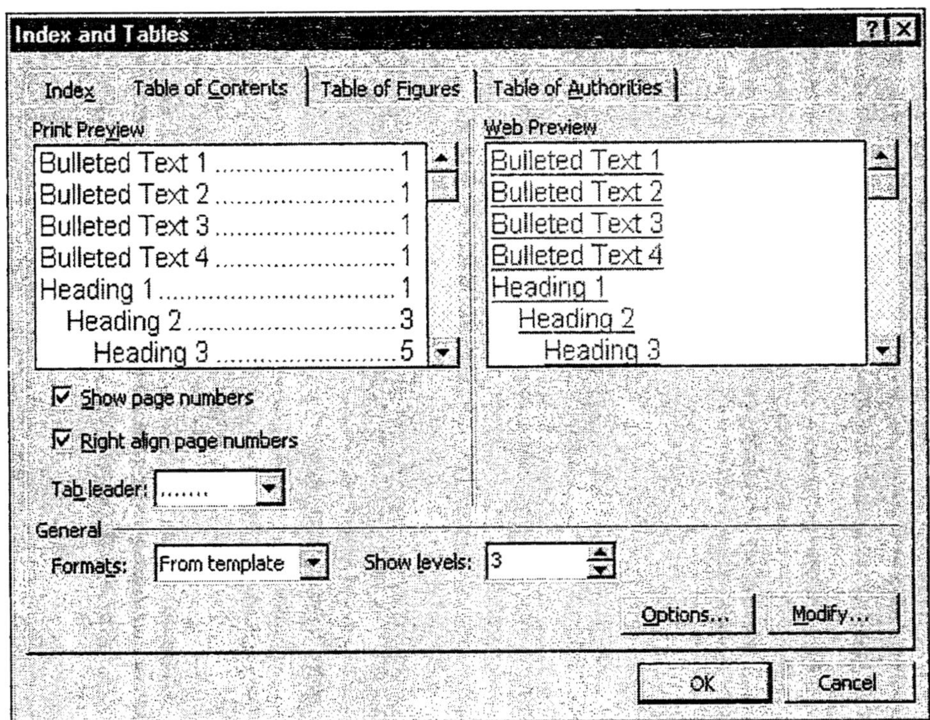

Figure 5.11: Table of Contents tab in the Index and Tables dialog box

3. Choose any of the following formats for your TOCs.

   - Check the **Show Page Number** box to have page numbers appear when the document is viewed in Print Layout view or when the document is printed.

   - Check the **Right Align Page Numbers** box to have displayed or printed page numbers aligned along the right margin of the page. Select **dots, dashes, or underline** as the character **leader** to appear before the page number.

   - Select the formatting you want for the table of contents in the **Formats drop-down** list. If you choose **From Template**, choose **Modify** to display the **Style** dialog box, and then make any necessary changes to the TOC headings.

   - Adjust the value in the **Show Levels** text box to display; the number of heading levels you want to appear in the table of contents.

4. Choose **OK** to generate the table of contents.

When you generate the table of contents, a page break is inserted above the insertion point and Word enters the TOC field code on the new page.

Embed TrueType Fonts in a Document

If you used TrueType fonts in a document, you can save or "embed" them in the document. That way, others can view, modify, and print the document with its original fonts even if they haven't installed the fonts on their computers.

1. On the **Tools** menu, click **Options** → **Save** Tab.

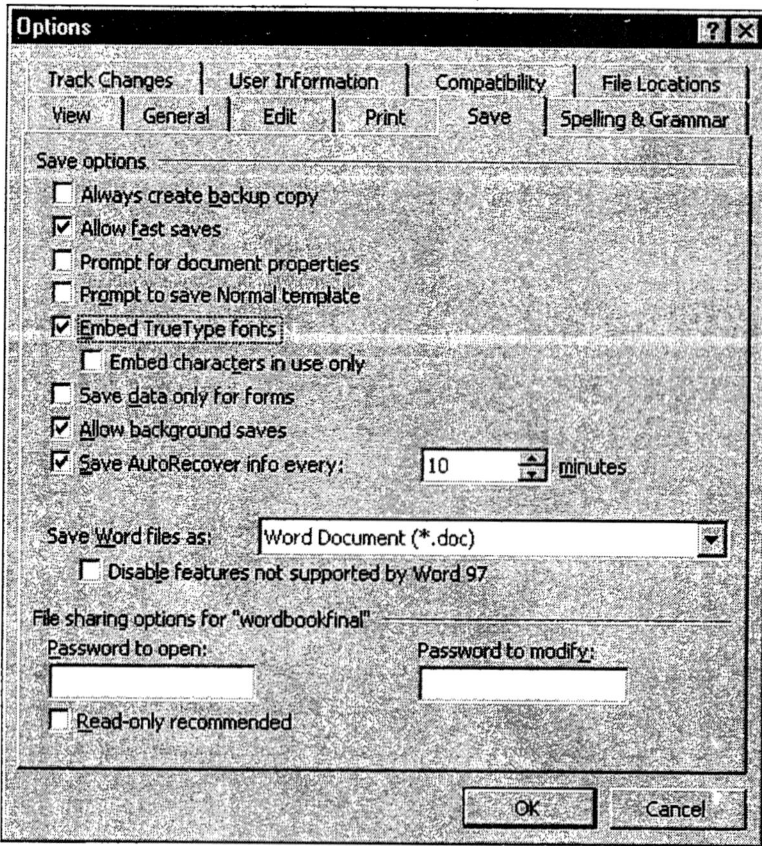

Figure 5.12: Save tab in the Options dialog box

2. Select the **Embed TrueType fonts** check box.

3. Save the document.

☞ *Notes: When you embed TrueType fonts, you may be able to reduce the file size of your document by selecting the Embed characters in use only check box. This option embeds only the font styles used in your document.*

Maintain a document's original appearance when other users View or Print it

Word provides several options for the documents to keep their original appearance no matter which computer or printer you use to view or print them. These options are especially helpful if you share documents with other users, or if you create documents on one computer and then print them from another computer.

For example, you can embed TrueType fonts in a document and preserve the document's layout and page breaks. That way, anyone can view or print the document with its original fonts and layout.

Macros

If you perform a task repeatedly in Word, you can automate the task using a macro. A macro is a series of Word commands and instructions that you group together as a single command to accomplish a task automatically. Instead of manually performing a series of time-consuming, repetitive actions in Word, you can create and run a single macro that accomplishes the task for you.

Some uses for macros:

- To speed up routine editing and formatting
- To combine multiple commands
- To make an option in a dialog box more accessible
- To automate a complex series of tasks

Word offers two ways for you to create a macro: the macro recorder and Visual Basic Editor. The macro recorder can help you get started creating macros. Word records a macro as a series of Word commands in Visual Basic for Applications programming language. You can open a recorded macro in Visual Basic Editor to modify the instructions. You can also use Visual Basic Editor to create very flexible, powerful macros that include Visual Basic instructions that you cannot record.

After you've assigned a macro to a toolbar, a menu, or shortcut keys, running the macro is as simple as clicking the toolbar button or menu item or pressing the shortcut keys. You can also point to Macro on the Tools menu, click Macros, and then click the name of the macro you want to run. You can store macros in templates or in documents. By default, Word stores macros in the Normal template so that they're available for use with every Word document.

Create and Record a New Macro

To record a macro in Word, start the macro recorder and perform a sequence of actions. You can then run the macro whenever you need to perform this sequence. For example, if you often need to insert a specifically formatted table in your documents, you can record a macro that inserts the table with the correct borders, size, and number of rows and columns.

When you're recording a macro, you can temporarily pause recording and then resume recording where you stopped.

Before you record or write a macro, plan the steps and commands you want the macro to perform. If you make a mistake when you record the macro, corrections you make will also be recorded. You can edit the macro later and remove unnecessary steps you recorded.

1. On the **Tools** menu, click **Macro → Record New Macro**.

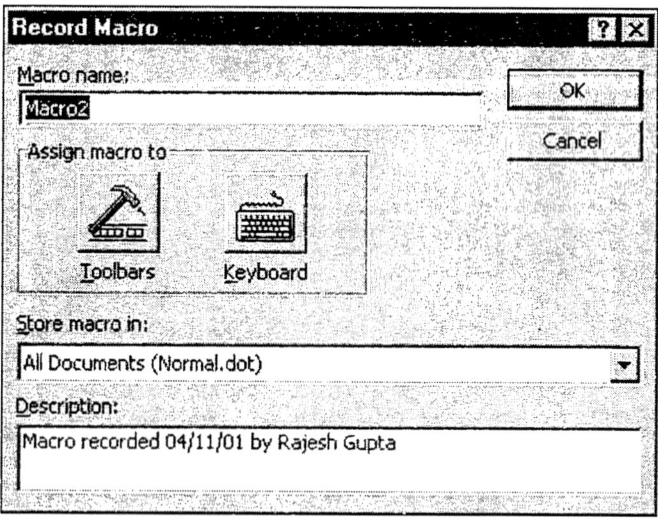

Figure 5.13: Record Macro dialog box

2. In the **Macro Name** box, type a name for the macro.

3. In the **Store Macro** in box, click the template or document in which you want to store the macro.

4. In the **Description** box, type a description for the macro.

5. If you don't want to assign the Macro to a toolbar, a menu, or shortcut keys, click **OK** to begin recording the macro.

To assign the macro to a toolbar or menu, click **Toolbars.** In the **Commands** box, click the macro you are recording, and drag it to the toolbar or menu you want to assign it. Click **Close** to begin recording the macro.

To assign the macro to shortcut keys, click **Keyboard.** In the **Commands** box, click the macro you are recording. In the **Press new shortcut key** box, type the key sequence. Click **Close** to begin recording the macro.

6. Perform the actions you want to include in your macro.

7. To stop recording your macro, click **Stop Recording.**

Once the macro is recorded, run it using the assigned button, shortcut key sequence, or by clicking the Run button in the **Tools → Macro → Macros** dialog box.

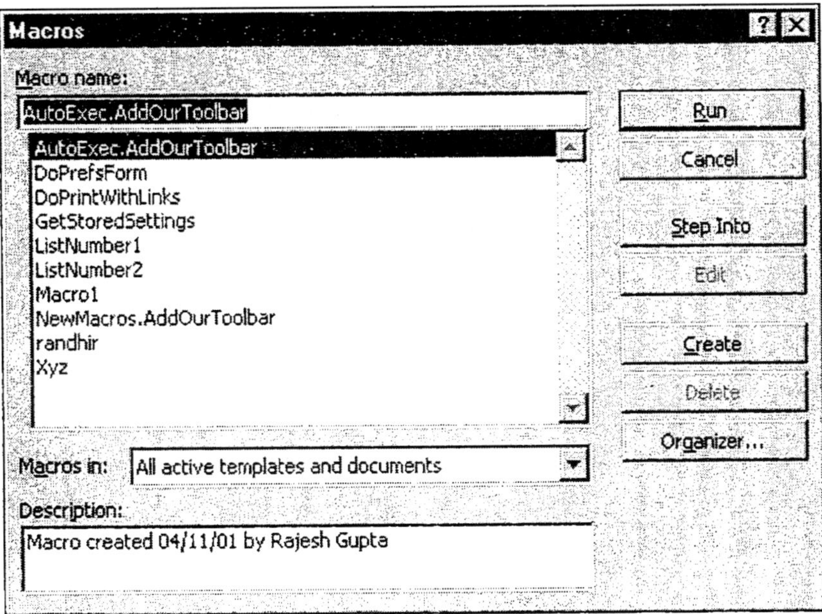

Figure 5.14: Run Macro dialog box

Shortcut Keys

When Formatting Characters	
To	**Press**
Change the font	CTRL+SHIFT+F
Change the font size	CTRL+SHIFT+P
Increase the font size	CTRL+SHIFT+>
Decrease the font size	CTRL+SHIFT+<
Increase the font size by 1 point	CTRL+]
Decrease the font size by 1 point	CTRL+[
Change the formatting of characters (Font command, Format menu)	CTRL+D
Change the case of letters	SHIFT+F3
Format letters as all capitals	CTRL+SHIFT+A
Apply bold formatting	CTRL+B
Apply an underline	CTRL+U
Underline words but not spaces	CTRL+SHIFT+W
Double-underline text	CTRL+SHIFT+D
Apply hidden text formatting	CTRL+SHIFT+H
Apply italic formatting	CTRL+I
Format letters as small capitals	CTRL+SHIFT+K
Apply subscript formatting (automatic spacing)	CTRL+EQUAL SIGN
Apply superscript formatting (automatic spacing)	CTRL+SHIFT+PLUS SIGN
Remove manual character formatting	CTRL+SPACEBAR
Change the selection to Symbol font	CTRL+SHIFT+Q
Display nonprinting characters	CTRL+SHIFT+* (asterisk)
Review text formatting	SHIFT+F1 (then click the text whose formatting you want to review)
Copy formats	CTRL+SHIFT+C
Paste formats	CTRL+SHIFT+V

Format Paragraphs when setting line spacing	
To	**Press**
Single-space lines	CTRL+1
Double-space lines	CTRL+2
Set 1.5-line spacing	CTRL+5
Add or remove one line space preceding a paragraph	CTRL+0 (zero)
When setting paragraph alignments and indents	
To	**Press**
Center a paragraph	CTRL+E
Justify a paragraph	CTRL+J
Left align a paragraph	CTRL+L
Right align a paragraph	CTRL+R
Indent a paragraph from the left	CTRL+M
Remove a paragraph indent from the left	CTRL+SHIFT+M
Create a hanging indent	CTRL+T
Reduce a hanging indent	CTRL+SHIFT+T
Remove paragraph formatting	CTRL+Q
When Applying Styles	
To	**Press**
Apply a style	CTRL+SHIFT+S
Start AutoFormat	ALT+CTRL+K
Apply the Normal style	CTRL+SHIFT+N
Apply the Heading 1 style	ALT+CTRL+1
Apply the Heading 2 style	ALT+CTRL+2
Apply the Heading 3 style	ALT+CTRL+3
Apply the List style	CTRL+SHIFT+L

Table 5.2: Shortcut Keys used in Word

 Test Your Knowledge

Students must solve the following assignment.

Multiple Choice Questions:

1. A misspelled word is marked by

   a. enclosing the word in a gray bar.
   b. changing the display to a blinking word.
   c. underlining the word with a solid black line.
   d. underlining the word with a wavy red line.

2. The Autocorrect feature does

   a. spelling corrections.
   b. grammar corrections
   c. automatic capitalizing of the first letter in a sentence.
   d. all of the above.

3. The footnote reference mark in a document appears as a

   a. subscript
   b. superscript
   c. number enclosed in parentheses
   d. letter enclosed in parentheses

4. Footnotes are located

   a. at the bottom of a page
   b. at the end of the document
   c. at the end of a paragraph
   d. at the end of a line.

5. What is the feature that copies format settings from one block of text to another?

   a. Format Painter
   b. Copy and Paste
   c. Style
   d. Customize

6. Two identical words in succession such as the the is detected by the feature

   a. Spell checker
   b. Thesaurus
   c. Edit
   d. Language

7. In looking for a specific file to open you can search for

   a. a specific word in the text
   b. a file last modified
   c. files modified in a certain period
   d. any of the above can used in specifying the search.

8. Clip Art is

   a. a library of graphics images.
   b. an area in which graphics images are placed when cut from a document.
   c. a feature of Word which allows you to draw a graphics figure.
   d. a feature of Word that allows graphics image editing.

9. How would you add text to an Autoshape graphics image?

   a. click inside the shape and enter text.
   b. click inside the shape and use the Edit command.
   c. double click in the shape and enter text.
   d. right click in the shape, and in the pop up menu select the add text command.

10. You can set the left and right margins in a document by

    a. dragging the margin markers in the Ruler bar.
    b. using the File, Page Setup... command
    c. using the Format, Paragraph... command
    d. any of the above will work.

11. A table created in Word

    a. allows additional columns or rows to be added later.
    b. does not allow additional rows to be added after the last existing row of a table.
    c. does not allow columns to be added after the last column.
    d. all of the above.

12. Word controls page breaks automatically by using

    a. manual page breaks
    b. word breaks
    c. soft page breaks
    d. line markers

13. Sometimes it is difficult to tell how many spaces are between words. It can be seen clearly by using the feature

    a. Print Preview
    b. Zoom
    c. Undo
    d. Show/Hide

14. The Page numbering feature

    a. automatically inserts page numbers in the center of the bottom line on a page.
    b. has an option to place page numbers on either the top or bottom of a page.
    c. has an option to conceal the number on the first page.
    d. b and c

15. Header is?

    a. Any text printed at the top of every page.
    b. Any graphics printed at the top of every page.
    c. Any text or graphics printed at the top of a particular page.
    d. Any text or graphics printed at the top of every page.

State whether True or False:

1. We cannot incorporate graphics in a word processor.

    a. True
    b. False

2. Word can also check the spelling and grammar in a document.

    a. True
    b. False

3. Word can also check the spelling and grammar in a document.

    a. True
    b. False

4. In word the search is case sensitive by default.

    a. True
    b. False

5. It is not possible to cancel the search in between a search operation.

   a. True
   b. False

6. One cannot change uppercase letters to lowercase and vice-versa.

   a. True
   b. False

7. The gutter margins for the odd pages is more than the gutter margins for the even pages.

   a. True
   b. False

8. Page layout view has WYSIWYG feature.

   a. True
   b. False

9. Pressing CTRL key on the ruler line displays measurement for the margin.

   a. True
   b. False

10. It is essential to be in page layout view before you view the header and footer.

    a. True
    b. False

11. We cannot give different headers and footers on even and odd pages.

    a. True
    b. False

12. Horizontal orientation is the other name of landscape orientation.

    a. True
    b. False

13. It is possible to limit the scope of spelling check to a part of a document.

    a. True
    b. False

14. Word processor list antonyms for all words it look for.

    a. True
    b. False

Fill in the Blanks:

1. The Margin dialog box is found using the menu item ______________________________.

2. One example of Toggle switch is ______________________.

3. I have typed some text on a page and I have filled about half a page. I want the next text to begin on page 2. I must insert a ____________________ .

4. If I type Teh, WORD 2000 changes it to The. This feature is called _________________.

5. I have written a ten-page essay and now realize that everywhere I have used the word himself, I should have used oneself. What command ______________ from the Edit menu shall I use?

6. The part of Microsoft Office containing clip art images, photographs, sound files and video clips is called ___________________

7. We can make search case sensitive by choosing ____________ option.

8. ____________ case converts first letter of each word to capital.

9. To copy character-format, click ___________ button.

An Introduction to Excel

Objectives

- Introduction
- Toolbars
- Office Assistant
- Starting and Exiting Excel
- Saving Workbook
- Printing

Introduction

Excel is a full-featured spreadsheet program that is used by millions of people around the world. Excel 2000 makes use of all the features available to programs designed specifically to run with a 32-bit operating system such as Windows 95/98/2000 and NT. This means your version of Excel runs faster and more realibly than the older 16-bit technology programs. When acquired as part of Office 2000, Excel uses a number of shared Office resources. These shared resources include fonts, Clip Art, spelling resources, AutoCorrect, AutoText and more.

Excel can integrate documents and information created by other Office and Windows programs. For example you can insert Word documents and Access tables directly into your Excel documents. You can put upto 32,000 bytes or characters in an Excel cell. You can cut a portion of a document created in another program and then paste it into your Excel worksheet. The worksheet is the primary document used in Excel. A worksheet is made up of cells in columns and rows and is always part of a workbook. You can also 'drag and drop' part of one document into another using your mouse.

You enter your data into a worksheet. It is nothing more than a large planning form made up of column and rows. The worksheets in turn are grouped together into a workbook. By default each workbook in Excel 2000 contains 3 worksheets which are identified by tabs displaying along the bottom of your screen which identify the individual worksheets making up the workbook. The first worksheet is called **Sheet1**, the next is **Sheet2** and so on, although you can insert more worksheet as well as delete which only contains one worksheet.

Figure 6.1: A sample worksheet

Within Excel 2000, you can have up to 65,536 rows in a worksheet and up to 256 columns. That's room for a lot of data!

The last few files that you opened are displayed in the File drop-down menu.

The Uses of Excel

- Formulae or calculations
- Storing information (database)
- Creating Tables
- Creating Charts

For Formulae or Calculations

Here is a very simple domestic budget using Excel:

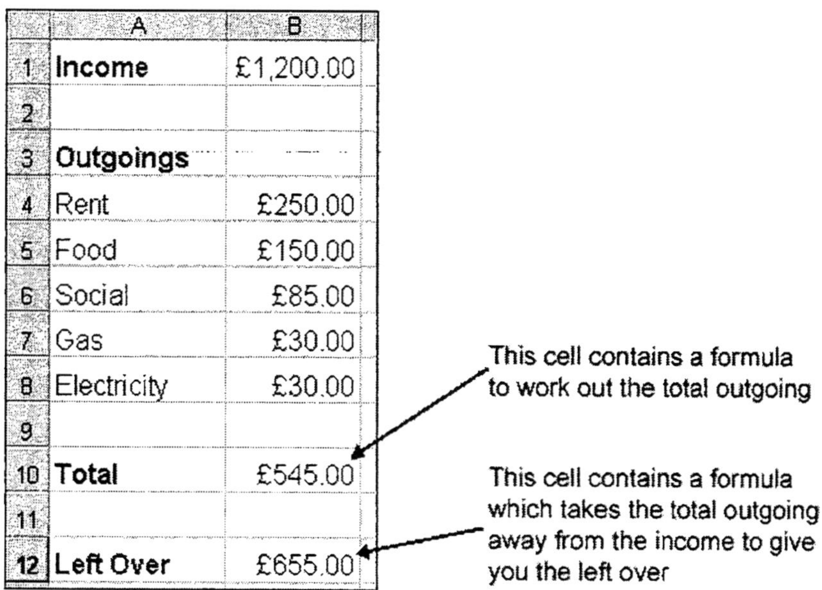

	A	B
1	**Income**	£1,200.00
2		
3	**Outgoings**	
4	Rent	£250.00
5	Food	£150.00
6	Social	£85.00
7	Gas	£30.00
8	Electricity	£30.00
9		
10	**Total**	£545.00
11		
12	**Left Over**	£655.00

Figure 6.2: Formulae Calculation

For Storing Information

The diagram below shows part of a database in Excel:

	B	C	D	E	F	G
1	**Title**	**Surname**	**First Name**	**Sex**	**Date of Birth**	**Start Date**
2	Dr.	Rubal	Abigeti	Female	23-May-60	23-Apr-93
3	Ms.	Ayesa	Ahlot	Female	12-Mar-58	6-Aug-90
4	Mr.	Alex	Hydel	Male	23-May-28	9-Aug-71
5	Mrs.	Richi	Kurian	Female	27-Mar-68	12-Sep-92
6	Mrs.	Surbhi	Singhal	Female	15-Jun-59	23-Jul-91
7	Mr.	Oleander	Paes	Male	21-Nov-67	1-Mar-94

Figure 6.3: Storing information as a database

Excel has a simple database facility that allows you to:

- Sort information into any order (e.g. by surname)
- Extract the information you wish to see (e.g. only the females)

For Creating Tables

Excel can also be used very much like Word processing tables, i.e. for laying information out neatly in rows and columns. Worksheets can then be formatted to look impressive.

	A	B	C
1	Competitor	Current Share	Share in 2 years
2	Largest Competitor	50%	30%
3	Second Competitor	25%	20%
4	Third Competitor	15%	12%

Figure 6.4: Creating Tables

For Creating Charts

Once you have created your tables, you can display the information in a chart. This gives you a visual interpretation of your figures.

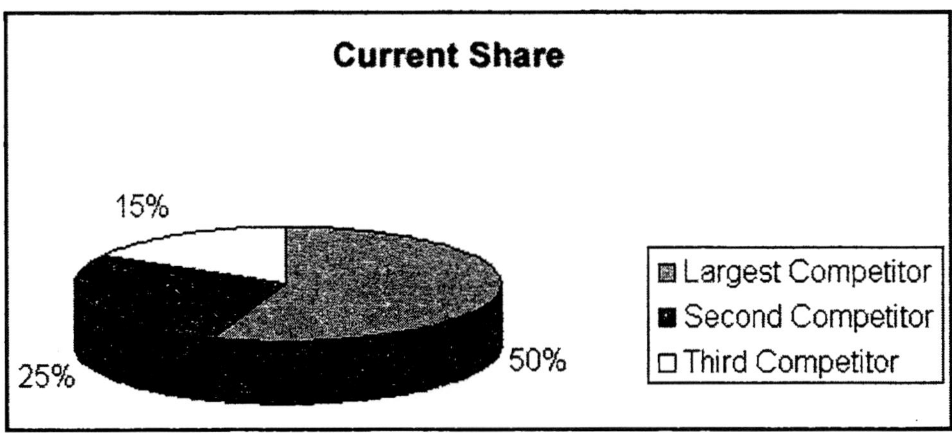

Figure 6.5: Creating Charts

What are workbooks and worksheets?

A workbook is made up of multiple worksheets whereas a worksheet is made up of the rows and columns into which you enter your data information.

Advantages of Using Excel

Excel 2000 is an advanced computer-based spreadsheet which combines immense power and flexibility with ease of use. You may never need to learn about the very advanced features such as Pivot Tables, yet you can still use the program to achieve your desired goal. The really big advantage of using any computer-based spreadsheet, as opposed to writing down all your figures on a piece of paper, is that you can change any particular piece of data. Providing you have used the correct functions and formulae within the spreadsheet, the computer will do all the work necessary to calculate all your end values.

Getting Started with Excel

Before creating or opening a document in Excel, first you will have to load / open MS-Excel in memory.

1. Click on **Start → Programs → Microsoft Office → Microsoft Excel** or click on the shortcut icon as shown in figure 6.6 below.

2. The Excel opening screen will appear as in figure below. The default name of the blank document is *book1*. The extension of a Excel file is *.xls*.

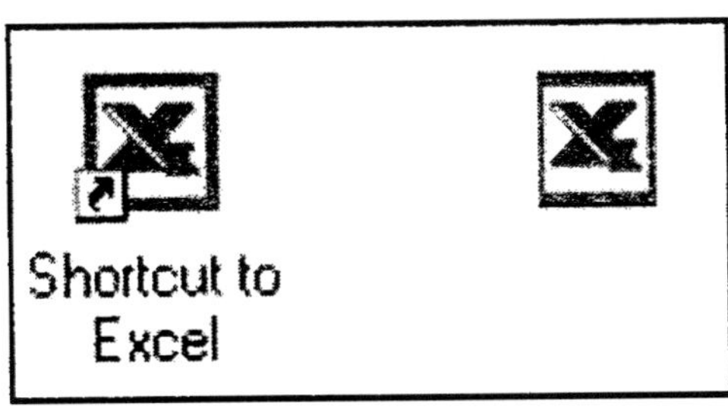

Figure 6.6: MS-Excel Icon

If you are using Excel for the first time, the Office Assistant welcome will appear. To Start using Excel, click the suitable option in the Assistant window.

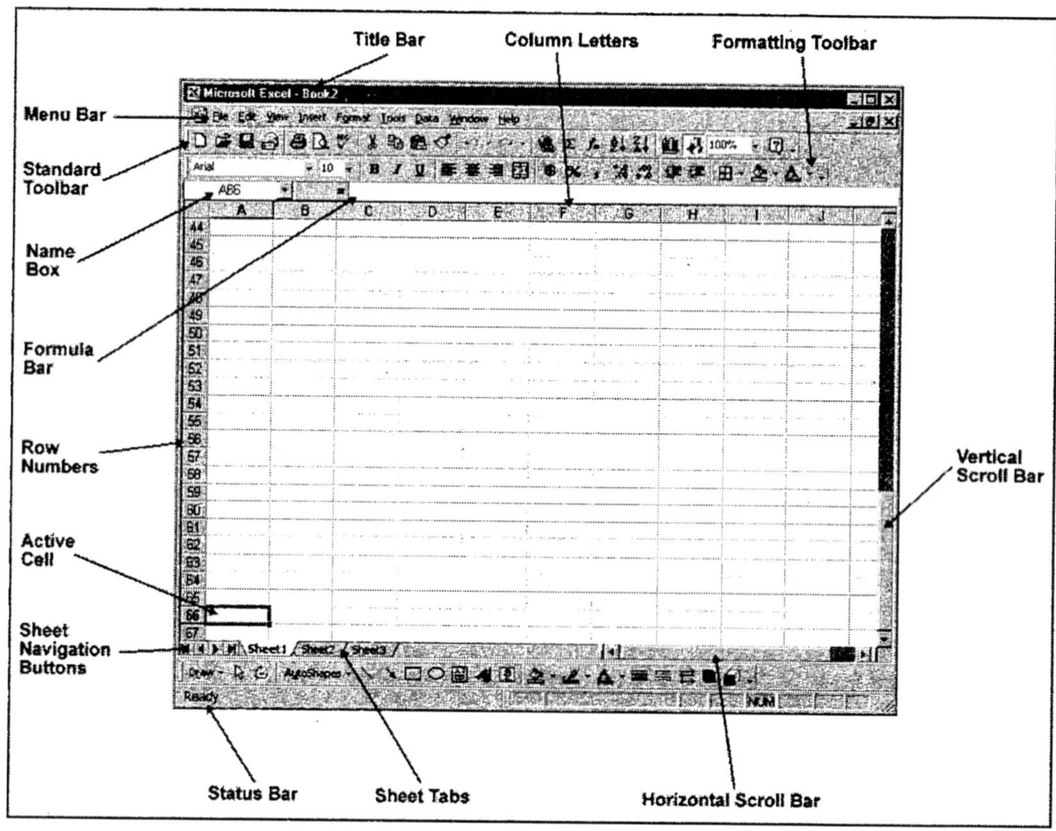

Figure 6.7: Excel 2000 Interface

Toolbars

Excel displays one or more toolbars containing a row of related buttons across the top of your screen. When you first start Excel, the Standard and Formatting toolbars are displayed; the Formula bar, which is used to enter and edit cell values, is also displayed. Each button to a toolbar offers a shortcut method of performing commonly used file and workbook operations. Use the toolbars list by clicking on the check boxes. Use Customize to display the Customize dialog box, where you can modify existing toolbars and even create new toolbars of your own.The Customize feature gives you a way to add shortcuts to frequently used items.

The Standard Toolbar: Displayed by default. Allows you to achieve common actions in Excel 2000 quickly and effectively.

The Formatting Toolbar: Allows you to achieve common formatting actions in Excel 2000 quickly and effectively. This includes: Changing the font type and size; Toggling bold, italics and underlining; Alignment; Applying borders and colors; Applying currency and decimal point.

To display other toolbars

From the **View** menu, select **Toolbars** to display a list of toolbars as shown in Figure 6.8. Then click on the toolbar you wish displayed or simply right-click on any toolbar to display a pop-up menu from which you can select the toolbar that you wish to display (or hide).

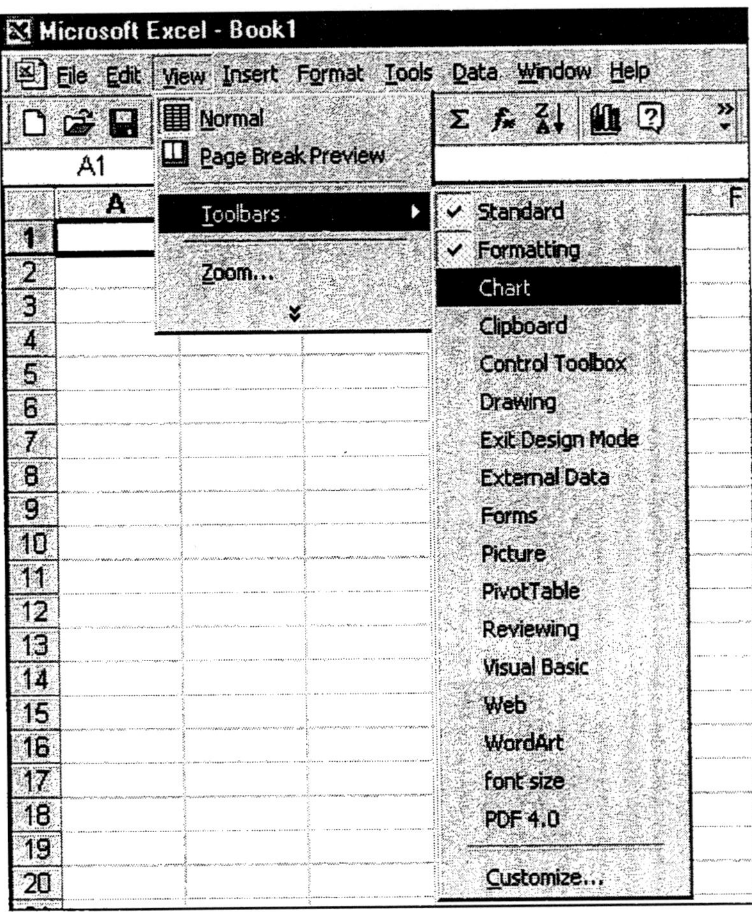

Figure 6.8: View menu

Toolbar	Function
Standard	Icons for basic Excel 2000 features.
Formatting	Icons for changing formats.
Chart	Includes icons used when creating charts.
Clipboard	Used when cutting/copying/pasting multiple items to/from the clipboard
Control Toolbox	Icons used when creating fill in forms.
Drawing	Icons for drawing rectangles, circles, ovals, and other shapes.
External Data	Icons used when querying external data.
Forms	Icons for creating list boxes, option buttons, etc.
Picture	Icons for creating and manipulating pictures.
Pivot Table	Icons useful data for pivot tables.
Reviewing	Icons for creating and manipulating comments.
Visual Basic	Includes Visual Basic icons.
Web	Icons for creating, manipulating and interacting with the Web.
WordArt	Icons for creating and manipulating WordArt objects.

Table 6.1: Toolbar and their function

Office Assistant

By default this friendly little creature will watch what you do and offer tips on how to work more productively. When you get stuck..... use the Office Assistant. Office Assistant will display information on the screen. If you are not sure about how to use this product you should always read the help offered.

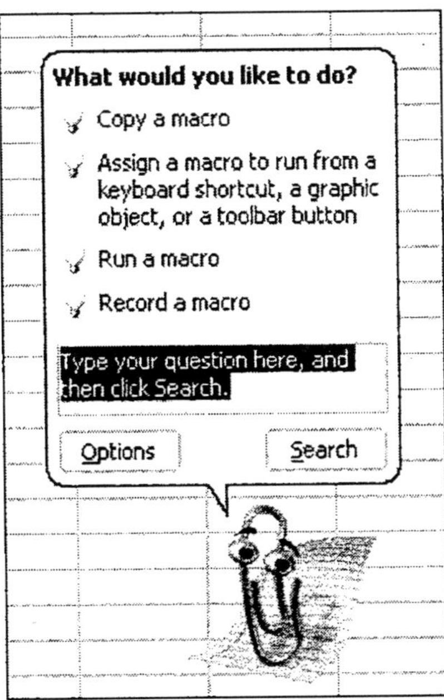

Figure 6.9: Office Assistant

By default Excel 2000 will display a tip of the day each time you start Excel. The Office Assistant will display a light bulb, as illustrated. If you click on the Assistant with the bulb displayed, then you will see a tip offering advice. If you take time to read these as they are displayed, then you will soon find that you are on the way to becoming a Excel 2000 expert!

Click on the **Office Assistant** icon located within the **Standard** Toolbar to display the Office Assistant. Right click on the Office Assistant, and from the pop-up menu displayed, select **Hide** to hide the Office Assistant.

Starting and Exiting Excel

1. Start Microsoft Windows 95/98/NT.

2. From the **Programs** group list or the Office 2000 toolbar, click **Microsoft Excel**.

3. Notice that a blank workbook named Book1 is displayed; the first worksheet tab labelled *Sheet1* is active and ready for your entries.

4. Press **<Alt+F4>** or use **<Alt, F, X>** to exit the worksheet program, returning to the Windows desktop.

Create a new workbook

1. Click on the **File** drop down menu, and then click on the **New** command. The New dialog box will be displayed.
2. To create a workbook based on a pre-defined template, click on the Workbook icon, located within the General tab.
3. Double-click the template for the type of workbook you want to create.
4. Click on the **OK** button to continue.

Open a Workbook

In Microsoft Excel, you can open workbooks that are stored on your hard disk or on network drives that you have connections to. If you want to make sure that a workbook remains unchanged, and you have permission to save files where the workbook is stored, you can create and work on a copy of the workbook instead of the original file, or you can open the workbook as read-only, regardless of its location.

1. From the **File** menu, click **Open**.
2. Locate the file that you wish to open and then double-click on the file name to open it.

Show/hide list of recently used workbooks on the File Menu

1. On the **Tools** menu, click **Options**, and then click the **General** tab.
2. **Select** or **clear** the Recently used file list check box.

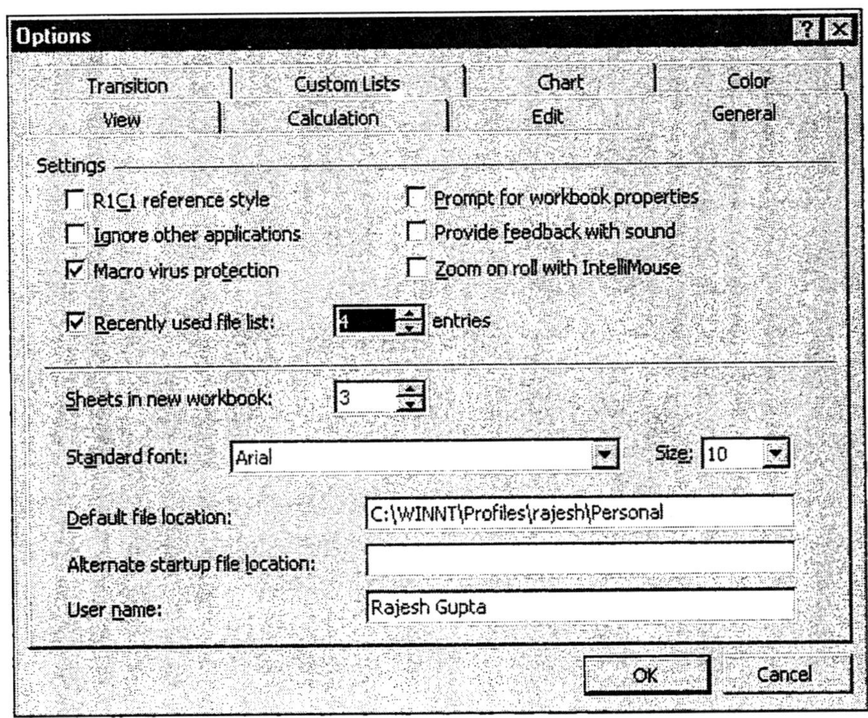

Figure 6.10: Options dialog box

3. To change the number of files listed on the menu, **select** the number of entries.

Default working folder in the Open and Save As dialog boxes

The first time you click the **Save As** command after starting Microsoft Excel, the *My Documents* folder is the default working folder whose contents are displayed in the dialog box. It is the default working folder in each Office program you install. If you use Microsoft Windows NT Workstation 3.51, the default working folder is the *Personal* directory. The My Documents folder is located at the root directory. The Personal directory is a subdirectory of the Windows NT Workstation directory. These folders are a good place to store documents, workbooks, presentations, databases, and other files you're working on.

If you haven't already changed the default working folder for an individual program, you can change the default working folder for all your Office programs and for the Open Office Document button and command by renaming the My Documents folder, by moving the folder to a new location, or both. You can change the default working folder only for Microsoft Excel on both Windows and Windows NT Workstation 3.51.

Finding files

- From the **File** menu, choose **Open** to display the **Open** dialog box.
- Click on the **Tools** drop down menu and select **Find.**
- By default the **Property** section of the dialog box will display **File Name.**

To search a file in the current folder, type the complete filename or the first part of the name into the **Value** text box and then click on the **Find Now** button.

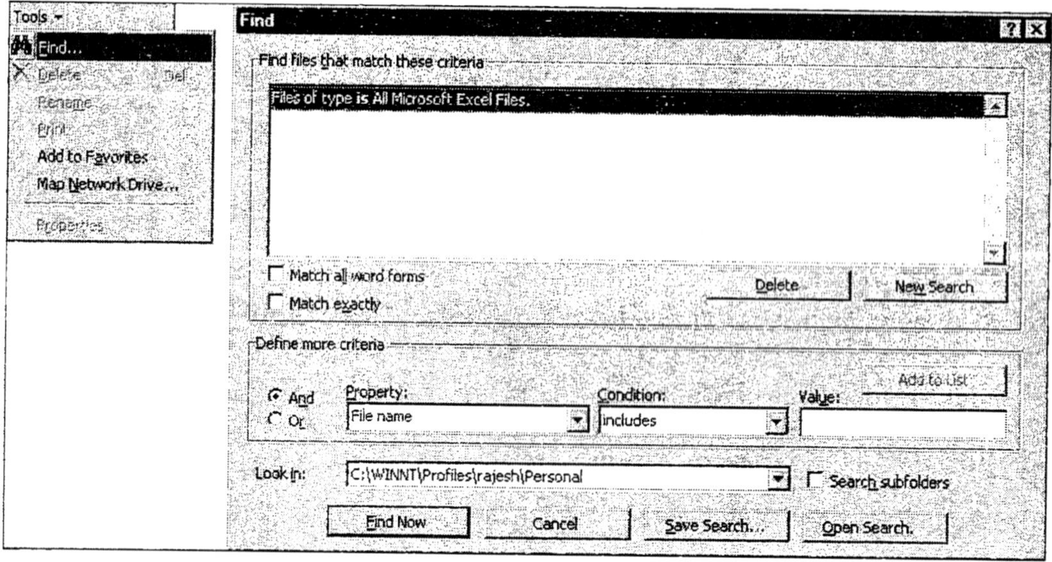

Figure 6.11: Finding Files dialog box

Entering Data

Select the cell into which you wish to enter data. By default Numbers will be right-aligned and text entries are left-aligned. Select the cell in which you want to enter a number and type in the number. If you want to make the number a negative, type a minus sign in front of it. To indicate decimal places, you type a full stop. If you wish to enter a number or formula as text, type an apostrophe before it. Select the cell in which you want to enter the text and then type in the text. Select the cell in which you want to enter the date or time and then type in the date or time. Separate the date with either hyphens or slashes. *To enter current date press CTRL+ ; and to enter current time press CTRL+ :*

There are a number of techniques to be aware of when carrying out data entry.

- Entering data into a range of cells
- Filling a range of cells with a single value
- AutoCorrect
- AutoComplete
- Pick Lists

Entering data into a range of cells

1. Use the mouse to drag across a range of cells into which you wish to enter numbers. This will highlight the selected range as shown in the following Figure 6.12.

B2 =

	A	B	C	D	E
1					
2					
3					
4					
5					
6					
7					

Figure 6.12: Range of cells selected

2. Type your first entry and press Enter, the active cell moves down one location.

3. Enter the remaining numbers following each with the Enter key. When you reach the bottom of each column (in the selected range) the active cell moves to the top of the next.

D2 =

	A	B	C	D	E
1					
2		20	91		
3		60	95		
4		54	17		
5		81	14		
6					
7					

Figure 6.13: Data entered in the selected range of cells

4. Highlight the cells you wish to fill. Enter the information that you wish to fill the selected range with. Press **Ctrl+Shift+Enter** and the range will be filled.

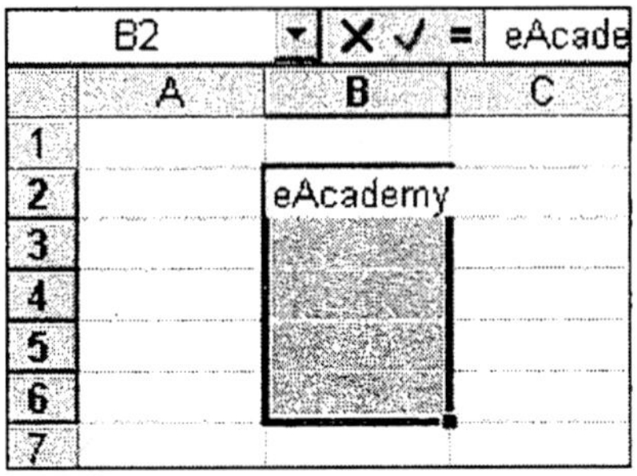

Figure 6.14: Using Ctrl+Shift+Enter to fill the range

AutoCorrect

AutoCorrect looks at the entry you are making and checks it against a pre-defined list of errors. If you make an error AutoCorrect command makes the required correction automatically.

Open the Tools menu and select the **AutoCorrect** option. Use the scroll bars to move through the items listed in the **Replace** and **With** section.

To add items to AutoCorrect

1. Open the **Tools** menu and select the **AutoCorrect** option.

2. Enter the incorrect spelling in the **Replace** box.

3. Enter the correct spelling in the **With** box.

4. Click the **Add** button. The entry is now in the AutoCorrect list as shown in Figure 6.15.

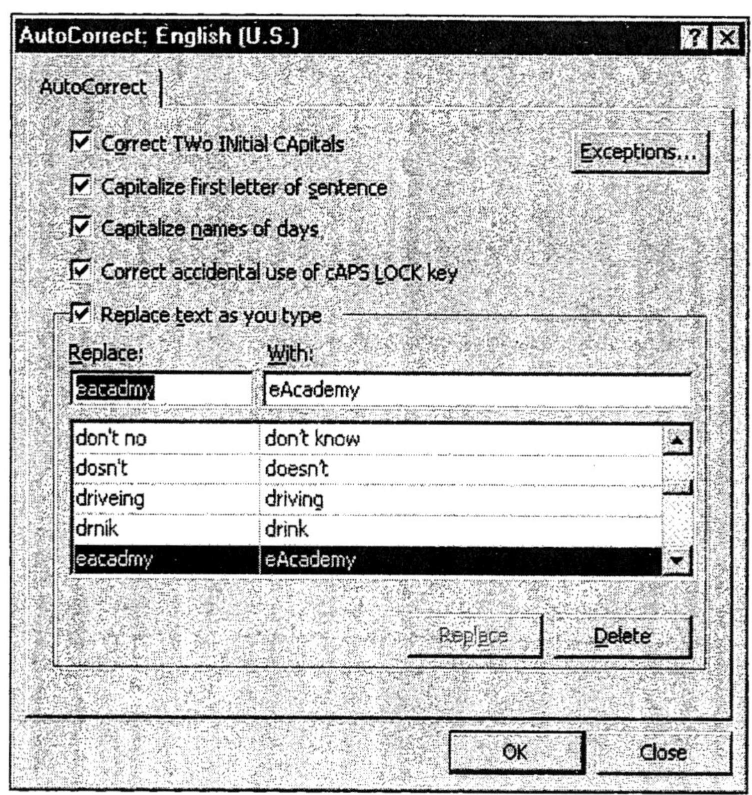

Figure 6.15: AutoCorrect dialog box

5. Click **OK** to finish.

AutoComplete command

When you start entering data into an empty cell, directly below an existing list, then excel will automatically offer you a match from the existing data above it.

Suppose you have entered the following data. Click on the cell directly below the existing list.

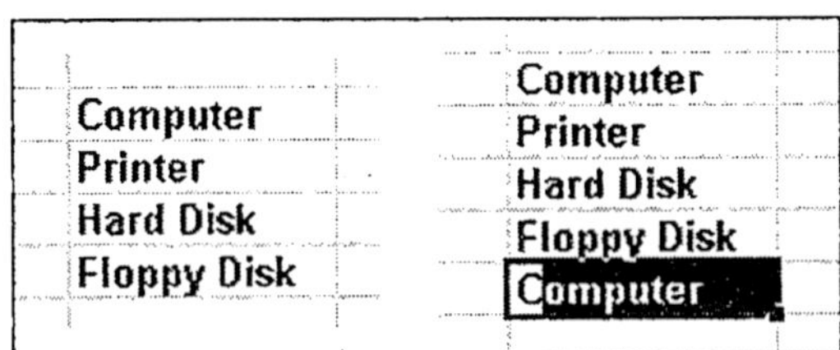

Figure 6.16: Using AutoComplete

In this case as soon as you enter the letter **C**, then Excel will offer the rest of the word **Computer**, as illustrated in Figure 6.16. At this point you can continue to enter the rest of a word and then press the **Enter** key or you can press the **Enter** key as soon as the AutoComplete offers to enter the word **Computer** and the word **Computer** will be inserted into the cell.

The Series Command

A series may be customized or you can create your own series. To do this, from the **Tools** drop down menu, select the **Options** command. In the **Options** dialog box select the **Custom Lists** tab and enter the required information to create your own series.

- If you were to enter the word January, Excel 2000 can automatically extend the series across selected cells to display the rest of the months of the year. The same can be done with week, dates, times and items such as Q2 and Qtr2.

Different types of Series are:

- **Linear:** Excel 2000 increases or decreases the values by a constant value.
- **Growth:** Excel 2000 will multiply the value by a constant factor.
- **AutoFill:** Excel 2000 can extend various types of data, such as Qtr1, Qtr2, Qtr3.

  AutoFill may be used directly on your worksheet using drag and drop techniques or may be applied using the Series command located under the **Edit → Fill** drop down menu.

To apply a series using drag and drop techniques

- Enter a value, such as **JANUARY**.
- Move the mouse cursor to the bottom right-hand corner of the selected cell, until the cursor changes to the shape of a fine cross-hair.

- While depressing the left-hand mouse button drag down the screen.
- When you release the mouse button, the selected cells will be filled with the series as shown in Figure 6.17.

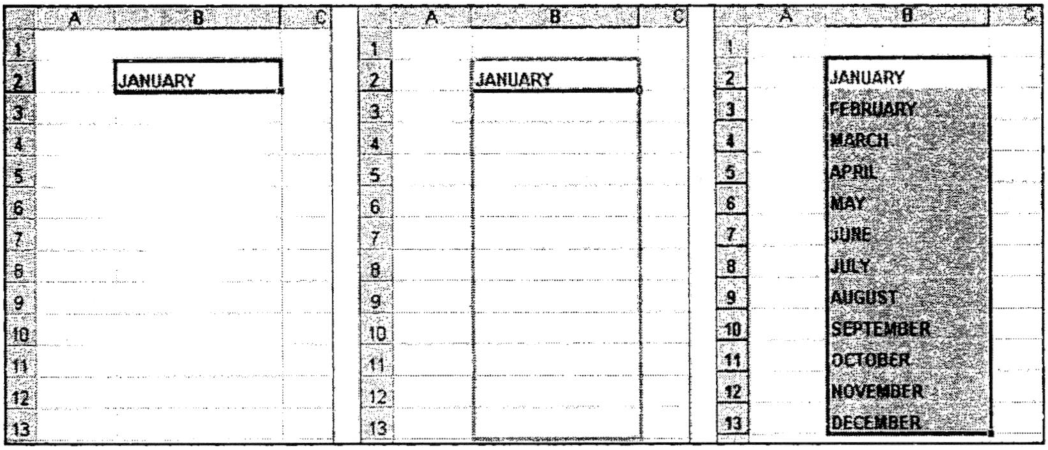

Figure 6.17: A Series Example

To apply a number series using drag and drop techniques

- Enter a number into cell 1 of the range.
- Enter another number into the adjacent cell of the range.
- Select both cells.
- Move the mouse cursor to the bottom right-hand corner of the selected cell, until the cursor changes to the shape of a fine cross-hair.
- While depressing the left-hand mouse button, drag down the screen.
- When you release the mouse button, the selected cells will be filled with the number series commencing with your first number.

☞ *Note: If the numbers are 1 and 2 the series will count 1, 2, 3, 4, 5 etc. If the numbers are 1 and 4 the series will count 1, 4, 7, 10, 13 etc.*

Freeze and Unfreeze Panes

This command enables you to see in which row or column you are working in when you are working on a large worksheet. You may wish to lock the row or column headings. From the **Window** menu, select **Freeze Panes** to freeze and select **Unfreeze Panes** to unfreeze rows and columns.

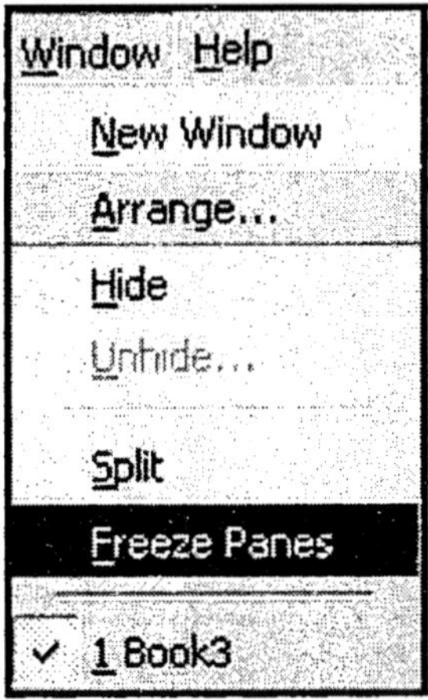

Figure 6.18: Freeze Panes Option

Navigating in the Worksheet

1. Use the mouse to click on the cell to which you wish to move.
2. Use keyboard shortcuts.
3. Use the **Go To** feature.

To move to a particular cell

- Enter the cell that you wish to jump to into the **Name Box**. When you press the **Enter** key you will jump to the cell you entered.

Moving with the Keyboard

Keyboard command	Action Perfomed
↑	Up one cell
↓	Down one cell
←	Left one cell
→	Right one cell
Ctrl + →	Goes to the furthest right column of the current worksheet
Ctrl + ←	Goes to the furthest left column of the current worksheet
Home	Goes to column A
Ctrl + Home	Goes to cell A1
Ctrl + End	Moves to the bottom right cell of the current worksheet
Page Up	Moves active cell up one screen
Page Down	Moves active cell down one screen

Table 6.2: Moving Cursor with the keyboard

Moving with the Mouse

1. Position the mouse over the middle of the cell you wish to move to
2. Click when your mouse looks like the big white cross.

Tips: To move, your mouse must look like the big white cross as shown in figure below.

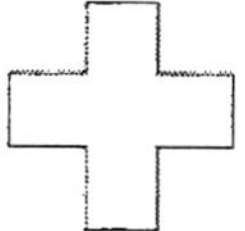

Figure 6.19: A white cross

To move using Go To feature

- From the **Edit** menu, choose **Go To** in order to display the **Go To** dialog box.
- In the **Reference** text box type the cell reference, or click a range name in the **Go To** list box and then select **OK** .

Selecting items within Excel 2000

- **You can select a single cell or a range of cells:** Just click on the cell you wish to select the single cell. Click on the first cell in the range. Hold down the left-hand mouse button and drag over the cells you wish to include in the selection.
- **You can select a non-contiguous range:** Select the first range and then select the next range in the same way but hold down the **Ctrl** key and keep it pressed while you click and drag with the mouse.
- **You can select a row or a column:** Click the row heading number or the column heading letter.
- **You can select an entire worksheet:** Click the **Select All** icon in the top, left-hand corner of the worksheet where the row heading and column heading meet or press **Ctrl+A**.
- **You can select a single sheet or several sheets:** Click on the first sheet tab. Click on other sheet tabs you wish to select while pressing the **Ctrl** key.
- **You can select all sheets:** Click on a sheet tab using the right-hand mouse button to display the shortcut menu. Choose **Select All Sheets**.

Inserting and Deleting Cells, Rows and Columns

- Insert cells, rows or columns using the Insert menu.
- Delete cells, rows or columns using the Edit menu.

To insert a row into a Worksheet

1. Select the row **below or after** where you require a new one
2. Click Insert

3. Click Rows. A new row will be inserted above the selection

   Or

1. Select the row **below or after** where you require a new one

2. Press CTRL & +

If you select row 6

	A	B	C	D	E
1	**No. of Courses Held at eAcademy**				
2					
3		**January**	**February**	**March**	**Total**
4					
5	*MS-Word*	10	15	25	**50**
6	*MS-Excel*	5	5	10	**20**
7	*MS-Powerpoint*	5	15	15	**35**
8	*MS-Access*	6	10	12	**28**
9					
10	**Total**	**26**	**45**	**62**	

A new row is inserted above row 6

	A	B	C	D	E
1	**No. of Courses Held at eAcademy**				
2					
3		**January**	**February**	**March**	**Total**
4					
5	*MS-Word*	10	15	25	**50**
6					
7	*MS-Excel*	5	5	10	**20**
8	*MS-Powerpoint*	5	15	15	**35**
9	*MS-Access*	6	10	12	**28**
10					
11	**Total**	**26**	**45**	**62**	

Figure 6.20: New Row Inserted above row 6

To insert columns into a Worksheet

1. Select the column to the **right of or after** where you require a new one

2. Click Insert

3. Click Columns. A new column will be inserted to the left of the selection

   Or

1. Select the column to the **right of or after** where you require a new one

2. Press CTRL & +

If you select column B

	A	B	C	D	E
1	**No. of Courses Held at eAcademy**				
2					
3		**January**	**February**	**March**	**Total**
4					
5	*MS-Word*	10	15	25	**50**
6	*MS-Excel*	5	5	10	**20**
7	*MS-Powerpoint*	5	15	15	**35**
8	*MS-Access*	6	10	12	**28**
9					
10	**Total**	**26**	**45**	**62**	

A new column is inserted to the left

	A	B	C	D	E	F
1	**No. of Courses Held at eAcademy**					
2						
3			**January**	**February**	**March**	**Total**
4						
5	*MS-Word*		10	15	25	**50**
6	*MS-Excel*		5	5	10	**20**
7	*MS-Powerpoint*		5	15	15	**35**
8	*MS-Access*		6	10	12	**28**
9						
10	**Total**		**26**	**45**	**62**	

Figure 6.21: New Column Inserted to the left

To delete a row or column

- Use the same techniques outlined above, but select the **Delete** command from the pop-up menu.

To insert cells or ranges

- Select the cell where you want to insert a new cell.
- From the **Insert** menu, select **Cells** to display the **Insert** dialog box.
- Select one of the following options:

Option	Description
Entire column	Moves all cells in the column to the right and inserts a new column.
Entire row	Moves all cells in the row down and inserts a new row.
Shift cells down	Moves existing cells down and inserts one cell.
Shift cells right	Moves existing cells to the right and inserts one cell.

Table 6.3: Insert cell or ranges Option

- Click **OK**.

To delete cells or ranges

- Select the cell(s) you want to delete.
- From the **Edit** menu, select **Delete** to display the **Delete** dialog box.
- Select one of the options.
- Click on the **OK** button.

Deleting and Inserting Worksheet

You can insert and delete worksheets using the Insert and Edit menus. It is much faster to select the relevant worksheet tab and then right-click on it to display a pop-up menu. From this menu, select either Delete or Insert.

To insert a worksheet using the Insert menu

- Click the sheet tab to select the worksheet where you want to insert a new one. The new worksheet will be inserted before this worksheet.
- From the Insert menu, select Worksheet *OR* press **Shift+F11**.

To delete a worksheet using the Edit menu

- Click the sheet tab to select the worksheet you wish to delete.
- From the Edit menu, select Delete Sheet.
- Click OK to permanently delete the selected sheet.

To insert or delete using right-clicking

- Click on the relevant worksheet tab with the right-hand mouse button.
- Select Insert or Delete as required.

Renaming Worksheet

- Double click on the worksheet tab you wish to rename. The worksheet name is highlighted, indicating that it is selected.
- Enter a new name for the worksheet.
- Press the **Enter** key.
- The new worksheet name will be displayed on the worksheet tab at the bottom of the screen.

☞ *Note: You can also rename a worksheet by clicking on the worksheet tab with the right-hand mouse button and selecting* ***Rename****.*

Grouping and Ungrouping Sheets

You can group sheets together to enable you to edit and format them at the same time. Every change you make to the active sheet will be reflected in all other sheets in the group.

- To select all worksheet tabs click the right-hand mouse button and choose **Select All Sheets** from the pop-up menu.
- To select contiguous sheets, click on the first tab you wish to select whilst holding down the **Shift** key and then click on the last tab you wish to select whilst holding down the **Shift** key and to select non-contiguous sheets, click on each sheet tab you wish to select whilst holding down the **Ctrl** key.
- Click on one of the grouped worksheet tabs and click with the right-hand mouse button. Select **Ungroup Sheets** from the pop-up menu or click on the active sheet tab whilst holding down the **Shift** key.

Saving Workbook

- From the **File** menu, select **Save** *or* press **Ctrl+S** *or* click on the **Save** button on the **Standard** toolbar.
- If it is a new file, the **Save As** dialog box will appear. If necessary select a different folder that you may wish to save the file in.
- Enter a name in the **File name** text box.
- Select **Save**.

To Save a Backup Copy

- From the **File** menu, select **Save As** to display the **Save As** dialog box.
- Insert a name for the file in the **File name** text box.
- Select **Save**. To work on the original file again, select it from the list displayed at the bottom of the **File** drop down menu.

To Save Summary Information

- From the **File** menu, select **Properties** .

- Enter the required information in the **Properties** dialog box.
- Select **OK** to save the information within the file.

Moving between Worksheet

- **To move to a visible worksheet within a workbook:** Click on the relevant worksheet tab displayed along the bottom of the worksheet.
- **To move to a worksheet that is not visible:** Click on the worksheet arrows using the left-hand mouse to move forwards or backwards through the worksheets or click on the worksheet. Arrows using the right-hand mouse button to display the list of available worksheets and click on the required worksheet.

Shortcut	Action
Ctrl + Page Up	To move one tab to the left
Ctrl + Page Down	To move one tab to the right

Table 6.4: Shortcut used for moving between worksheet

Using the Spelling Checker

- Select a single cell to check the entire worksheet and then from the **Tools** menu, select **Spelling**.
- If no incorrect words are found, the **Spelling** dialog box will not appear. A box will appear to tell you that Excel 2000 has finished checking the spelling. If the **Spelling** dialog box is displayed, select one of the following options:

Option	Description
Add	Will add the word to the current custom dictionary.
Cancel	Will stop the spelling check
Change	Will change this occurrence of the word to the word displayed in the Change to text box.
Change All	Will change all occurrences of the word to the word displayed in the Change to text box.
Ignore	Will ignore the word and continue.
Ignore All	Will ignore all further occurrences of the word in the document.

Option	Description
Suggest	Will suggest alternative words from the dictionary.
AutoCorrect	The misspelled word and its correct spelling is added to the list of words and phrases that are corrected automatically by AutoCorrect

Table 6.5: Spell check Options

- If you began the spelling check in the middle of the worksheet, you may be asked whether you want to continue checking at the beginning of the sheet. Select **Yes**. When the spelling check is complete a box will appear. Select **OK**.

Closing an Excel Workbook

- **To Close an Excel 2000 workbook:** From the File menu, select Close or double click on the Control menu in the top left-hand corner of the workbook window. You will be asked if you wish to save any changes you have made to the file. Select **Yes** to save or **No** to ignore the changes. If you are saving a new file, the **Save As** dialog box will be displayed. In the **File name** text box, enter a name and click on the **Save** button.

- **To close all open workbooks:** Press the **Shift** key and click on the File drop-down menu and then release the shift key. Close command changes and Close All command is displayed.

- **To minimize a workbook window:** Click on the **Minimize** button in the top right-hand corner of the workbook window. If the workbook is maximized, restore it first by clicking the **Restore** button which appears in the top right-hand corner of the workbook window.

Selecting Worksheet Views

Allows you to customize how Excel 2000 components will be displayed on your screen. You can set default **View** option using the **Tools → Options** command.

Cancel, Undo and Repeat

This command allows you to cancel, undo or repeat an action.

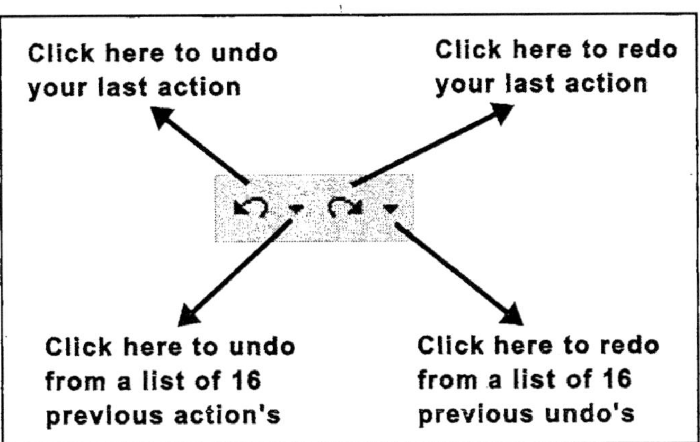

Figure 6.22 Undo and Redo

- The Esc key is used to back out of a process and return to the worksheet.
- **To undo an action:** Click the Undo button on the Standard toolbar or press Ctrl+z or select Undo from the Edit menu to restore it. Excel maintains upto 16 undo levels.
- **To repeat and action:** Click the Repeat button on the Standard toolbar or press F4 or select Repeat from the Edit menu.

Printing

From the File menu, choose Page Setup to display the Page Setup dialog box. Options are: Orientation, Page numbering, Paper size, Print quality, Scale of the page.

To select a printer

- From the **File** menu, select **Print** to display the **Print** dialog box.
- From the **Printer Name** list box, choose the printer you wish to use.
- Click **OK**.

To change the printer settings

- From the **File** menu, choose **Page Setup** to display the **Page Setup** dialog box.
- Choose the **Options** button to display the **Properties** dialog box for the printer.
- Change the options required. The options will vary depending on what type of printer you have.
- Select **OK**, and then select **OK** to close the **Page Setup** dialog box.

To set the print area

- From the **File** menu, choose **Page Setup** to display the **Page Setup** dialog box.
- Select the **Sheet** tab.
- In the **Print area** text box, enter the print area, or select the worksheet range by clicking in the **Print area** text box and dragging through the worksheet to select the areas you wish to print.
- Select **OK**.

To print

- From the **File** menu, select **Print** to display the **Print** dialog box.
- Select what you want to print in the **Print what** area, i.e. **Selection**, **Active sheet(s)**, or **Entire workbook**.
- Specify the number of copies you want to print in the **Number of Copies** spin box.
- In the **Page range** area, select whether you want to print **All** pages in a range, or enter the starting and ending page numbers in the **From** and **To** spin boxes. Select **OK**.

To print column or row titles on every page

- From the **File** menu, choose **Page Setup** to display the **Page Setup** dialog box.
- Select the **Sheet** tab.
- Click the **Rows to repeat at top** text box and then select the rows you want to repeat by dragging over the rows in the worksheet. Click on the **Columns to repeat at left** text box and select the columns to repeat in the same way. Select **OK**.

To print multiple files

- Click on the **File** drop down menu.
- Click on the **Open** command.
- Whilst holding down the **Ctrl** key select the files to be printed.
- Right-click on the files to display a pop-up menu.
- Select the **Print** command from the pop-up menu.

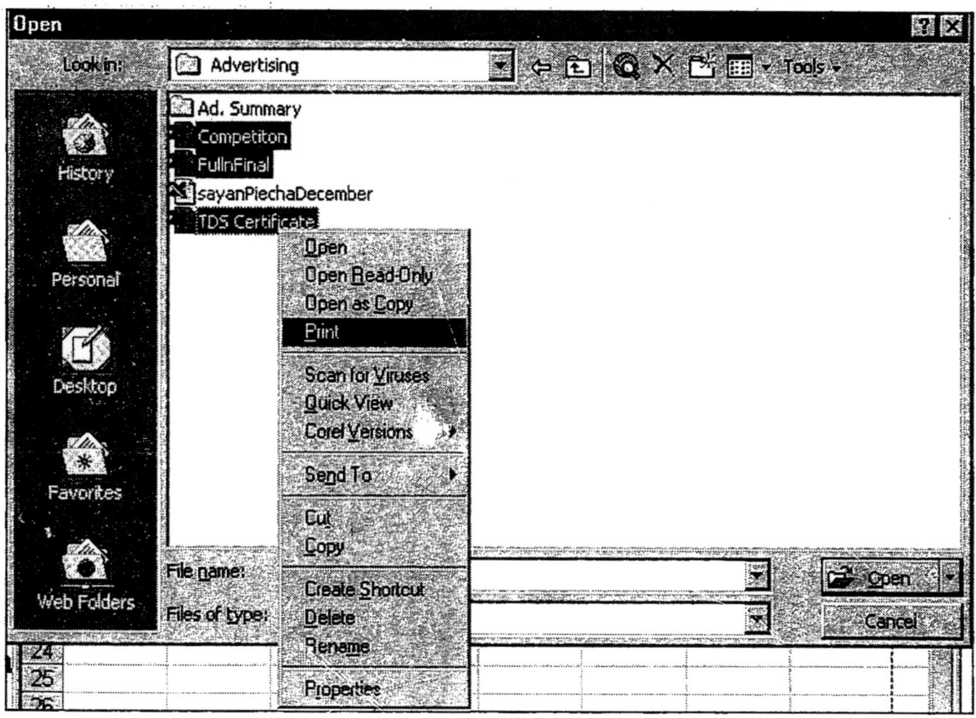

Figure 6.23: Printing Multiple files

Page Setup

To change page setup, choose **File → Page Setup** from the menu bar to open the Page Setup dialog box. The Page Setup dialog box splits page layout into four tabbed pages that contain Page, Margins, Header/Footer and Sheet settings.

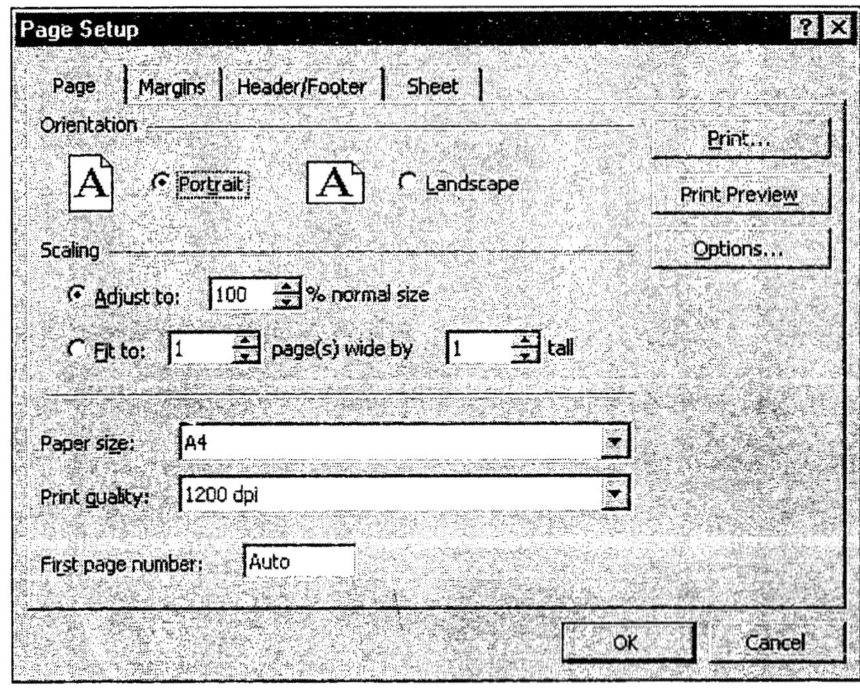

Figure 6.24: Page tab in Page Setup dialog box

- From the **File** drop down menu, choose **Page Setup** to display the **Page Setup** dialog box as shown in Figure 6.24.
- Click on the **Page** tab. Make changes to any of the following:
  - **Orientation:** Select Portrait or Landscape by clicking the option button in the Orientation area.
  - **Page numbering:** To begin page numbering with a different number, select the First page number text box and enter the number you want to use.
  - **Paper size:** Display the Paper size drop-down list box and select the size you require.
  - **Scaling:** This is used to reduce or enlarge the print. If you simply need to make the print larger, use the Adjust To control and choose a size greater then 100%. The Fit To control instructs Excel to reduce a worksheet that exceeds a specific number of pages so it will fit.
- Display the **Print quality** drop-down list box and choose the quality you require.

- Choose the **Adjust to** option button.
- Enter a percentage to scale in the **Adjust to** spin box, or choose the **Fit To** option and enter the dimensions of the pages in the tall and wide spin boxes.
- Click **OK** to apply the settings.

Margins

From the File menu, choose Page Setup to display the Page Setup dialog box and then select the Margins tab. Options are: Changing the margins, Changing header and footer margins, Changing margins in Print Preview.

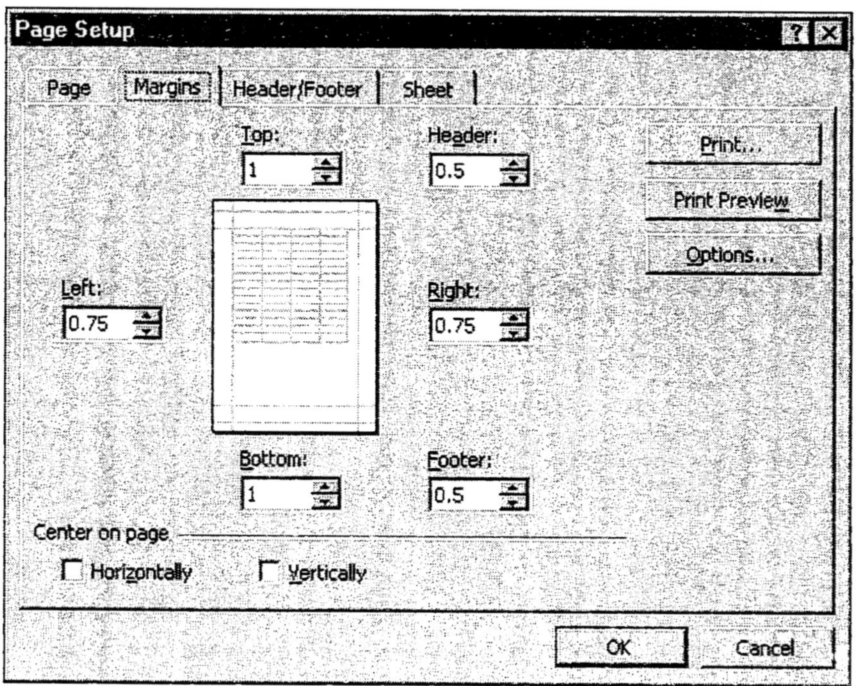

Figure 6.25: Margins tab in Page Setup dialog box

To change the margins

- From the **File** menu, choose **File → Page Setup** to display the **Page Setup** dialog box as shown in Figure 6.25.
- Select the **Margins** tab and click on the margin spin box you want to change, **Top, Bottom, Left** or **Right**.
- Click on the spin box arrows to change the settings and click **OK** to apply the changes.

Margins in Print Preview

- From the **File** menu, choose **File → Print Preview** to display the **Print Preview** window and click on the **Margins** button. Dotted guidelines will appear to indicate each margin.
- Click and drag the margin guideline you wish to change to a new location.

Centering a report on a page

- From the **File** menu, choose **Page Setup** to display the **Page Setup** dialog box as in Figure 6.26.
- Select the **Margins** tab.
- Click the **Horizontally** and/or **Vertically** check boxes in the **Center on page** area. An example of how your selection will print is displayed on the preview page.
- The print block will be centered between the margins which you establish.
- When you have selected your options, choose the **Print** button to display the **Print** dialog box.
- Choose **OK** to print the report.

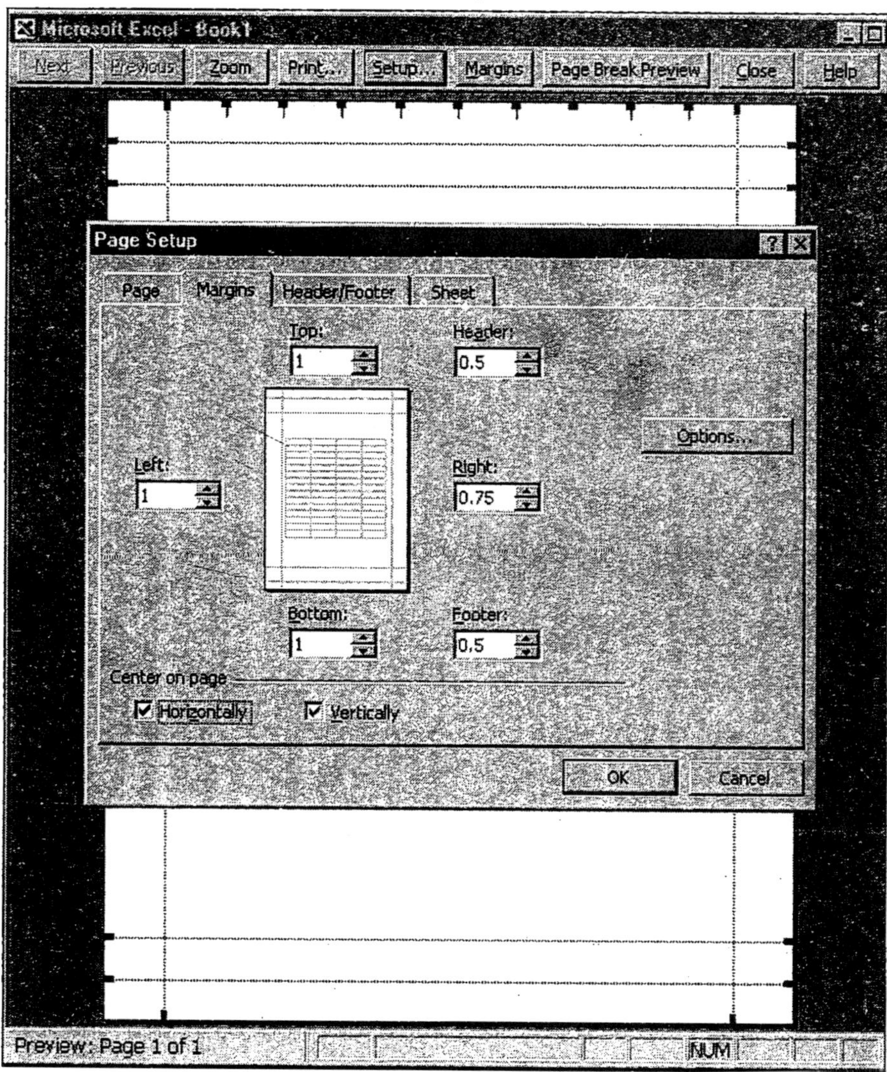

Figure 6.26: Setting the Page Margin in the Preview

Header and Footer

- Excel 2000 provides standard header and footer options as well as you can create your own custom header and footer, which can be selected from the drop down menus in the **Page Setup** dialog box. Make sure the **Header/Footer** tab is displayed as shown in Figure 6.27.

- Click on the **down arrow** to the right of the **Header** list box to reveal a list of available headers. Click on the header required to select it.

- Click on the **down arrow** on the right of the **Footer** list box to reveal a list of available footers. Click on the footer required to select it.

- Click on the **Custom Header** or **Custom Footer** button to display the **Header** (or **Footer**) dialog box. In the **Left section** box, enter any data you want to appear at the left margin of the header or footer. In the **Center section** box, enter any data you want to appear at the center of the header or footer. In the **Right section** box, enter any data you want to appear at the right margin of the header or footer. You can also add the date and time to your header or footer using the **Date** and **Time** icons, include file and sheet names in the header or footer using the **File** and **Sheet name** icons, and determine which pages the header and footer will appear on using the **Page** buttons. When you have finished, click on **OK** to close the dialog box. Your new header (or footer) will be displayed in the **Page Setup** dialog box in the **Header** or **Footer** list box. Choose **OK** to close the **Page Setup** dialog box.

- Click on **OK** to accept the header and footer and close the dialog box.

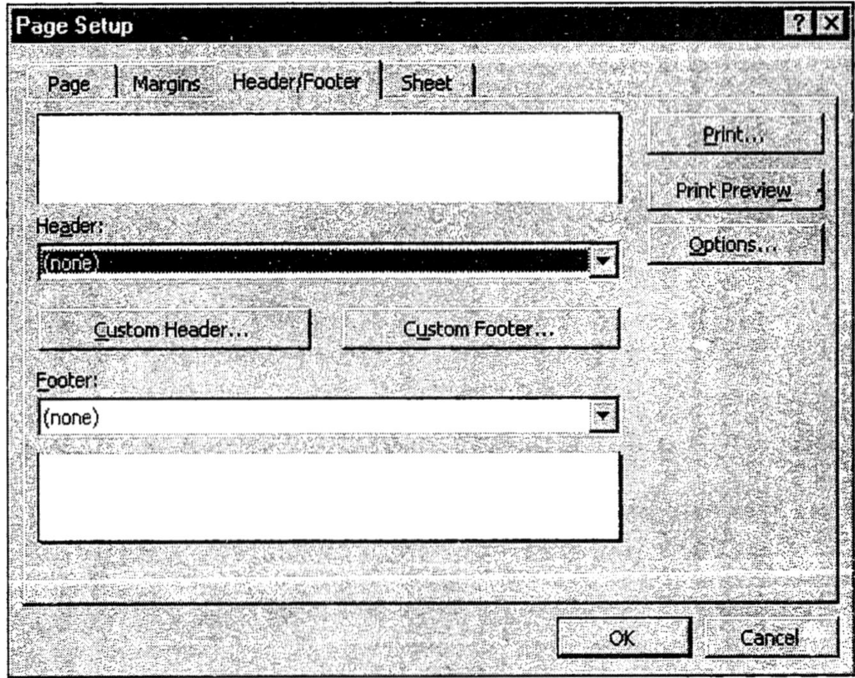

Figure 6.27: Header/Footer tab in Page Setup dialog box

Sheet Options

- From the **File** drop down menu, click on the **Page Setup** command to display the **Page Setup** dialog box.
- Select the **Sheet** tab as in Figure 6.28 and then make changes to any of the following:
    - **Columns or rows to repeat:** Click on the icon in the right of the Rows to repeat at top text box in the Print titles area and drag over the rows you wish to repeat at the top of the page. Click on the icon in the right of the Columns to Repeat at Left text box, and drag over the columns you wish to repeat at the left of the page.
    - **Elements that will print:** Select the elements you wish to print, i.e. Gridlines, Comments, Draft Quality, Black and White, Row and Column Headings.
    - **Order of pages to print:** Select Down, then over, or Over, then down.
    - **Print range:** In the Print Area text box, enter the worksheet range you want to print, or click on the icon in the right of the Print Area text box and drag through the worksheet areas you wish to print.

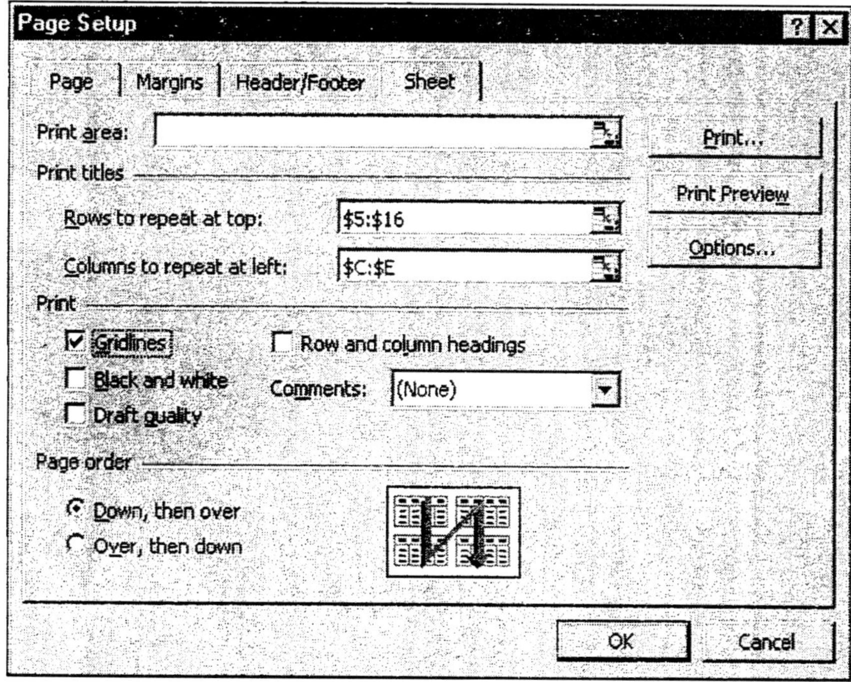

Figure 6.28: Sheet tab in Page Setup dialog box

Hands on Exercise

Exercise 1: A Series Example

1. Create a new worksheet.
2. Fill the cell A2: A13 with the month series.
3. Fill cell B2:B8 with the weekday series.
4. Fill the cell C2:C13 with number series (**Hint:** enter 1 in cell C2 and 3 in cell C3).
5. Select the cell A4:C7 and go to the cell A18 and paste.
6. Final output is shown in the Figure 6.29.

TableChair Details

	A	B	C	D
1				
2	JANUARY	MONDAY	1	
3	FEBRUARY	TUESDAY	3	
4	MARCH	WEDNESDAY	5	
5	APRIL	THURSDAY	7	
6	MAY	FRIDAY	9	
7	JUNE	SATURDAY	11	
8	JULY	SUNDAY	13	
9	AUGUST		15	
10	SEPTEMBER		17	
11	OCTOBER		19	
12	NOVEMBER		21	
13	DECEMBER		23	
14				
15				
16				
17				
18	MARCH	WEDNESDAY	5	
19	APRIL	THURSDAY	7	
20	MAY	FRIDAY	9	
21	JUNE	SATURDAY	11	
22				
23				

Sheet1 / Sheet2 / Sheet3

Figure 6.29: A sample worksheet

Test Your Knowledge

Students must solve the following assignment.

Multiple Choice Questions:

1. What is the name of the package which permits people to quickly create, manipulate and analyse data arranged in rows and columns ?

   a. Spreadsheet package
   b. Wordprocessing package
   c. Outline processors
   d. Application package

2. What does an electronic spreadsheet consist of ?

   a. Rows
   b. Columns
   c. Cells
   d. All of the above.

3. To change the name of a sheet, ______ the sheet tab and then enter the new name.

   a. double-click
   b. single-click
   c. left-click

4. Many Excel spreadsheets are printed in _______________orientation which means the printout is printed across the length of the page (sideways

   a. Portrait
   b. Landscape

5. The mouse pointer changes to a(n) ______ when you point to the boundary of a column heading or row heading.

   a. Magnifying glass
   b. an arrow
   c. a cross hair
   d. a split double-arrow

6. The cell having bold boundary is the ________ cell.

   a. Active
   b. In-active

State Whether True or False:

1. If you enter 127A in a cell it will be treated as a number because it stars with a digit.

   a. True
   b. False

2. You cannot open two different workbooks in Excel simultaneously.

   a. True
   b. False

Write cell references for the following:

1. Cell formed by intersection of row 18, and column Z.
2. The right most cell in row 32 in a worksheet.
3. If you select on entire worksheet, Which range of cells gets selected.

Short Questions:

1. What are the three types of Series command?
2. What is the use of Freeze Panes command and how will you lock it?
3. What is Grouping Sheets and how will you select All Sheets and Contiguous Sheets?
4. How will you print multiple files. Write down the steps involved?

Formatting and Customizing Data

Objectives

- Introduction
- Alignment
- Data Indentation and Rotation
- Using Fonts
- Formatting Numbers
- Adding, Editing and Removing Borders
- Formatting with Style

Introduction

There are many ways to format an Excel 2000 spreadsheet and a large number of different items that can be formatted separately including the fonts, colors, borders, printer formatting option. Within Excel 2000 there are many levels at which formatting can be applied. You can format individual characters, paragraphs, worksheet or entire workbook.

Many different formatting effects can be applied such as alignment of data. You can add color effects. You can even use the AutoFormat option to automatically apply formatting to a table.

Alignment

Data can be aligned with any or all four sides of a cell.

Text can be aligned to the left, right, top or bottom of a cell. You can also change the orientation in a cell, i.e., from top to bottom, bottom to top, left to right or stacked.

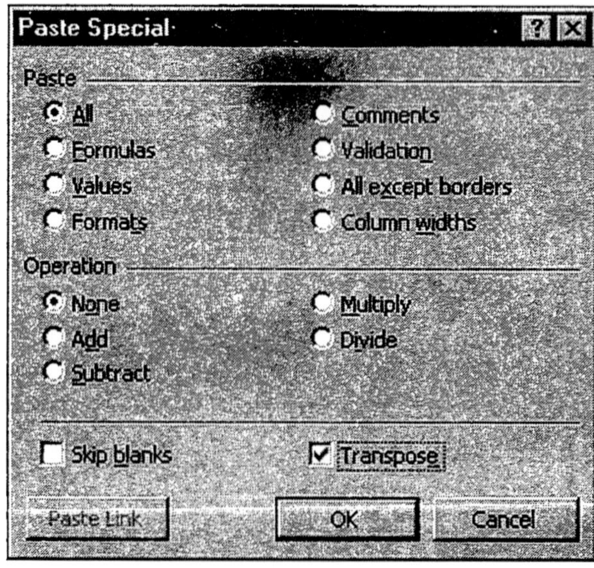

Figure 7.1: Alignment tab in Format Cells dialog box

To align data between the left and right sides of a cell

- Select the cell, or cells, you wish to align. On the **Formatting** toolbar, click the **Align Left** icon to align data with the left edge of the cell.
- Click the **Align Right** icon to align data with the right edge of the cell.
- Click the **Center** icon to center the data in the cell.

To align data between the top and bottom of a cell

- Select the cell, or cells, you wish to align. From the **Format** menu, select **Cells** to display the **Format Cells** dialog box. To view the **Alignment** options, click on the **Alignment** tab at the top of the dialog box. Choose the **Top**, **Center** or **Bottom** option in the **Vertical** area to align the data in the cell.
- To make the lines of data fit evenly within the height of a cell, choose the **Justify** option and click on **OK**.

To change the orientation of data in cells

- Select the cell, or cells, you wish to change and from the **Format** menu, choose **Cells** or press **Ctrl+1**, to display the **Format Cells** dialog box. To view the **Alignment** options, click on the **Alignment** tab at the top of the **Format Cells** dialog box.
- Click the option you require in the **Orientation** area and click on **OK**.

To wrap multiple lines of data in a cell

- Type the data you require into the cell and press **Enter**. The entry will appear as one long line and select the cell, or cells, you wish to format.
- From the **Format** menu, choose **Cells** or press **Ctrl+1** to display the **Format Cells** dialog box.
- Click on the **Alignment** tab to display the **Alignment** options.
- Select the **Wrap text** check box and click on **OK**.

To center a heading over multiple columns

- Type a heading at the top of the left-hand column.
- Place the cell pointer on the heading cell and highlight it along with all the cells across the columns or rows.
- On the **Formatting** toolbar, click the **Merge and Center**  icon.

Data Indentation and Rotation

Works in a way similar to indenting when using a word processor. Use to set the horizontal and vertical alignment of selected values. The Wrap Text check box is used to wrap text within the current cells. Text can also be rotated to any angle you require.

To indent data within a cell

- First select the cell or cells that you wish to apply the indenting formatting to.
- Right click to display the pop-up box, and from the list displayed, select **Format Cells** This will display the **Format Cells** dialog box. Select the **Alignment** tab.
- Select **Left (Indent)** from the **Text Alignment/Horizontal** list, and then use the spinner controls to add the required indent.
- Select **OK**.

To rotate text to any angle

- First select the cell or cells that you wish to apply the rotation formatting to.
- Right click to display the pop-up box, and from the list displayed, select **Format Cells**. This will display the **Format Cells** dialog box. Select the **Alignment** tab.
- From the **Orientation** section either enter the exact amount of rotation required into the **Degrees** box, or drag the **Text** dial to give the desired level of rotation as shown in Figure 7.2.
- Select **OK**.

Figure 7.2: Text Orientation in degrees

Using Fonts

Used to select a font name, style, size, color and special effect.

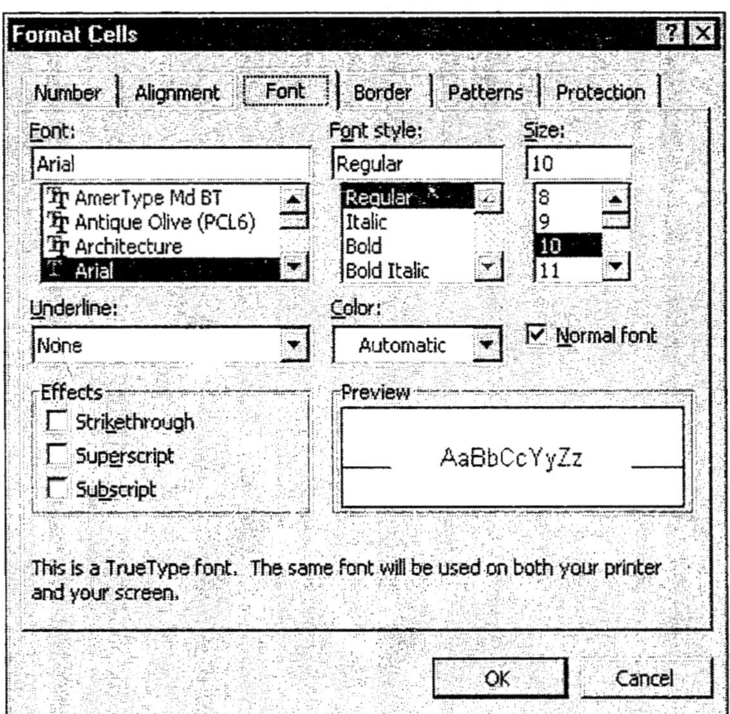

Figure 7.3: Font tab in the Format Cells dialog box

To change the default font of the current workbook

- From the **Format** menu, select **Style** to display the **Style** dialog box.
- From the **Style name** drop down list, choose **Normal**.
- Select **Modify** to display the **Format Cells** dialog box.
- Choose the **Font** tab and make the changes you require.
- Choose **OK** to return to the **Style** dialog box.
- Choose **OK** again.

To change the font used in a cell or range

- Select the cell or range you wish to change.
- On the **Formatting** toolbar choose a font from the **Font** drop down list.

To change other font characteristics

- Select the cell or range you wish to change.
- From the **Format** menu, choose **Cells** or press **Ctrl+1** to display the **Format Cells** dialog box.
- Select the **Font** tab to change the **Font**, **Style** or **Size**.
- Select the **Underline** drop down list box to select a style of underline or **None** to remove the underlining.
- Select the **Color** drop down list box to choose a font color.
- Select **Effects** to choose **Strikethrough**, **Superscript** or **Subscript**.
- To change all the settings in the dialog box back to the **Normal** style which is set in the **Style** dialog box, select the **Normal Font** check box.
- Select **OK** to close the **Format Cells** dialog box.

Using Colors

Used to change the color of text, fill colors and patterns into cells.

To change the color of your text

- Select the cell or range of cells containing the data you want to color.
- In the **Format** menu, click **Cells → Font → Font Color** or on the **Formatting** toolbar, click the down arrow next to the **Font Color** icon.
- Choose a color from the **Font Color** palette.

☞ *Note: The color you selected from the **Color** palette will be displayed on the new icon. Click on the face of the icon to apply the color again.*

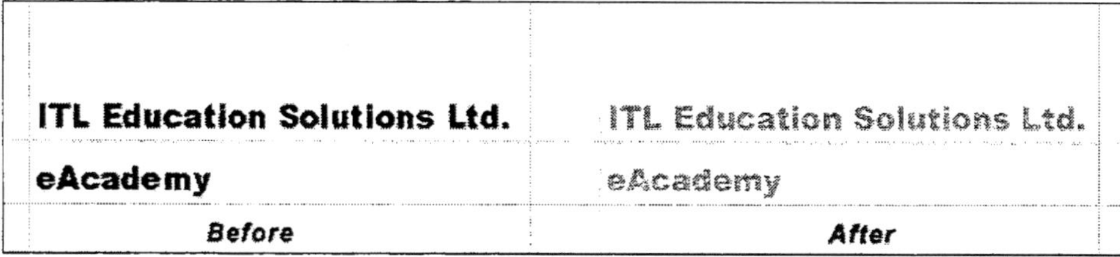

Figure 7.4: Changing the color of text

To apply colors to cells

- Select the range of cells you wish to color (one cell or the entire worksheet).
- On the **Formatting** toolbar, click the down arrow next to the **Fill Color** icon.
- Select the color from the palette you wish to aply.

To apply patterns to cells

- Select the cells you wish to fill patterns.
- From the **Format** drop down menu, select **Cells** (or press **Ctrl+1**) to display the **Format Cells** dialog box.

- Select the **Patterns** tab as shown in Figure 7.5.

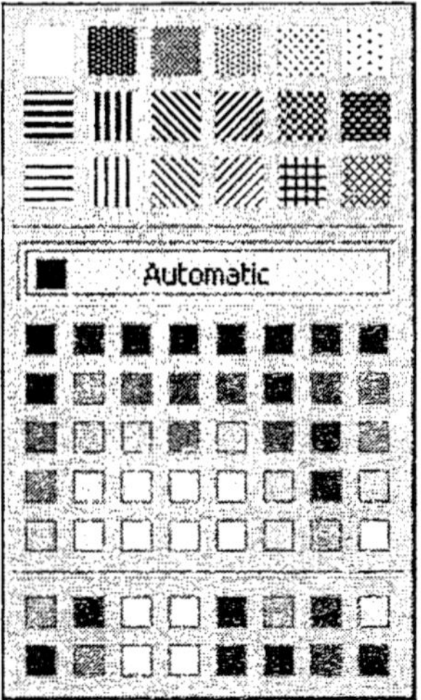

Figure 7.5: Patters and Colors

- From the **Pattern** drop-down list, choose from the available patterns and the standard colors.
- Select the pattern you want to apply it to the selected range.
- Click **OK** to apply.

To change colors based on the values

- Select the cells you wish to change, which contains numeric values. Click **Format → Cells** (or **CTRL+1**) to display the **Format Cells** dialog box. Click the **Number** tab.
- From the **Category** list box choose **Custom**. To view what custom number formats are available use the scroll bars in the **Type** section of the dialog box. To force all negative numbers to be displayed in Red, select the required option. Click **OK** to apply.

To turn the gridlines on/off

- From the **Tools** menu, click **Options** to display the **Options** dialog box.
- Select the **View** tab as shown in the Figure 7.6.

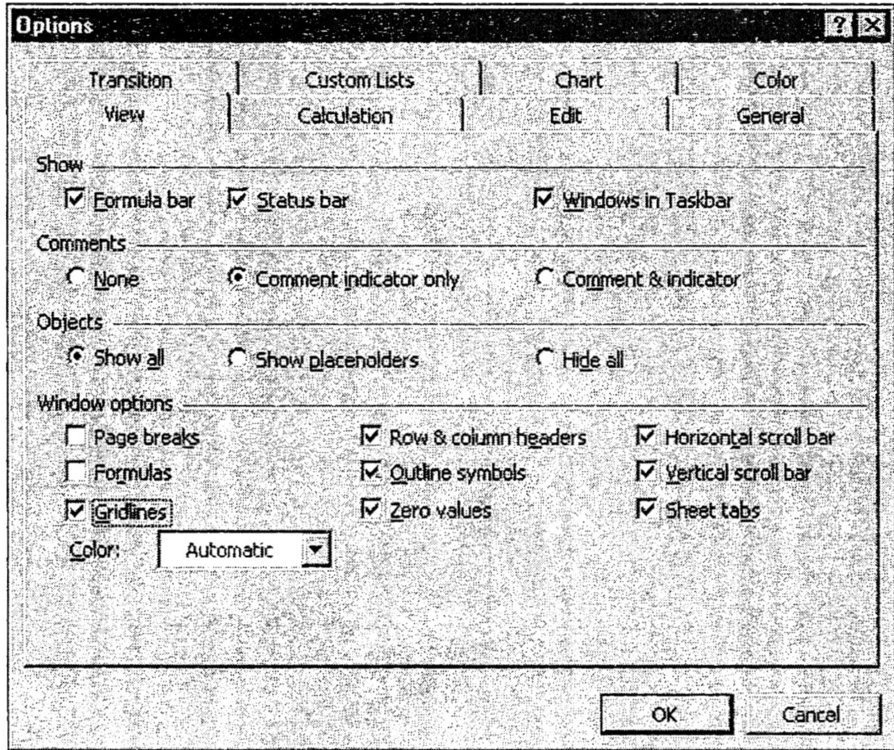

Figure 7.6: View tab in the Options dialog box

- Uncheck the **Gridlines** check box in the **Window options** area.
- Click **OK**. The gridlines will not appear on the screen.

Formatting Numbers

When you enter data in a format that resembles one of Excel's built-in formats, Excel automatically applies formatting to the cell. If you enter a number that contains a slash (/) or hyphen (-) and matches any of Windows date and time formats, Excel converts the entry to a date value and formats the cell using the closest matching Date format. If the date you enter includes only the month and date, Excel uses the current year. To change number formatting in Excel 2000 use the **Formatting** toolbar. You can change Currency, Percent, Comma, Decimal point. If you enter a number preceded by a dollar sign, Excel applies the Currency style with two decimal places, regardless of how many decimal places you entered.

When you enter number that contains a color (:) or if the number is followed by a space and the letter A or P, Excel converts it to a time format. If you enter a number that includes a comma to set off thousands or millions, Excel applies the Number format using the default separator.

You can quickly change the formatting of a cell or selected range by using the shortcut icons on the **Formatting** toolbar.

To apply a custom format to numbers in a cell or range

- Click the cell or select the range you want to format.
- From the **Format** menu, choose **Cells** to display the **Format Cells** dialog box.
- Select the **Number** tab and click the **Custom** format in the **Category** list box on the left.
- Select the format the one you wish to create by clicking other items in the **Type** list box.
- Edit the code in the **Type** text box if required.
- Click **OK** to accept the settings.

To format a number as a percentage

- Select the range you wish to format.
- From the **Format** menu, select **Cells** to display the **Format Cells** dialog box.
- Select the **Number** tab and select **Percentage** in the **Category** list box.
- Select the number of decimal places you require by using the **Decimal places** spin box arrows.
- Click **OK** to accept the settings.

☞ *Notes: Select the range and click the **Percent Style** icon on the **Formatting** toolbar if you want a percentage with no decimal places.*

To round numbers using a numeric format

To squeeze data so that it fits in a cell, Excel rounds numbers and truncates cell contents, usually without telling you.

- Select the range you wish to format.
- From the **Format** menu, select **Cells** to display the **Format Cells** dialog box.
- Select the **Number** tab and select **Number** in the **Category** list box.
- Select the number of decimal places you require by using the **Decimal places** box arrows.
- Click on the **OK** button to accept the settings.

Example:

1. Enter the data as shown in the Figure 7.7. Select the range B3:F6 and select the **Number** tab in the **Format Cells** dialog box and select **Number** in the **Category** list box. Select 2 decimal places.

2. Now select the row G3:G6 and select the **Number** tab in the **Format Cells** dialog box and select **Percentage** in the **Category** list box. Select 2 decimal places. Now click OK.

South East Sales

	A	B	C	D	E	F	G	H
1	Eastern Region Sales							
2	*Product Sales*	*Qtr 1*	*Qtr 2*	*Qtr 3*	*Qtr 4*	*Total*	*Percent*	
3	Retailers	55	60	58	65	238	0.518519	
4	Distributors	59	38	44	41	182	0.396514	
5	Other	4	9	12	14	39	0.084967	
6	Total Sales	118	107	114	120	459	1	
7								
8								
9								

South East Sales

	A	B	C	D	E	F	G	H
1	Eastern Region Sales							
2	*Product Sales*	*Qtr 1*	*Qtr 2*	*Qtr 3*	*Qtr 4*	*Total*	*Percent*	
3	Retailers	55.00	60.00	58.00	65.00	238.00	51.85%	
4	Distributors	59.00	38.00	44.00	41.00	182.00	39.65%	
5	Other	4.00	9.00	12.00	14.00	39.00	8.50%	
6	Total Sales	118.00	107.00	114.00	120.00	459.00	100.00%	
7								
8								

Sheet1 Sheet2 Sheet3

Figure 7.7: Example of Percent and Numeric format

Decimal Points

Select the cell, or range, you wish to format with a fixed number of decimal places. To add a decimal points, click on the **Increase Decimal** icon on the **Formatting** toolbar. Continue to click to add as many decimals as required. To remove a decimal point from the selection, click on the **Decrease Decimal** icon on the **Formatting** toolbar.

To set decimal places for numeric values on the workbook

- From the **Tools** menu, choose **Options** to display the **Options** dialog box. Select the **Edit** tab and select the **Fixed Decimal Places** check box as shown in Figure 7.8.

- Enter the number of decimal places required in the box. Select **OK**. You will not need to type in the decimal point when you are entering numbers in the workbook. This does not affect data which already exists.

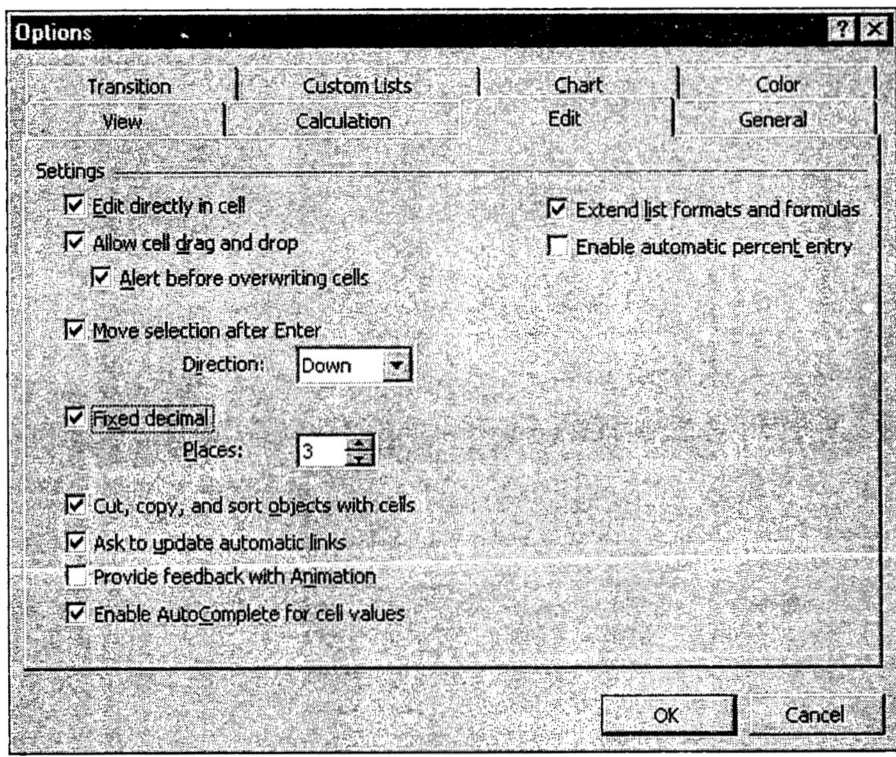

Figure 7.8: Edit tab in the Options dialog box

Formatting Columns and Rows

If you enter text which exceeds the column width, it will spill over into the next column as long as the cell does not contain any data. If it contains data the entry will be truncated at the edge of the cell. Although the entire entry does not appear, it will still be intact. If you enter a number which exceeds the width of a column, #### signs will be displayed in the cell to let you know that the column is not wide enough.

To change the width of a column

- On the right-hand border of the column you wish to change and follow it to the top of the worksheet into the area of the column heading.
- When the mouse pointer is moved in this area, it changes to a thick crosshair.
- Click on the right-hand column heading border and drag the mouse to the right to increase the column, or to the left to reduce the column size.

To set new default column widths

- From the **Format** menu, choose **Column Standard Width** to display the **Standard Width** dialog box.
- Enter a new width for standard columns.
- Select **OK** to accept the settings.

To change the height of a row

- Select the row(s) you wish to change.
- From the **Format** menu, select **Row** and choose **Height** from the **Format Row** menu. The **Row Height** dialog box is displayed.
- Enter the value you want in the **Row Height** text box. The value represents the row height in points.
- Click **OK** to apply the settings.

Adding, Editing and Removing Borders

To apply a border to a cell or range of cells

- Select the cell(s) or ranges to which you want to add a border.
- To view border options, click on the down arrow next to the **Borders** icon on the **Formatting** toolbar.
- Select the option you require. Once you have added a border using the **Borders** icon, the border you selected will appear on the **Borders** icon. You can add the same border simply by clicking on the icon after you have selected the cell(s) or ranges to which you wish to apply the border.

To remove a border from a cell or range of cells

- Select the cell(s) or ranges that contain the border you wish to remove. If you have a border that appears to be on the left side of a cell, but may actually be on the right side of the adjacent cell, select both of the cells.
- To reveal the border options, click the arrow next to the **Borders** icon on the **Formatting** toolbar.
- Click on the first border option i.e., **no border** selection and all highlighted borders will be removed.

To change the style and color of borders

- Select the cell that contain a border and then from the **Format** menu, choose **Cells**, or press **Ctrl+1** to display the **Format Cells** dialog box.
- To display the border options, click the **Border** tab on the top of the **Format Cells** dialog box.
- Select the border style you require by clicking on it.
- From the **Color** drop-down palette, select the color you require.
- Click on the **Border** options to determine where you want the colored borders to appear on the selected cells. Click on **OK**.

Format a Table using the AutoFormat command

AutoFormat command allows you to automatically format a table.

- Place the insertion cell within a table of information.
- From the **Format** drop down menu, select the **AutoFormat** command.
- From the list displayed in the **Table format** section of the dialog box as shown in Figure 7.9, select the required format say **Classic 3** and click on the **OK** button to apply the formatting information.

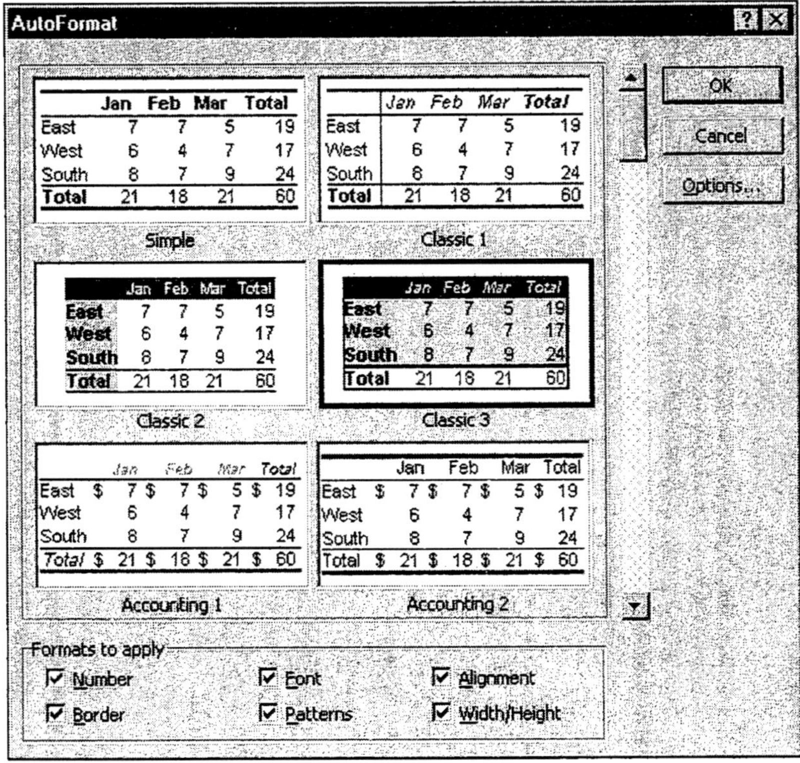

Figure 7.9: AutoFormat dialog box

☞ *Notes: Clicking on the* ***Options*** *button within the dialog box allows you to specify the following customization options:*

- Checking any of the above boxes applies the appropriate elements when AutoFormat is applied.
- If you do not wish to apply a format to a particular element uncheck the appropriate box.

To copy data to different location on the same page

- Select the cell or range you wish to copy.
- Click on the border edge of the highlighted range with the mouse pointer, while holding down the **Ctrl** key. Before you click, the mouse pointer turns into an arrow.
- While holding down the mouse button, drag the selection to the required location.
- Release the mouse button to insert the selection.

To view the Clipboard toolbar

As Microsoft Office supports upto 12 items on the Clipboard, when you have copied 12 items you will see a message similar to that illustrated. To copy multiple items, simply select each item and copy it to the clipboard.

- If the Clipboard toolbar is not displayed, then you can display it by clicking on the **View** drop down menu, selecting **Toolbars**, and then selecting **Clipboard**. Icons on this toolbar includes **Copy**, **Paste All** and **Clear Clipboard**.
- If the Clipboard toolbar is not displayed, then you can display it by clicking on the **View →** **Toolbars → Clipboard**.
- If you move the mouse over one of the icons held within the Clipboard toolbar, then you will see the first 50 characters displayed. If the item is a picture, then the pictures will be labeled in the order in which they were copied to the Clipboard.

To use the Clipboard to copy an object between pages, workbooks or programs

- Click on the object to select it and choose **Copy** from the **Edit** menu (or press **Ctrl+C**, or click on the **Copy** icon on the **Standard** toolbar).
- Move to a different application, or move to the new sheet or workbook.
- Select a location for the top left-hand corner of the object.
- From the **Edit** menu, choose **Paste** (or press **Ctrl+V**, or click on the **Paste** icon on the **Standard** toolbar).

To move and copy data to another worksheet

- Select the cell or range that contains the data to be copied.
- Press and hold the **Alt** key and drag any edge of the selected range to the required worksheet tab.
- Place the range where required and release the mouse button.
- To copy the data carry out the above procedure holding down both the **Ctrl** and **Alt** keys.

To copy data to another workbook

- Open the other workbook.
- Select the **Window** menu and choose **Arrange**.
- Choose **Tiled** and click on the **OK** button.
- Select the cell range you wish to copy.
- Press and hold the **Ctrl** key and drag any edge of the selected range to the required position in the destination workbook.
- Release the mouse button.

To insert new cells to make space for the copied data

- Select the cell or range you wish to copy.
- Click and drag on the border edge of the selected range whilst holding down the **Ctrl** and **Shift** keys.
- As you drag, the insert indicator shows you where the copied cells will be inserted. A vertical indicator shows that the cells to the right will be moved to make room, a horizontal indicator shows that cells below will be moved to make room.
- When you release the mouse button, the copy will be inserted into the worksheet at the desired location. Existing data will move to make space for the copied data.

To copy a numeric value down a column

- In the first cell of the column, enter the first numeric value or formula.
- Select the second cell in the column.
- To copy the data in the selected cell, press **Shift+Ctrl+"**.
- Press **Enter** to insert the value into the selected cell.

☞ *Notes: If there is already a formula in the original cell, the copied version will only contain the value for the formula. If you want to copy the whole formula, press* ***Ctrl + '***.

To copy a column of text into a row

- Select the range of data you wish to copy and transpose.
- From the **Edit** menu, choose **Copy** or click on the **Copy** icon on the **Standard** toolbar.
- Highlight the cell where you want to place the range.
- Select **Paste Special** from the **Edit** menu, to display the **Paste Special** dialog box.
- Select the **Transpose** check box and select **OK**.

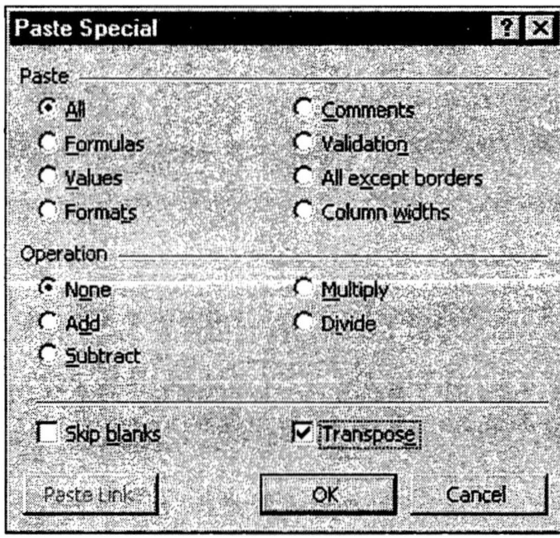

Figure 7.10: Paste Special dialog box

Formatting with Style

AutoFormats are composed of styles that is specifications about one or more formatting options. AutoFormats may include several styles like:

- Arial 18-point bold for the title
- Arial 12-point accounting format for the numbers
- Arial 14-point bold with a top and bottom border for totals

To apply several formats in one step and ensure that cells have consistent formatting, you can apply a style to the cells. Microsoft Excel has styles that you can use to format numbers as currency, as percentages, or with commas that separate thousands. You can create your own styles to apply a font and font size, number formats, cell borders, and shading and to protect cells from changes.

To create a style

Follow these steps to create a style:

- Select the cell whose formatting is the same as you want to use several times.
- Choose **Format** → **Style** from the menu bar to display the **Style** dialog box as shown in Figure 7.11.

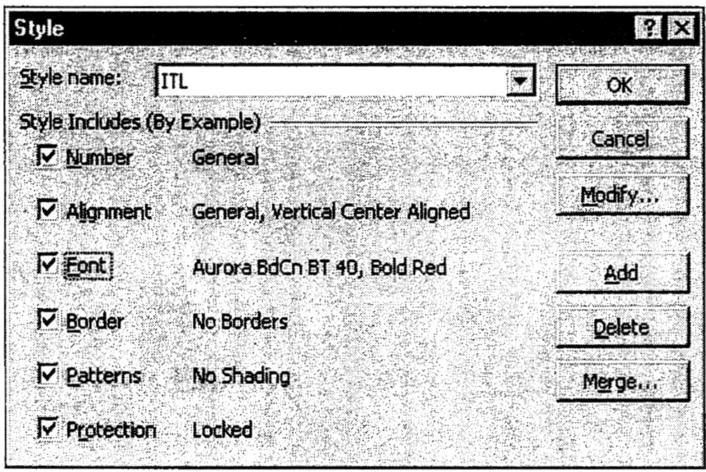

Figure 7.11: Style dialog box

- Enter a new name for the style in the **Style name** drop-down list box and click on the **Add** button.
- Click on the **OK** button to close the dialog box.

To apply a style to selected cells

- Select the cell(s) that you wish to apply a style to.
- Choose **Format → Style** from the menu bar to display the **Style** dialog box
- Click on the down arrow in the **Style name** part of the **Style** dialog box and select the required style.
- Click **OK** to apply the style.

Conditional Formatting

With conditional formatting you can apply formats to selected cells based on a condition. A condition is an expression that when evaluated is either true or false. Allows you to highlight data if it meets a specified criteria. You can also find cells that meets a specified criteria.

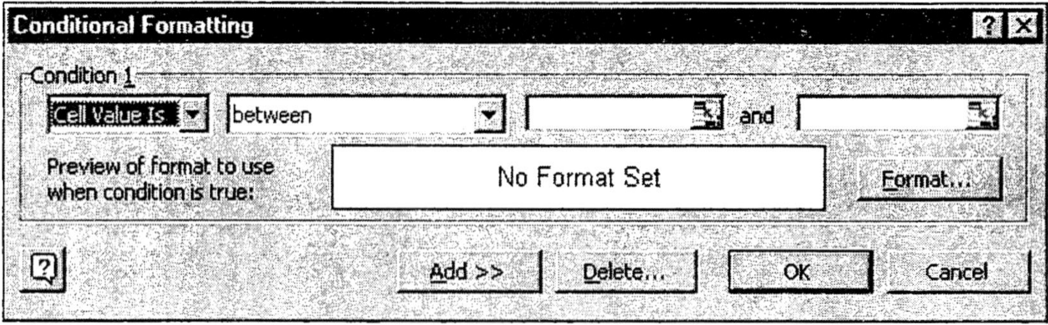

Figure 7.12: Conditional Formatting dialog box

To format a range of cells using conditional formatting

- If we enter the data as shown in diagram 7.13, we can then apply conditional formatting.

	A	B	C
1	11	16	2
2	15	3	18
3	9	12	3
4	12	17	13
5	18	14	22

Figure 7.13: Data used in the conditional formatting

- Select the range of cells to which you wish to apply conditional formatting. Here the range would be **A1:C5**.

- Click on the **Format** drop down menu and select the **Conditional Formatting** command. This will display the **Conditional Formatting** dialog box as shown in Figure 7.14.

  Lets say we wish to highlight all values between 15 and 22, then we would enter the numbers in the correct fields, as illustrated in Figure 7.14.

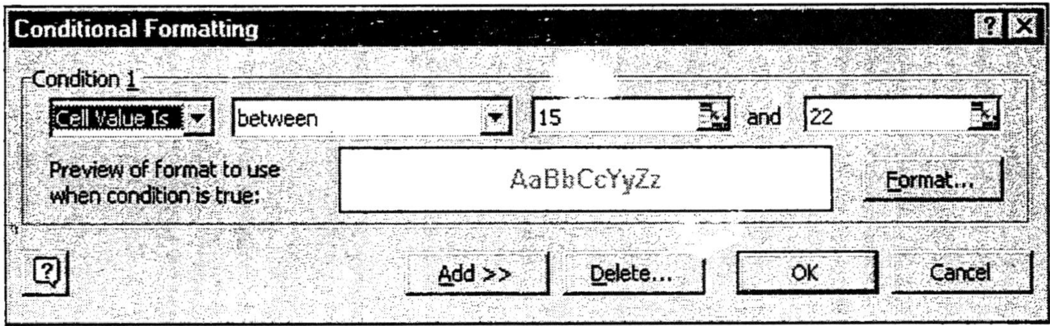

Figure 7.14: Conditional Formatting dialog box

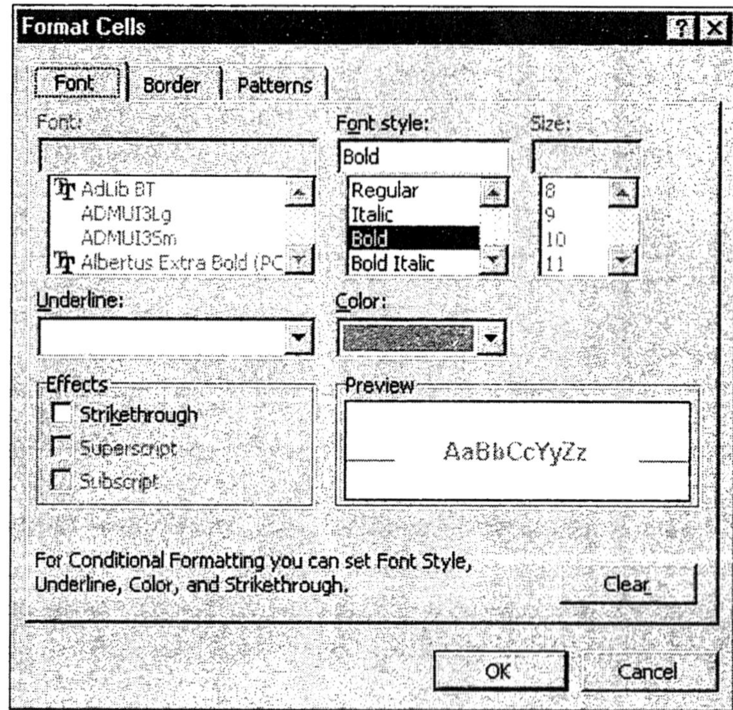

Figure 7.15: Font tab in Format Cell dialog box

- Click on the **Format** button within this dialog box. The normal **Formal Cells** dialog box is displayed as shown in Figure 7.15. Here we can specify how data meets the specified criteria is displayed. We could choose bold formatting and pink colored font. Now click on the **OK** button to close this dialog box, which returns you to the **Conditional Formatting** dialog box. Then click on **OK** to close this dialog box. The output is shown in Figure 7.16.

> **Tips:** By clicking on the **Add** button in the **Conditional Formatting** dialog box you can define other criteria for formatting.

	A	B	C
1	11	[illegible]	2
2	[illegible]	3	[illegible]
3	9	12	3
4	12	[illegible]	13
5	[illegible]	14	[illegible]

Figure 7.16: Output after conditional formatting

To hide columns/rows

- Click the column/row heading to select the column/row you wish to hide. If you wish to select other columns/row, press the **Ctrl** key whilst clicking on each column/row heading.
- From the **Format** menu, select **Column** to hide columns or select **Row** to hide rows.
- Choose **Hide** from the sub-menu as shown in Figure 7.17.

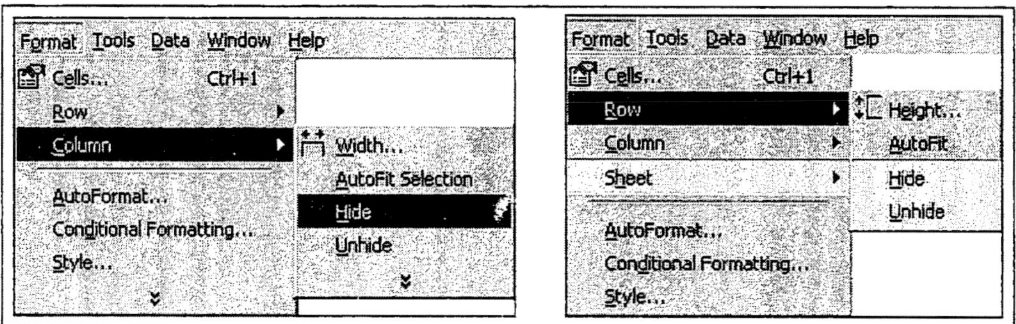

Figure 7.17: Row and column tab in the Format menu

To re-display hidden columns/rows

- Select the columns/rows either side of the hidden column/rows.
- From the **Format** menu, choose **Column** to re-display column or choose **Row** to re-display rows.
- Select **Unhide** from the **Format Column/Row** sub-menu.

To hide worksheets

- Click on the sheet tab on the left bottom corner of the worksheet to select the sheet you wish to hide.
- From the **Format** menu, select **Sheet**.
- Choose **Hide** from the **Format Sheet** sub-menu as shown in Figure 7.18.

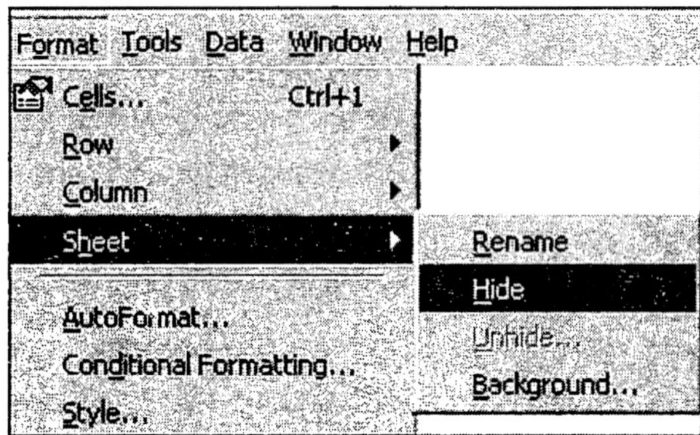

Figure 7.18: Sheet tab in the Format menu

To re-display hidden worksheets

- From the **Format** menu, choose **Sheet**.
- Select **Unhide** from the **Format Sheet** menu. The **Unhide** dialog box is displayed listing the hidden sheets.
- Click the sheet you want to un-hide in the **Unhide sheet** list box.
- Select **OK**.

 Hands on Exercise

Exercise 1: Term End Marks

Create a worksheet having Term End Marks Scored by the students exactly as shown in the Figure 7.19 below.

	A	B	C	D	E	F	G
1	Term End Marks						
2	**Name / Month**	**January**	**April**	**July**	**October**	**December**	
3	**Vipul Singh**	20	34	65	76	80	
4	**Rajesh Sinha**	21	45	56	36	32	
5	**Tanuja**	22	22	45	32	22	
6	**Niraj Kumar**	32	32	32	32	76	
7	**Prem Thakur**	43	45	76	43	45	
8	**Radha Krishnan**	66	45	56	32	66	
9	**Jayant Singh**	24	24	32	24	32	
10							
11							

Sheet1 / Sheet2 / Sheet3

Figure 7.19: A sample worksheet

Exercise 2: Advertising Summary Sheet

Create Advertisement Summary Sheet as shown in the Figure 7.20 below.

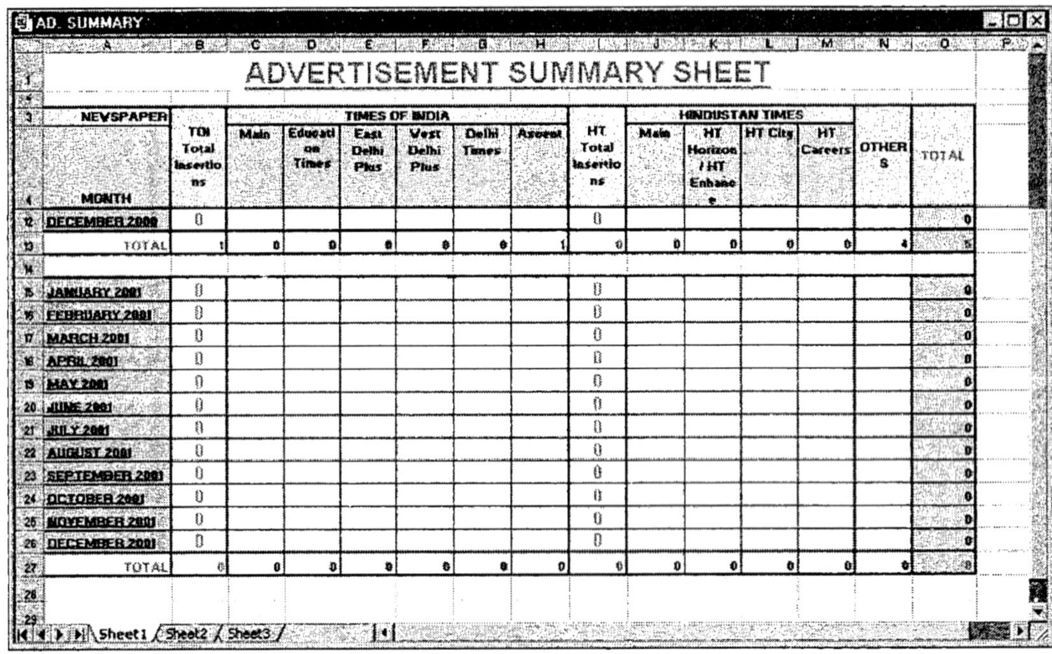

AD. SUMMARY

ADVERTISEMENT SUMMARY SHEET

NEVSPAPER		TIMES OF INDIA							HINDUSTAN TIMES					
MONTH	TOI Total Insertions	Main	Education Times	East Delhi Plus	Vest Delhi Plus	Delhi Times	Ascent	HT Total Insertions	Main	HT Horizon / HT Enhance	HT City	HT Careers	OTHERS	TOTAL
DECEMBER 2000	0							0						0
TOTAL	1	0	0	0	0	0	1	0	0	0	0	0	4	5
JANUARY 2001	0							0						0
FEBRUARY 2001	0							0						0
MARCH 2001	0							0						0
APRIL 2001	0							0						0
MAY 2001	0							0						0
JUNE 2001	0							0						0
JULY 2001	0							0						0
AUGUST 2001	0							0						0
SEPTEMBER 2001	0							0						0
OCTOBER 2001	0							0						0
NOVEMBER 2001	0							0						0
DECEMBER 2001	0							0						0
TOTAL	0	0	0	0	0	0	0	0	0	0	0	0	0	0

Sheet1 / Sheet2 / Sheet3

Figure 7.20: A sample worksheet

Test Your Knowledge

Students must solve the following assignment.

Multiple Choice Questions:

1. When Excel automatically sets the width of a column based on the widest entry in the column, it is called ______.

    a. custom fit
    b. choice fit
    c. best fit
    d. best guess

2. To start a new line in a cell, press __________ after each line.

    a. Ctrl+Enter
    b. Shift+Enter
    c. Alt+Enter
    d. Enter

Fill in the Blanks:

1. Excel worksheets are given ________ extension.

2. The keyboard shortcut for copy is ________ and for paste is ________.

3. When you ________ or ________, the selected range gets surrounded by a moving border.

4. The ________ operation copies data from the source range to target range and erases it from the source range.

5. Address of the cell at 20th column and 30th row is ________.

6. The formula in cell A2 is =B2 + C3. On copying this formula to cell C2, the formula in cell C2 will be ________.

State Whether True or False:

1. Cancel button can be used to undo a cell entry after it has been completed.

   a. True
   b. False

2. When you clear only the contents of a cell, all the formats and contents are deleted.

   a. True
   b. False

3. Once you copy data on to the clipboard, it can be copied to multiple ranges even after pressing Enter key.

   a. True
   b. False

4. When you increase the font size, the row height is automatically adjusted.

   a. True
   b. False

5. By default, the numbers are left aligned and text values are right aligned.

   a. True
   b. False

6. You can't spell-check a spreadsheet.

   a. True
   b. False

Formulas and Functions

Objectives

- Introduction
- Operator Evaluation Order
- Date() Function
- Average() Function
- The IF() Function
- Other commonly used function
- Array Formulas
- Totaling Rows and Columns Automatically
- Naming Cells and Ranges

Introduction

Functions are special commands which are used to make complex operations simple and to perform mathematical processes. Formulas add intelligence to a workbook. Functions can only be used in formulas. They always include parentheses after them [()].

Formula is the term used for a calculation in a worksheet. The diagrams below show an example formula being entered.

To work out the surplus, we need to do a calculation by taking away the expenditure from the salary. You can see this being entered on the left hand side. On the right hand side, you can see what happens after the formula has been entered.

Entering the Formula

COUNT X ✓ = =B3-B12

	A	B
1	**Home Budget**	
2		
3	***Income***	£2,000.00
4		
5	***Expenditure***	
6	Rent	£200.00
7	Food	£150.00
8	Social	£35.00
9	Bills	£50.00
10	Loan	£100.00
11		
12	***Total***	**£535.00**
13		
14	***Surplus***	=B3-B12

Completed Formula

B14 = =B3-B12

	A	B
1	**Home Budget**	
2		
3	***Income***	£2,000.00
4		
5	***Expenditure***	
6	Rent	£200.00
7	Food	£150.00
8	Social	£35.00
9	Bills	£50.00
10	Loan	£100.00
11		
12	***Total***	**£535.00**
13		
14	***Surplus***	**£1,465.00**

Figure 8.1: Formula

How is the Formula Made Up?

- Formulae always start with an equals sign - that's how Excel knows it's a formula.
- Cell references are used in the calculation instead of numbers. This means that if the number inside the cell changes - the answer to the formula will update.
- A mathematical symbol is used to denote the type of calculation.

Here is the formula from the example above, which found us the surplus or money left over.

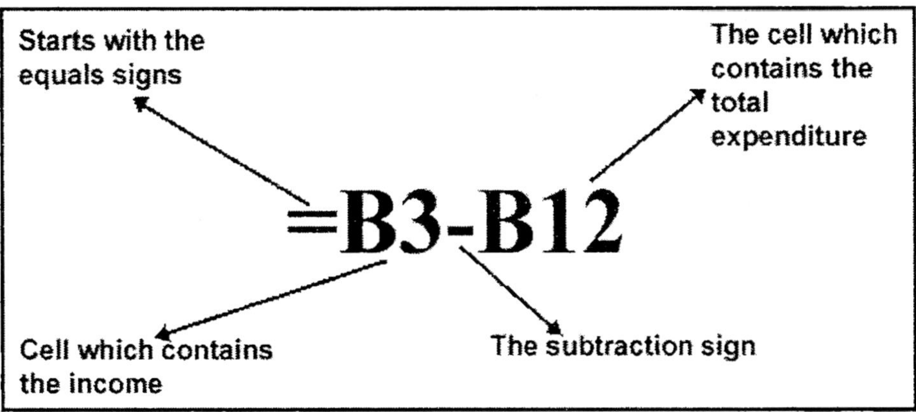

Figure 8.2: Composition of Formula

A formula can be as simple as a reference to another cell, or it can go on for hundreds of characters, with as many as seven functions nested within other functions; regardless of its complexity, however, a formula must begin with an equal sign. Formula consist of three basic building blocks:

- **Operands:** The data to be calculated in a formula can include any combination of constant values, cell or range references, labels that define the intersection of a specific row and column used in natural language formulas or worksheet functions.
- **Operators:** Formulas can use any six basic arithmetic operators – addition (+), subtraction (-) multiplication (*), division (/), percent (%), exponentiation (^). You can also use comparison operators to compare two values and produce the logical result. Comparison operators consists of equal to (=), greater than (>), less than (<), greater than or qual to (>=), less than or equal to (<=) and not equal to (<>). Use an ampersand (&) to combine two pieces of text into a single value.
- **Worksheet functions:** These are predefined formulas that allow you to perform calculations on worksheet data by entering a constant value or cell or range reference. You can also use a worksheet function as a complete contents of a cell or you can use a function as an operand in another formula.

Worksheet functions handle a broad array of tasks, from simple arithmetic to complex financial calculations and intricate statistical tests. Regardless of its complexity, every function consists of two parts - the function name and its arguments. The syntax of a function defines what type of arguments it uses for example, text, numbers, dates and logical values. Excel 2000 contains a built-in list of worksheet functions which are categorized to make it easy to search. You can also define your own functions for calculations. Excel 2000 uses commas to separate multiple arguments.

TODAY() is one of the simplest of all worksheet functions. Whenever you open, save or otherwise recalculate a worksheet that contains this function, Excel updates the value of the cell that contains this formula to display the current date, as stored in your computer.

AVERAGE() accepts upto 30 arguments and calculates the arithmetic mean of all values in the list, ignoring text and logical values. If you calculate a year's worth of monthly sales totals in cells B25 through M25, for example, =AVERAGE(B25:M25) displays the average of the 12 monthly totals.

To calculate the amount of interest you pay each month on a mortgage, use the *IPMT* function. As the syntax description shows, you must supply a minimum of four values as arguments. This function requires the interest rate per period (rate), the specific payment period for which you want to calculate interest (per, a number between 1 and nper), the number of payment periods (nper), and the present value (pv, the amount of the loan).

Operator Evaluation Order

The order of the operators is vital, they are executed in this order:

AND, OR, NOT functions
+ or - (unary)
^
*** or /**
+ or -
&
= < > <= >= <>

To enter functions directly into the worksheet cell

- Select the cell into which the formula will be entered.
- Insert an equal (=) sign to begin the formula. The formula toolbar buttons will appear.
- Enter the name of the function, followed by an opening parenthesis [( ], any arguments required for the function and closing parenthesis [ )].
- Press **Enter**. If there are no errors in the formula, the result of the function will be entered in the cell. If you activate the cell again, the function will be displayed in the formula bar.

Date() Function

Spreadsheets users often requires dates to carry out tasks based on it. To do this Excel 2000 has a number of date related functions.

Microsoft Excel stores dates as sequential numbers known as serial values. Excel stores times as decimal fractions because time is considered a portion of a day. Dates and times are values and, therefore, can be added, subtracted, and included in other calculations. For example, to determine the difference between two dates, you can subtract one date from the other. You can view a date as a serial value and a time as a decimal fraction by changing the format of the cell that contains the date or time to General format.

Excel supports two date systems: the 1900 and 1904 date systems. The default date system for Microsoft Excel for Windows is 1900. To change to the 1904 date system, click **Options** on the **Tools** menu, click the **Calculation** tab and then select the **1904 date system** check box.

How the dates are stored?

Excel 2000 stores dates as a serial number giving each day of the year a unique number starting "Day 1" as 1st January 1900, "Day 2" as 2nd January 1900, "Day 3" as 3rd January 1900.

To enter the current date

If you want the sheet to always show the current date use the **TODAY()** function which will return the serial number for now. When formatted as a date this will show the current date.

To separate the year from a date

To separate the year from a date use the **YEAR()** function. If you have two dates entered you can use the YEAR() function to calculate the number of years between each date. Excel stores January 1, 1904, as serial number 0 (January 2, 1904, is serial number 1). For example, in the 1900 date system, Excel stores January 1, 1998, as serial number 35796 because it is 35,795 days after January 1, 1900. For example, in the 1900 date system, Excel stores January 1, 1998, as serial number 35796 because it is 35,795 days after January 1, 1900.

Example: If you are using the 1900 date system, then:

YEAR(0.007) equals 1900
YEAR(35981.007) equals 1998

To show the day of the week

To show the day of the week for a given date use the **WEEKDAY()** function.

WEEKDAY("2/14/1998") equals 7
WEEKDAY("2/14/1998",2) equals 6

If you are using the 1900 date system, then:
WEEKDAY(35981.007) equals 1

Commands to calculate the difference between two dates in weeks

- In cell A10 (or any other cell) enter the first date say "12/25/1999".
- In cell A12 (or any other cell) enter the second date say "12/25/2000".
- In cell A14 (or any other cell) enter the formula **=A12-A10** to calculate the difference between the second date and the first date.
- This formula calculates the difference between the two dates in days. Output is 366.

To calculate the difference in weeks use the following command:

=(A12-A10)/7
Output is 52

To add days or weeks to a date

- In cell A10 (or any other cell) enter a date say "12/25/1999".
- In cell A12 (or any other cell) enter the following formula: **=A10+180**. This adds 180 days to the date. Output is 22nd June, 2000.

To add weeks to a date, multiply the number of weeks by seven to calculate the number of days,

=A10+(4*7) adds four weeks to the date.
Output is 36547.

To add months to a date

- In cell A10 (or any other cell) enter a date say "12/25/1999".
- In cell A12 (or any other cell) enter the following formula:

=DATE(Year(A10),MONTH(A10)+1,DAY(A10))
Output is 01/25/2000.

If you change the **+1** value to **+2** or **+3**, you will add two months or three months on respectively.

To find out the last day of the month

- In cell A10 (or any other cell) enter a date say "12/25/1999".
- In cell A12 (or any other cell) enter the following formula:

  =DATE(YEAR(A10),MONTH(A10)+1,1)-1
  Output is 31st December.

This will give you a date that represents the last day of the month found in cell A10.

Average() Function

Returns the average of the arguments.

Syntax: AVERAGE(number1,number2, ...)

Number1, number2, ... are 1 to 30 numeric arguments for which you want the average.

The arguments must be either numbers or names, arrays, or references that contain numbers. If an array or reference argument contains text, logical values, or empty cells, those values are ignored; however, cells with the value zero are included.

☞ *Note: When averaging cells, keep in mind the difference between empty cells and those which contain the value zero, if you have cleared the* ***Zero values*** *check box on* ***Tools → Options → View*** *tab. Zero values are counted and empty cells are not counted.*

Examples:

If A1:A5 is named Scores and contains the numbers 10, 7, 9, 27, and 2, then:

AVERAGE(A1:A5) equals 11
AVERAGE(Scores) equals 11
AVERAGE(A1:A5) equals SUM(A1:A5)/COUNT(A1:A5) equals the same result 11

If C1:C3 is named OtherScores and contains the numbers 4, 18 and 7 then:

AVERAGE(Scores, OtherScores) equals 10.5

The easiest way to create and apply functions is the Paste Function.

- Select the cell where you want the formula to appear and insert an equal (=) sign to start the formula.

- Enter any expression that appears before the function.
- Click the **Paste Function** button on the **Standard** toolbar to display the **Paste Function** dialog box when you are ready to enter the function.
- From the **Function category** list box, choose a function category.
- From the **Function name** list box, choose the function you require, say AVERAGE. Use the down arrow to select other functions. Select the **OK** button.
- A second **Paste Function** dialog box appears as shown in figure 8.3 containing the function's arguments. Use the **Tab** key to move through the various arguments.

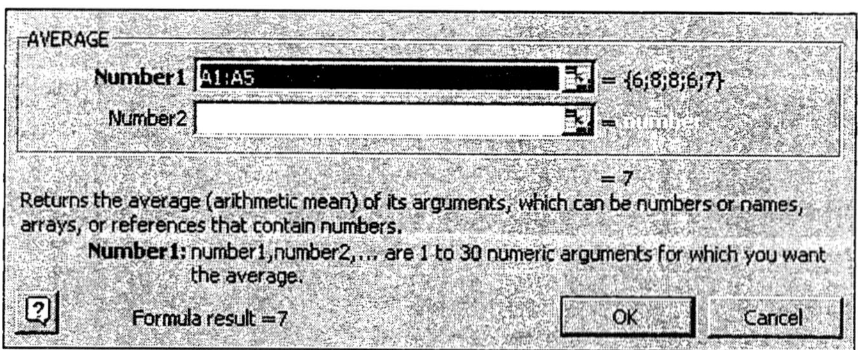

Figure 8.3: Paste function dialog box

- When all the arguments are satisfied, click the **OK** button to enter the function into the cell.
- If you want to make further changes, do so in the formula bar. Press **Enter** to complete the entry.
- Enter 6,8,8,6,7 in the cells A1,A2,A3,A4,A5. Thus the average of A1:A5 is 7.

The IF() Function

This function is used to make a decision based upon a value within the Spreadsheet. Excel 2000 has a number of functions that allow us to evaluate values and make decisions based on the result of the evaluation.

Syntax: IF(Logical_test, value_if_true, value_if_false)

Logical_test: The logical_test is any value or expression that can be evaluated to TRUE or FALSE.

Logical Operators	Values for Evaluation A=10, B=5, C=15, D=10	Result
= (Equal to)	A=B	FALSE
	A=D	TRUE
> (Greater than)	A>B	TRUE
	A>C	FALSE
< (Less than)	A<B	FALSE
	A<C	TRUE
>= (Greater than or Equal to)	A>=B	TRUE
	A>=D	TRUE
	A>=C	FALSE
<= (Less than or Equal to)	A<=B	FALSE
	A<=C	TRUE
	A<=D	TRUE

Table 8.1: Logical test options

Value_if_true: Value_if_true is the value that is returned if Logical_test is TRUE. If omitted, TRUE is returned. You can nest upto seven IF functions.

Value_if_false: Value_if_false is the value that is returned if Logical_test is FALSE. If omitted, FALSE is returned.

Example:

A company offers a 20% discount to its customers if the value of purchase is above Rs. 1000 and if the purchase is below Rs. 1000 there is no discount.

If the purchase value is greater than Rs. 1000 give 20% discount otherwise no discount. IF( ) function for the above statement looks like the following:

IF(PurchaseValue>1000,PurchaseValue * 20%,0)

B4	= =IF(A4>1000,A4*20%,0)	
A	B	C
1		
Purchase Value	DiscountValue	PurchaseValue-Discount
1000	0	1000
1500	300	1200
1250	250	1000
600	0	600
2000	400	1600

Figure 8.4: A sample worksheet showing the IF function

Follow the steps given below to use the IF( ) function

- Click on the cell where you want the IF( ) function to appear.
- Click the **Paste Function** icon.
- Select the **IF** option from the **Paste Function** dialog box and then click **OK**.
- Enter the required expression to be evaluated into the **logical_test** text area.
- Press the **Tab** key.
- Enter the required expression to be evaluated into the **value_if_true** text area.
- Again press the **Tab** key.
- Enter the required expression to be evaluated into the **value_if_false** text area and then click **OK**.

Excel 2000 has a family of functions starting with the letters "IF", such as IFNUMBER, IFTEXT, which are commonly used for data validation. They are especially useful when designing templates for other users.

Example:

IF(ISTEXT (A1), "", "Please enter your Department Name")

Means if text is entered into the **cell A1** then no message is displayed, otherwise the user will see the message "Please enter your Department Name".

IF(ISNUMBER (A1), "", "Please enter your Department Number")

Means if a number is entered into the **cell A1** then no message is displayed, otherwise the user will see the message "Please enter your Department Number".

To build a function from scratch, follow these steps:

1. Click in the cell in which you want to add a formula, and then click the Edit Formula button. Excel inserts an equal sign in the Formula bar, positions the insertion point to the right and opens the Formula Palette just below the formula bar.

2. If the name of the function you want to use appears in the Function box, click to enter it into the Formula bar.

3. If the function you want to use is not on the Top 10 list, choose More Functions. The **Paste Function** dialog box appears as shown in figure 8.5.

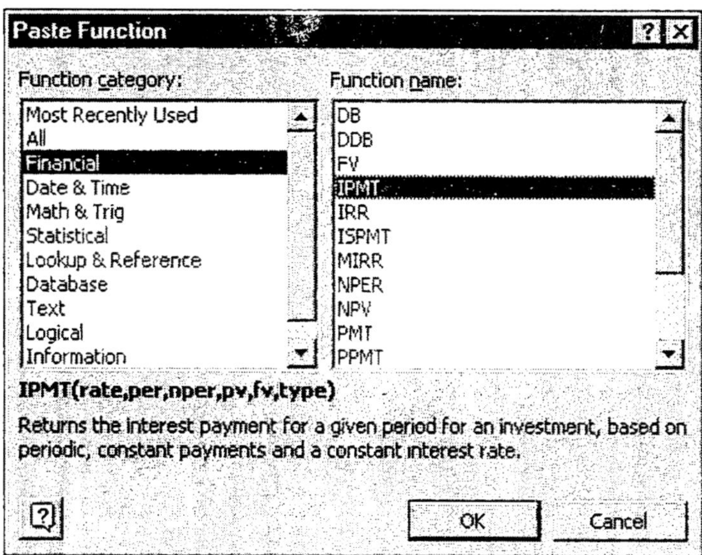

Figure 8.5: Paste Function dialog box

4. Select a category from the list on the left and choose a function from the matching list on the right. The text at the bottom of the Paste Function dialog box offers a brief explanation of the selected function and its syntax. When you have selected the correct function click **OK**. Excel adds the function to the Formula bar and expands the Formula Palette to show separate input boxes for each arguments as shown in figure 8.6.

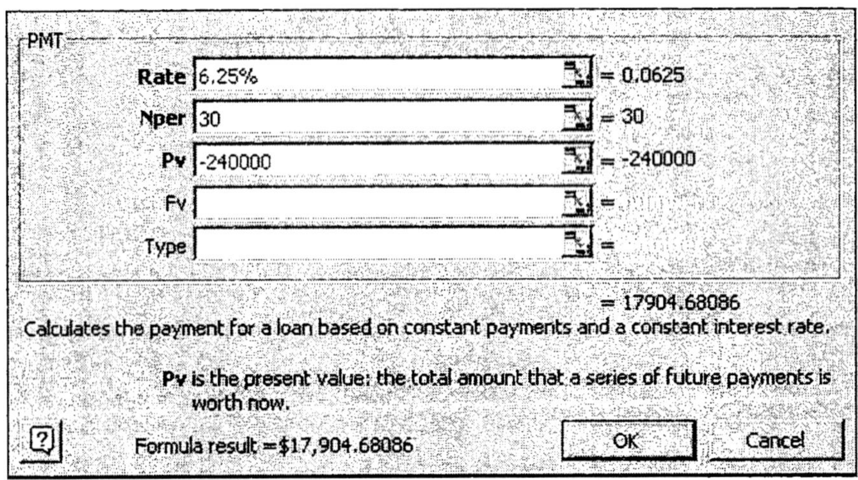

Figure 8.6: Formula Palette showing separate input boxes

5. Click within the first argument box and fill in the required data. The help text at the bottom of the dialog box is specific to the argument you are currently working with, and the data type required for each argument appears to the right of the input box.

   - Type text, numbers, and other constants directly in the input box.
   - To add cell references by pointing and clicking, first click the Collapse dialog button to roll most of the Formula Palette up and out of the way. Next select the cell or range to use for the selected argument and then click the Collapse dialog button again to continue.
   - When entering constants values, you can include the percent operator (%) and minus sign (-) with numeric data. Look to the right of the input box to see the current value of each argument you enter. If the data is not of the type required by the argument, Excel displays the word invalid to the right of the input box.

6. Repeat step 5 for other required and optional arguments. Look to the right of the equal sign for each argument to see its current value, using the data you have entered so far.

7. After entering all required arguments, click **OK** to paste the complete function into the current cell, or click Cancel to start over again.

Other commonly used function

Commonly used function include:

Function	Uses
AVERAGE	Displays the average number of the selected cells.
COLUMNS	Used to return the number of columns within a reference.
COUNT	Used to count how many numbers are in the list of arguments.
MAX	Displays the maximum number from a list of arguments.
MIN	Displays the minimum number from a list of arguments.
ROUND	Used to round off numbers to a specified number of decimal points.
SUM	Used to add the contents of selected cells.

Table 8.2: Most Recently used function

The CHOOSE() Function

This function is a means of choosing from a list of upto 29 options. If value1 through value7 are the days of the week, CHOOSE returns one of the days when a number between 1 and 7 is used as index_num.

Syntax: CHOOSE(Index_num,Value1,Value2,Value3, etc.)

Index_num: This specifies which of the set of values is returned by this function. Index_num must be a number between 1 and 29, or a formula or reference to a cell containing a number between 1 and 29.

If index_num is 1, CHOOSE returns value1; if it is 2, CHOOSE returns value2; and so on. If index_num is less than 1 or greater than the number of the last value in the list, CHOOSE returns the #VALUE! error value. If index_num is a fraction, it is truncated to the lowest integer before being used.

Value1,value2,... are 1 to 29 value arguments from which CHOOSE selects a value or an action to perform based on index_num. The arguments can be numbers, cell references, defined names, formulas, functions or text.

Example 1:

CHOOSE(A1, "Sales", "Purchasing", "Accounts", Personnel", "Export", "Maintenance")

If A1 = 3 the value "Accounts" is returned to the cell.

Example 2:

SUM(CHOOSE(2,A1:A10,B1:B10,C1:C10))

evaluates to:

SUM(B1:B10)

which then returns a value based on the values in the range B1:B10.

The CHOOSE function is evaluated first, returning the reference B1:B10. The SUM function is then evaluated using B1:B10, the result of the CHOOSE function, as its argument.

ABS

Returns the absolute value of a number. The absolute value of a number is the number without its sign.

Syntax: ABS(number)

Where, *number* is the real number of which you want the absolute value.

Examples:

ABS(2) equals 2

ABS(-2) equals 2

If A10 contains -16, then:

SQRT(ABS(A1)) equals 4, where *SQRT* is the square root of a number.

COUNTIF

Counts the number of cells within a range that meet the given criteria.

Microsoft Excel provides additional functions that can be used to analyze your data based on a condition. To calculate a sum based on a string of text or a number within a range, use the **SUMIF** worksheet function. To have a formula return one of two values based on a condition, such as a sales bonus based on a specified sales amount, use the **IF** worksheet function.

Syntax: COUNTIF(range,criteria)

Where, *range* is the range of cells from which you want to count cells and *criteria* is the criteria in the form of a number, expression, or text that defines which cells will be counted. For example, criteria can be expressed as 32, "32", ">32", "apples".

Examples:

Suppose A3:A6 contain "apples", "oranges", "peaches", "apples", respectively:

COUNTIF(A3:A6,"apples") equals 2

Suppose B3:B6 contain 32, 54, 75, 86, respectively:

COUNTIF(B3:B6,">55") equals 2

MOD

Returns the remainder after number is divided by divisor. The result has the same sign as divisor.

The MOD function can be expressed in terms of the INT function:

MOD(n, d) = n - d*INT(n/d)

Syntax: MOD(number,divisor)

Where, *number* is the number for which you want to find the remainder and *divisor* is the number by which you want to divide number. If divisor is 0, MOD returns the #DIV/0! error value.

Examples:

MOD(3, 2) equals 1
MOD(-3, 2) equals 1
MOD(3, -2) equals -1
MOD(-3, -2) equals –1
MOD(14, 5) equals 4

SUBTOTAL

Returns a subtotal in a list or database. It is generally easier to create a list with subtotals using the **Subtotals** command in the **Data** menu. Once the subtotal list is created, you can modify it by editing the SUBTOTAL function.

Syntax: SUBTOTAL(function_num,ref1,ref2,...)

Where, *function_num* is the number 1 to 11 that specifies which function to use in calculating subtotals within a list and ref1, ref2,..... are 1 to 29 ranges or references for which you want the subtotal.

Function_num	Function
1	AVERAGE
2	COUNT
3	COUNTA
4	MAX
5	MIN
6	PRODUCT
7	STDEV
8	STDEVP
9	SUM
10	VAR
11	VARP

Table 8.3: Function_num options

Example:

SUBTOTAL(9,C3:C5) will generate a subtotal of the cells C3:C5 using the SUM function

SUM

Adds all the numbers in a range of cells.

Syntax: SUM(number1,number2, ...)

Number1, number2, ... are 1 to 30 arguments for which you want the sum.

Numbers, logical values and text representations of numbers that you type directly into the list of arguments are counted.

Example 1:

SUM(3, 2) equals 5

SUM("3", 2, TRUE) equals 6 because the text values are translated into numbers, and the logical value TRUE is translated into the number 1.

If an argument is an array or reference, only numbers in that array or reference are counted. Empty cells, logical values, text, or error values in the array or reference are ignored.

Arguments that are error values or text that cannot be translated into numbers cause errors.

Example 2:

If cell A1 contains "3" and B1 contains TRUE, then:

SUM(A1, B1, 2) equals 2 because references to non-numeric values in references are not translated.

If cells A2:E2 contain 5, 15, 30, 40, and 50:

SUM(A2:C2) equals 50
SUM(B2:E2, 15) equals 150

SUMIF

Adds the cells specified by a given criteria.

Syntax: SUMIF(range,criteria,sum_range)

Where, *Range* is the range of cells you want to evaluate, *Criteria* is the criteria in the form of a number, expression or text that defines which cells will be added and *Sum_range* are the actual cells to sum. The cells in sum_range are summed only if their corresponding cells in range match the criteria. If sum_range is omitted, the cells in range are summed.

For example, criteria can be expressed as 32, "32", ">32", "apples".

Microsoft Excel provides additional functions that can be used to analyze your data based on a condition. For example, to count the number of occurrences of a string of text or a number within a range of cells, use the COUNTIF function. To have a formula return one of two values based on a condition, such as a sales bonus based on a specified sales amount, use the IF worksheet function.

Example:

Suppose A1:A4 contain the following property values for four homes: $200,000, $400,000, $800,000, $1200,000, respectively. B1:B4 contain the following sales commissions on each of the corresponding property values: $14,000, $28,000, $56,000, $84,000.

SUMIF(A1:A4,">210000",B1:B4) equals $168,000

SUMPRODUCT

Multiplies corresponding components in the given arrays and returns the sum of those products.

Syntax: SUMPRODUCT(array1,array2,array3, ...)

array1, array2, array3, ... array30 are 2 to 30 arrays whose components you want to multiply and then add.

The array arguments must have the same dimensions. If they do not, SUMPRODUCT returns the #VALUE! error value.

SUMPRODUCT treats array entries that are not numeric as if they were zeros.

Example:

The following formula multiplies all the components of the two arrays on the preceding worksheet and then adds the products — that is, 3*2 + 4*7 + 8*6 + 6*7 + 1*5 + 9*3.

SUMPRODUCT(A1:A6,B1:B6) equals 156

Using arrays provides a more general solution for doing operations similar to SUMPRODUCT. For example, you can calculate the sum of the squares of the elements in A1:B3 by using the formula SUM(A1,B3^2) entered as an array.

COUNT

Counts the number of cells that contain numbers. Use COUNT to get the number of entries in a number field in a range or array of numbers.

Syntax: COUNT(value1,value2, ...)

value1, value2, ... are 1 to 30 arguments that can contain or refer to a variety of different types of data, but only numbers are counted.

If an argument is an array or reference, only numbers in that array or reference are counted. Empty cells, logical values, text, or error values in the array or reference are ignored. If you need to count logical values, text, or error values, use the COUNTA function.

Examples:

COUNT(A1:A7) equals 3
COUNT(A4:A7) equals 2

COUNTA

Counts the number of cells that are not empty. Use COUNTA to count the number of cells that contain data in a range of cells or an array.

value1, value2, ... are 1 to 30 arguments representing the values you want to count. If an argument is an array or reference, empty cells within the array or reference are ignored. A value is any type of information, including empty text ("") but not including empty cells.

Syntax: COUNTA(value1,value2, ...)

Examples:

COUNTA(A1:A7) equals 6
COUNTA(A4:A7) equals 4
COUNTA(A1:A7, 2) equals 7
COUNTA(A1:A7, "Two") equals 7

ROUND

Rounds a number to a specified number of digits.

Syntax: ROUND(number,num_digits)

Number is the number you want to round, *Num_digits* specifies the number of digits to which you want to round number.

If num_digits is greater than 0 then number is rounded to the specified number of decimal places, if num_digits is 0, then number is rounded to the nearest integer and if num_digits is less than 0, then number is rounded to the left of the decimal point.

Examples:

ROUND(2.15, 1) equals 2.2
ROUND(2.149, 1) equals 2.1
ROUND(-1.475, 2) equals -1.48
ROUND(21.5, -1) equals 20

ROUNDUP

Rounds a number up, away from 0 (zero).

Syntax: ROUNDUP(number,num_digits)

Number is any real number that you want rounded up and *Num_digits* is the number of digits to which you want to round number.

ROUNDUP behaves like ROUND, except that it always rounds a number up. If num_digits is greater than 0 then number is rounded up to the specified number of decimal places. If num_digits is 0 or omitted, then number is rounded up to the nearest integer. If num_digits is less than 0, then number is rounded up to the left of the decimal point.

Examples:

ROUNDUP(3.2,0) equals 4
ROUNDUP(76.9,0) equals 77
ROUNDUP(3.14159, 3) equals 3.142
ROUNDUP(-3.14159, 1) equals -3.2
ROUNDUP(31415.92654, -2) equals 31,500

MAX

Returns the largest value in a set of values.

Syntax: MAX(number1,number2,...)

number1,number2,... are 1 to 30 numbers for which you want to find the maximum value.

You can specify arguments that are numbers, empty cells, logical values, or text representations of numbers. Arguments that are error values or text that cannot be translated into numbers cause errors.

If the arguments contain no numbers, MAX returns 0 (zero).

Examples:

If A1:A5 contains the numbers 10, 7, 9, 27, and 2, then:

MAX(A1:A5) equals 27
MAX(A1:A5,30) equals 30

MIN

Returns the smallest number in a set of values.

Syntax: MIN(number1,number2, ...)

number1, number2,... are 1 to 30 numbers for which you want to find the minimum value.

You can specify arguments that are numbers, empty cells, logical values, or text representations of numbers.

If an argument is an array or reference, only numbers in that array or reference are used. Empty cells, logical values or text in the array or reference are ignored.

If the arguments contain no numbers, MIN returns 0.

Examples:

If A1:A5 contains the numbers 10, 7, 9, 27, and 2, then:

MIN(A1:A5) equals 2
MIN(A1:A5, 0) equals 0

LOWER

Converts all uppercase letters in a text string to lowercase.

Syntax: LOWER(text)

Text is the text you want to convert to lowercase. LOWER does not change characters in text that are not letters.

Examples:

LOWER("E. E. Cummings") equals "e. e. cummings"
LOWER("Apt. 2B") equals "apt. 2b"

UPPER

Converts text to uppercase.

Syntax: UPPER(text)

Text is the text you want converted to uppercase. Text can be a reference or text string.

Examples:

UPPER("grand total") equals "GRAND TOTAL"

If E5 contains "education", then:

UPPER(E5) equals "EDUCATION"

T

Returns the text referred to by value.

Syntax: T(value)

Value is the value you want to test. If value is or refers to text, T returns value. If value does not refer to text, T returns "" (empty text).

You do not generally need to use the T function in a formula because Microsoft Excel automatically converts values as necessary. This function is provided for compatibility with other spreadsheet programs.

Examples:

If B1 contains the text "eAcademy":

T(B1) equals " eAcademy "

If B2 contains the number 222:

T(B2) equals ""
T("True") equals "True"
T(TRUE) equals ""

TEXT

Converts a value to text in a specific number format.

Syntax: TEXT(value,format_text)

Value is a numeric value, a formula that evaluates to a numeric value, or a reference to a cell containing a numeric value. *Format_text* is a number format in text form. Format_text cannot contain an asterisk (*) and cannot be the General number format.

Formatting a cell with an option on the **Cells** command (Ctrl+1) **Number** tab changes only the format, not the value. TEXT function converts a value to formatted text, and the result is no longer calculated as a number.

Examples:

TEXT(2.715, "$0.00") equals "$2.72"
TEXT("4/15/91", "mmmm dd, yyyy") equals "April 15, 1991"

TRIM

Removes all spaces from text except for single spaces between words. Use TRIM on text that you have received from another application that may have irregular spacing.

Syntax: TRIM(text)

Text is the text from which you want spaces removed.

Example:

TRIM(" ITL   Education   Solutions   Limited   ") equals "ITL Education Solutions Limited "

VALUE

Converts a text string that represents a number to a number.

Syntax: VALUE(text)

Text is the text enclosed in quotation marks or a reference to a cell containing the text you want to convert. Text can be in any of the constant number, date, or time formats recognized by Microsoft Excel. If text is not in one of these formats, VALUE returns the #VALUE! error value.

Example:

VALUE("$1,000") equals 1,000

VALUE("16:48:00")-VALUE("12:00:00") equals "16:48:00"-"12:00:00" the serial number equivalent to 4 hours and 48 minutes.

Array Formulas

An array formula can perform multiple calculations and then return either a single result or multiple results. Array formulas act on two or more sets of values known as array arguments. Each array argument must have the same number of rows and columns. You create array formulas in the same way that you create other formulas, except you press CTRL+SHIFT+ENTER to enter the formula.

Enter an Array formula

When you enter an array formula, Microsoft Excel automatically inserts the formula between { } (braces).

1. If the array formula will return one result, click the cell in which you want to enter the array formula.
2. If the array formula will return multiple results, select the range of cells in which you want to enter the array formula.
3. Type the array formula.
4. Press CTRL+SHIFT+ENTER.

Example:

- **To calculate a single result:** Sometimes Microsoft Excel must perform several calculations to generate a single result. For example, the following figure 8.7 shows that a company has regional offices in South Africa and Russia and that each region has three product divisions. To find the average revenue per product division for Russia in 1995, you would need to use an array formula.

	A	B	C	D	E	F
1						
2				1995	2000	
3		**Electronics**				
4			South Africa	100,600	161,000	
5			Russia	133,100	198,200	
6		*Electronics Total*		233,700	359,200	
7		**Acoustics**				
8			South Africa	129,200	160,700	
9			Russia	150,500	190,100	
10		*Acoustics Total*		279,700	350,800	
11		**Pro Studio Equipment**				
12			South Africa	89,900	153,900	
13			Russia	112,300	190,700	
14		*Pro Studio Equipment Total*		202,200	344,600	
15						
16			=AVERAGE(IF(C3:C14="Russia",D3:D14))			
17						

Figure 8.7: Calculate a single result using array formula

Cell C16 contains the array formula =AVERAGE(IF(C3:C14="Russia",D3:D14)), which finds the cells in the range C3:C14 that contain the text "Russia" and then averages the corresponding cells in the range D3:D14.

♦ **Calculate a result using constant values:** You can also use an array formula to calculate single or multiple results for a series of values that have not yet been entered on the worksheet. Array formulas accept constants in the same way that non-array formulas do, but you must enter the array constants in a certain format. For example, given the same three sales figures in row 5 for a series of three months in row 3, as shown in figure 8.8, you can project the sales figures for the next two months.

	C	D	E	F	G
3	**June**	**July**	**August**		
4					
5	500	1000	2000	=TREND(C5:E5,,{4,5}	
6					

Figure 8.8: Calculate a result using constant values

Use the formula =TREND(C5:E5,,{4,5}) to project the fourth and fifth values in the monthly sequence based on the first three values.

- **To calculate multiple results:** You must enter the array into a range of cells that has the same number of rows and columns as the array arguments. In the following example, suppose a businessman wants to purchase an area of land in July, the start of the next financial year. The businessman collects cost information of the land for the past 12 months in the desired area. Known_y values are in cells B1:B12; the known_y values are $133,890, $135,000, $135,790, $137,300, $138,130, $139,100, $139,900, $141,120, $141,890, $143,230, $144,000, $145,290.

  When entered as a vertical array in the range C1:C5, the following formula returns the predicted prices for March, April, May, June, and July:

  TREND(B1:B12,,{13;14;15;16;17}) equals {146155;147169;148184;149198;150212}

  The businessman can expect the cost to about $150,212 if it waits until July 2001. The array {13;14;15;16;17} corresponds to the next five months.

Values that do not change in array formulas

A basic, single-value formula produces a single result from one or more arguments or values; you can enter either a reference to a cell that contains a value or the value itself. In an array formula, where you usually use a reference to a range of cells, you can instead type the array of values contained within the cells. The array of values you type is called an **array constant** and generally is used when you do not want to enter each value into a separate cell on the worksheet. To create an array constant, you must do the following:

- Enter the values directly into the formula, enclosed in braces ({ })
- Separate values in different columns with commas (,)
- Separate values in different rows with semicolons (;)

What an array constant can contain?

- Array constants can contain numbers, text, logical values such as TRUE or FALSE, or error values such as #N/A.
- Numbers in array constants can be in integer, decimal, or scientific format.
- Text must be enclosed in double quotation marks - for example, "Tuesday".
- You can use different types of values in the same array constant.
- The values in an array constant must not be a formula, cell references, columns or rows of unequal length.

Totaling Rows and Columns Automatically

The most commonly used function (SUM) is also the easiest to enter. To insert a formula that adds a column or row of numbers automatically, click in a blank cell beneath any column of numbers and then click the **AutoSum** button. Excel inserts the SUM function with the argument already filled in and selected. Adjust the selected range and click the Enter box in the Formula bar or press Enter to store the formula in the active cell.

To sum numbers automatically

- Select the cell you want to contain the sum formula.
- Click the **AutoSum** icon on the **Standard** toolbar. Excel 2000 will create a sum formula, along with the range it thinks you want to sum.
- If the range is correct, press **Enter**. If it is incorrect, select the range you want to sum and press **Enter**.

Naming Cells and Ranges

Range names normally begin with a letter or underscore character. This must NOT contain hyphens or spaces and have a limit of 255 characters.

It is possible to navigate to named cells and ranges in a single workbook. It is also possible to automatically name cells/ranges using text labels that exist within the worksheet.

Follow these steps to name the cells

- Highlight and select the cell(s) to be named.
- Open the **Insert** menu and select the **Name** option.
- Select the **Define** option.
- The **Define Name** dialog box is displayed as shown in figure 8.9 below.

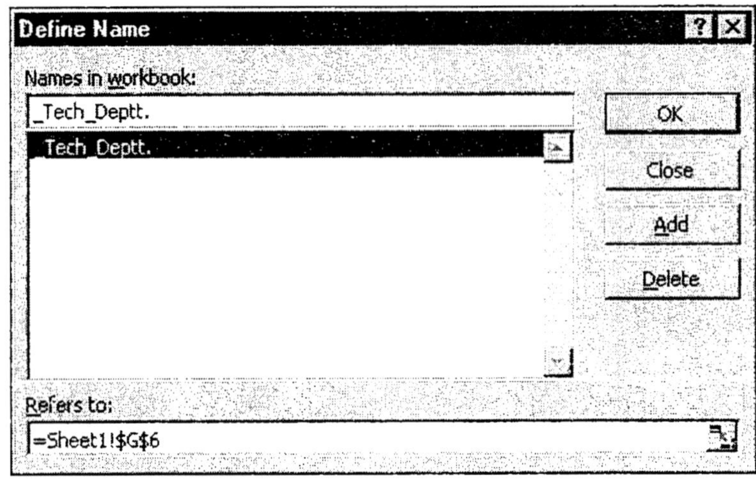

Figure 8.9: Naming cells dialog box

- Enter the name you wish to give to the cell or range.
- Click **Add** to add the name to the list of named ranges.
- Click **OK** to complete the name definition.
- The name of the cell is displayed in the **Name Box** at the top left of the formula bar.

To delete named cells/ranges

- Open the **Insert** menu, click **Name** → **Define** .
- The **Define Name** dialog box is displayed.
- Select the range name you wish to delete.
- Click the **Delete** button to remove that name from the available list.
- When you have deleted the names required click **OK** to exit.

Using Named Ranges with Formulas

Use named ranges within your formulas, as it is easier to understand, modify at a later date or to find your way around your spreadsheet such as:

=unit_price*no_of_units

than a formula of the type shown below:

=A30*B42

 Hands on Exercise

Exercise 1: Create a Travel Expense worksheet

1. Type a worksheet title: **Travelling Expense Details**. Font – Arial Bold, 14 points, left aligned, all caps, color – automatic.

2. Type the column headings A3 to E3 as shown in the figure 8.10 by clicking on cell A3, holding the mouse button down, and dragging to the cell E3. Make it Arial Bold, 10 points and center aligned.

Book2

	A	B	C	D	E	F
1	TRAVELLING EXPENSE DETAILS					
2						
3	Description	Empl	Comp	Total	Comments	
4						

Sheet1 / Sheet2 / Sheet3 / Sheet4

Figure 8.10: Column Heading

3. Increase the width of column A to 25, B, C, D to 10 and E to 14.

4. Move to A5 to A17 and type the row headings as shown in the figure 8.11.

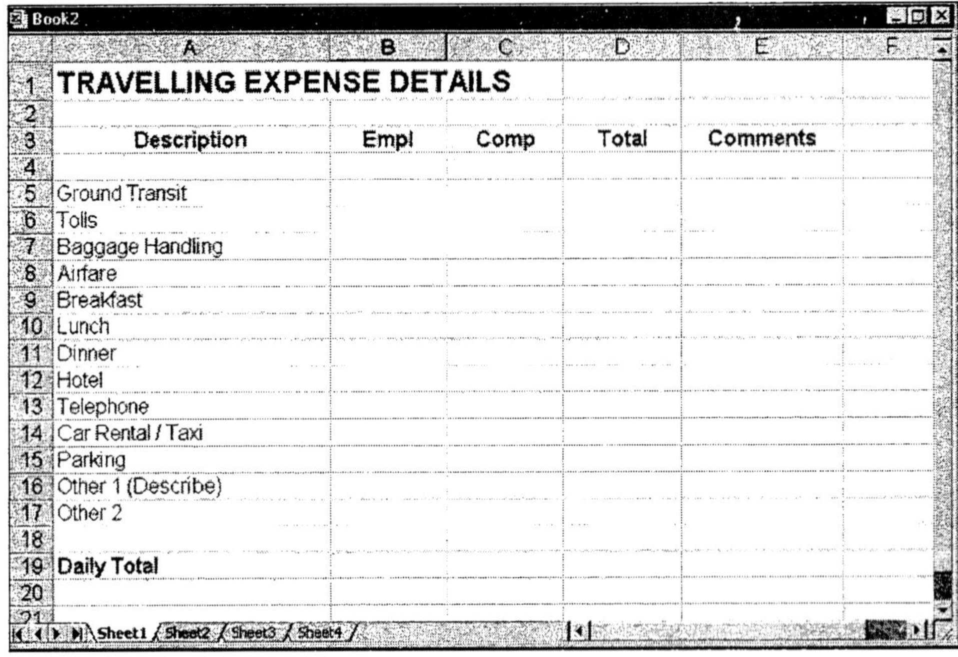

Figure 8.11: Inserting Row Heading

5. Enter the formula =B5+C5 in cell D5.

6. Copy the D5 formula to the cells D6:D17.

7. Enter formula =SUM(B5:B17) in cell B19.

8. Copy the formula in B19 to C19:D19.

9. Check the worksheet against the figure 8.12.

	A	B	C	D	E
1	**TRAVELLING EXPENSE DETAILS**				
2					
3	**Description**	**Empl**	**Comp**	**Total**	**Comments**
4					
5	Ground Transit			=B5+C5	
6	Tolls			=B6+C6	
7	Baggage Handling			=B7+C7	
8	Airfare			=B8+C8	
9	Breakfast			=B9+C9	
10	Lunch			=B10+C10	
11	Dinner			=B11+C11	
12	Hotel			=B12+C12	
13	Telephone			=B13+C13	
14	Car Rental / Taxi			=B14+C14	
15	Parking			=B15+C15	
16	Other 1 (Describe)			=B16+C16	
17	Other 2			=B17+C17	
18					
19	**Daily Total**	=SUM(B5:B17)	=SUM(C5:C17)	=SUM(D5:D17)	
20					

Book2 — Sheet1 / Sheet2 / Sheet3 / Sheet4

Figure 8.12: Filling the details

10. Format the block B5:D19 to two decimal places.

11. Copy the range A1:E19 containing the daily details information to the range A1:E19 of Sheet2 through Sheet4.

12. Rename the Sheet1 through Sheet4 to Tue 7-5, Wed 7-6, Thu 7-7, Total.

13. Move to cell A7 of each of the four sheet and make it AutoFit Selection to adjust the width of column A.

14. Now move to the Total sheet and enter the formulas for the grand totals.

15. In cell B5 type the formula, ='Tue 7-5'!B5+'Wed 7-6'!B5+'Thu 7-7'!B5.

16. Copy the B5 formula to cell B5:D5.

17. Then copy the range B5:D5 and paste into the range B6:B17 and B19.

18. Type Grand Total in cell A19 and Travelling Expense Totals in cell A1.

19. Compare your output with the following Figure 8.13.

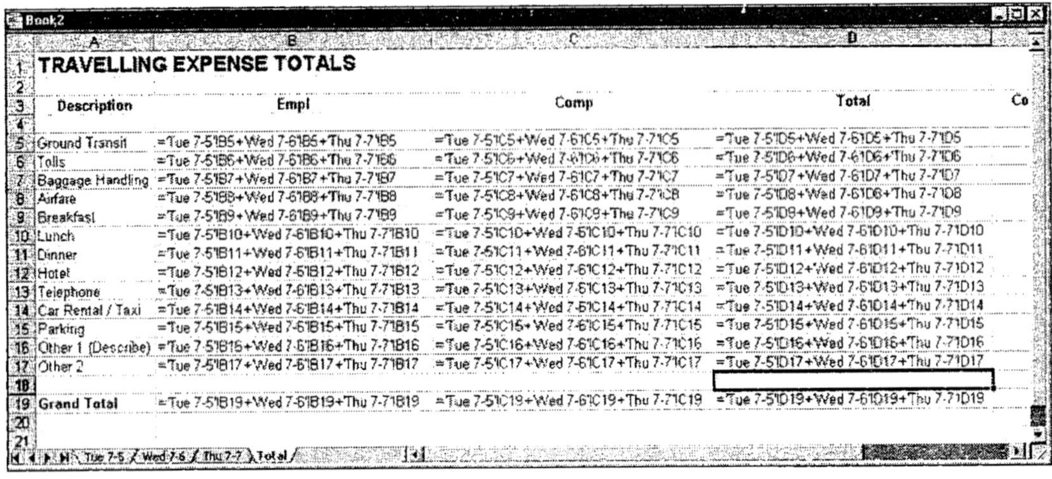

Book2

TRAVELLING EXPENSE TOTALS

	A	B	C	D
3	**Description**	**Empl**	**Comp**	**Total**
4				
5	Ground Transit	=Tue 7-5'!B5+Wed 7-6'!B5+Thu 7-7'!B5	=Tue 7-5'!C5+Wed 7-6'!C5+Thu 7-7'!C5	=Tue 7-5'!D5+Wed 7-6'!D5+Thu 7-7'!D5
6	Tolls	=Tue 7-5'!B6+Wed 7-6'!B6+Thu 7-7'!B6	=Tue 7-5'!C6+Wed 7-6'!C6+Thu 7-7'!C6	=Tue 7-5'!D6+Wed 7-6'!D6+Thu 7-7'!D6
7	Baggage Handling	=Tue 7-5'!B7+Wed 7-6'!B7+Thu 7-7'!B7	=Tue 7-5'!C7+Wed 7-6'!C7+Thu 7-7'!C7	=Tue 7-5'!D7+Wed 7-6'!D7+Thu 7-7'!D7
8	Airfare	=Tue 7-5'!B8+Wed 7-6'!B8+Thu 7-7'!B8	=Tue 7-5'!C8+Wed 7-6'!C8+Thu 7-7'!C8	=Tue 7-5'!D8+Wed 7-6'!D8+Thu 7-7'!D8
9	Breakfast	=Tue 7-5'!B9+Wed 7-6'!B9+Thu 7-7'!B9	=Tue 7-5'!C9+Wed 7-6'!C9+Thu 7-7'!C9	=Tue 7-5'!D9+Wed 7-6'!D9+Thu 7-7'!D9
10	Lunch	=Tue 7-5'!B10+Wed 7-6'!B10+Thu 7-7'!B10	=Tue 7-5'!C10+Wed 7-6'!C10+Thu 7-7'!C10	=Tue 7-5'!D10+Wed 7-6'!D10+Thu 7-7'!D10
11	Dinner	=Tue 7-5'!B11+Wed 7-6'!B11+Thu 7-7'!B11	=Tue 7-5'!C11+Wed 7-6'!C11+Thu 7-7'!C11	=Tue 7-5'!D11+Wed 7-6'!D11+Thu 7-7'!D11
12	Hotel	=Tue 7-5'!B12+Wed 7-6'!B12+Thu 7-7'!B12	=Tue 7-5'!C12+Wed 7-6'!C12+Thu 7-7'!C12	=Tue 7-5'!D12+Wed 7-6'!D12+Thu 7-7'!D12
13	Telephone	=Tue 7-5'!B13+Wed 7-6'!B13+Thu 7-7'!B13	=Tue 7-5'!C13+Wed 7-6'!C13+Thu 7-7'!C13	=Tue 7-5'!D13+Wed 7-6'!D13+Thu 7-7'!D13
14	Car Rental / Taxi	=Tue 7-5'!B14+Wed 7-6'!B14+Thu 7-7'!B14	=Tue 7-5'!C14+Wed 7-6'!C14+Thu 7-7'!C14	=Tue 7-5'!D14+Wed 7-6'!D14+Thu 7-7'!D14
15	Parking	=Tue 7-5'!B15+Wed 7-6'!B15+Thu 7-7'!B15	=Tue 7-5'!C15+Wed 7-6'!C15+Thu 7-7'!C15	=Tue 7-5'!D15+Wed 7-6'!D15+Thu 7-7'!D15
16	Other 1 (Describe)	=Tue 7-5'!B16+Wed 7-6'!B16+Thu 7-7'!B16	=Tue 7-5'!C16+Wed 7-6'!C16+Thu 7-7'!C16	=Tue 7-5'!D16+Wed 7-6'!D16+Thu 7-7'!D16
17	Other 2	=Tue 7-5'!B17+Wed 7-6'!B17+Thu 7-7'!B17	=Tue 7-5'!C17+Wed 7-6'!C17+Thu 7-7'!C17	=Tue 7-5'!D17+Wed 7-6'!D17+Thu 7-7'!D17
18				
19	**Grand Total**	=Tue 7-5'!B19+Wed 7-6'!B19+Thu 7-7'!B19	=Tue 7-5'!C19+Wed 7-6'!C19+Thu 7-7'!C19	=Tue 7-5'!D19+Wed 7-6'!D19+Thu 7-7'!D19

Tue 7-5 / Wed 7-6 / Thu 7-7 / Total

Figure 8.13: Worksheet after applying formula

20. Save the workbook as *TravExp.xls.*

21. Type the expense information in columns B, C and E as shown in each worksheet.

    a. Type in the Tue 7-5 sheet as shown below:

Description	**Empl**	**Comp**
Ground Transit	18.40	
Tolls	10.50	
Baggage Handling	12.00	
Airfare		2576.00
Breakfast		
Lunch		
Dinner		85.40
Hotel		324.42
Telephone		
Car Rental/Taxi	216.00	
Parking		
Other 1 (Describe)		
Other		

b. Type in the Wed 7-6 sheet as shown below:

Description	Empl	Comp
Ground Transit		
Tolls		
Baggage Handling		
Airfare		
Breakfast	13.80	
Lunch	88.85	
Dinner	86.40	
Hotel		324.42
Telephone		63.80
Car Rental/Taxi	194.40	
Parking		
Other 1 (Describe)		
Other		

c. Type in the Thu 7-7 sheet as shown below:

Description	Empl	Comp
Ground Transit	18.40	
Tolls		
Baggage Handling	12.00	
Airfare		
Breakfast		16.65
Lunch	86.00	
Dinner		
Hotel		
Telephone		
Car Rental/Taxi	218.00	
Parking	18.00	
Other 1 (Describe)		
Other		

22. Click the total worksheet tab to view the total expense amounts and it should be as shown in Figure 8.14.

	A	B	C	D	E
1	**TRAVELLING EXPENSE TOTALS**				
2					
3	**Description**	**Empl**	**Comp**	**Total**	**Comments**
4					
5	Ground Transit	36.80	0.00	36.80	
6	Tolls	10.50	0.00	10.50	
7	Baggage Handling	24.00	0.00	24.00	
8	Airfare	0.00	2576.00	2576.00	
9	Breakfast	13.80	16.65	30.45	
10	Lunch	174.85	0.00	174.85	
11	Dinner	86.40	85.40	171.80	
12	Hotel	0.00	648.84	648.84	
13	Telephone	0.00	63.80	63.80	
14	Car Rental / Taxi	628.40	0.00	628.40	
15	Parking	18.00	0.00	18.00	
16	Other 1 (Describe)	0.00	0.00	0.00	
17	Other 2	0.00	0.00	0.00	
18					
19	**Grand Total**	992.75	3390.69	4383.44	
20					
21					

TravExp — Tue 7-5 / Wed 7-6 / Thu 7-7 / Total

Figure 8.14: The final output

23. Save the workbook.

Exercise 2: Create a furniture details worksheet

1. Open a blank worksheet and create it as shown in the Figure 8.15.

Book1

	A	B	C	D
1	Item	Quantity	Price	Totals
2	Table, 30x60	6	132	=B2*C2
3	Table, Conf	2	389	=B3*C3
4	Chair, Side	28	68	=B4*C4
5	Chair, Exec	4	158	=B5*C5
6	Chair, Steno	2	105	=B6*C6
7	Desk, 30x60	3	225	=B7*C7
8	Desk, Steno	2	286	=B8*C8
9	Desk, Exec	2	349	=B9*C9
10	Credenza	2	248	=B10*C10
11	Cabinet, File	8	78	=B11*C11
12	Cabinet, Storage	4	141	=B12*C12
13	Grand Total			=SUM(D2:D12)
14				
15				

Sheet1 / Sheet2 / Sheet3

Figure 8.15: A sample worksheet

2. Format cells B2:B12 to 2 decimal places, cells C2:D13 to currency and 2 decimal places and cell D13 to scientific and 2 decimal places.

3. Format cell D13 back to currency.

4. Format the labels in A1:D1 to Times New Roman 12 points bold.

5. Select A1:D1 and draw a thick rule, red colored using the **Border** tab in the **Format Cells** as shown in Figure 8.16.

Book1

	A	B	C	D	E
1	Item	Quantity	Price	Totals	
2	Table, 30x60	6.00	$132.00	=B2*C2	
3	Table, Conf	2.00	$389.00	=B3*C3	
4	Chair, Side	28.00	$68.00	=B4*C4	
5	Chair, Exec	4.00	$158.00	=B5*C5	
6	Chair, Steno	2.00	$105.00	=B6*C6	
7	Desk, 30x60	3.00	$225.00	=B7*C7	
8	Desk, Steno	2.00	$286.00	=B8*C8	
9	Desk, Exec	2.00	$349.00	=B9*C9	
10	Credenza	2.00	$248.00	=B10*C10	
11	Cabinet, File	8.00	$78.00	=B11*C11	
12	Cabinet, Storage	4.00	$141.00	=B12*C12	
13	Grand Total			=SUM(D2:D12)	
14					
15					

Sheet1 / Sheet2 / Sheet3

Figure 8.16: Worksheet after applying formulas

6. Format cells B2:B12 to flush right.

7. Select the cells A1:D13 and use Format → AutoFormat and the 3D Effects 2 selection.

8. Enter the present date in the cell E1 using the *today()* function.

9. Save the workbook as *Table Chair Details.xls*.

10. Compare your workbook as shown in Figure 8.17.

TableChair Details

	A	B	C	D	E
1	**Item**	**Quantity**	**Price**	**Totals**	5/26/01
2	Table, 30x60	6.00	$132.00	$792.00	
3	Table, Conf	2.00	$389.00	$778.00	
4	Chair, Side	28.00	$68.00	$1,904.00	
5	Chair, Exec	4.00	$158.00	$632.00	
6	Chair, Steno	2.00	$105.00	$210.00	
7	Desk, 30x60	3.00	$225.00	$675.00	
8	Desk, Steno	2.00	$286.00	$572.00	
9	Desk, Exec	2.00	$349.00	$698.00	
10	Credenza	2.00	$248.00	$496.00	
11	Cabinet, File	8.00	$78.00	$624.00	
12	Cabinet, Storage	4.00	$141.00	$564.00	
13	**Grand Total**			$7,945.00	
14					
15					

Sheet1 Sheet2 Sheet3

Figure 8.17: Final Output

11. Enable workbook protection by the command **Alt+T+P+P**. Do not enter password.

12. Move to the Cell B3 and enter a number say 10. A message comes saying number could not be entered, it is protected and therefore read-only, as shown in Figure 8.18.

Figure 8.18: A Message

13. Now disable worksheet protection by the same command **Alt+T+P+P**.

14. Unlock B2:C12 to enable typed entries by the command **Alt+O+E**, click the **Protection** tab, click **Locked** to clear the check box and click **OK**.

15. Enable worksheet protection again and change the value in B3 from 2 to 10. Now you will notice that the cell is unlocked as shown in Figure 8.19.

TableChair Details

	A	B	C	D	E
1	**Item**	**Quantity**	**Price**	**Totals**	5/26/01
2	Table, 30x60	6.00	$132.00	$792.00	
3	Table, Conf	10.00	$389.00	$3,890.00	
4	Chair, Side	28.00	$68.00	$1,904.00	
5	Chair, Exec	4.00	$158.00	$632.00	
6	Chair, Steno	2.00	$105.00	$210.00	
7	Desk, 30x60	3.00	$225.00	$675.00	
8	Desk, Steno	2.00	$286.00	$572.00	
9	Desk, Exec	2.00	$349.00	$698.00	
10	Credenza	2.00	$248.00	$496.00	
11	Cabinet, File	8.00	$78.00	$624.00	
12	Cabinet, Storage	4.00	$141.00	$564.00	
13	**Grand Total**			$11,057.00	
14					
15					

Sheet1 / Sheet2 / Sheet3

Figure 8.19: Disabling Protection

16. Again type Table in the cell A3. The message comes that the cell is protected and therefore it is read-only.

Exercise 3: Create a worksheet to organize your monthly expenses and calculate the balance.

Make up data for this assignment. Your worksheet should include the following data:

1. A title such as "My Monthly Expenses"
2. Expenses
   - at least four items (e.g. Rent, Utilities, Food, Parking, Payroll, Phone Bill, etc.)
   - during a period of four months
3. Income
   - At least two sources (e.g. Loan, Family Support, Student Work, Other, etc.)
   - During a period of four months

☞ *Note: The data related to currency should have the dollar sign, with 2 decimal places*

You will need to do the following:

1. Compute the total
   - Compute the total expense for each of the months
   - Compute the total expense for each of the items during the four months
   - Compute the total income for each of the months
   - Compute the total income for each of the source during the four months
2. Compute the average
   - Compute the average for each of the items during the four months
   - Compute the average monthly expenses
   - Compute the average income for different sources
   - Compute the average monthly income
3. Compute the balance
   - between the income and the expense for each of the months
   - between the total income and the total expense for the four months
4. Take a Print and should be as shown in the following Figure 8.20.

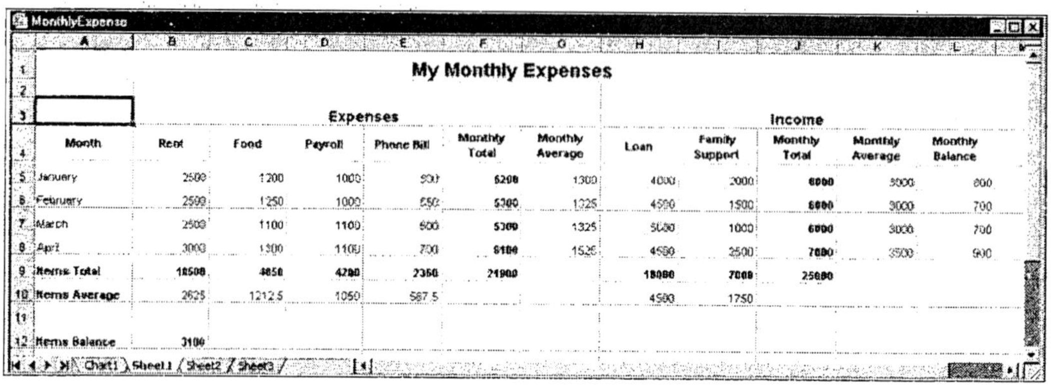

MonthlyExpense

	A	B	C	D	E	F	G	H	I	J	K	L
1						My Monthly Expenses						
2												
3				Expenses						Income		
4	Month	Rent	Food	Payroll	Phone Bill	Monthly Total	Monthly Average	Loan	Family Support	Monthly Total	Monthly Average	Monthly Balance
5	January	2500	1200	1000	500	**5200**	1300	4000	2000	**6000**	3000	800
6	February	2500	1250	1000	550	**5300**	1325	4500	1500	**6000**	3000	700
7	March	2500	1100	1100	600	**5300**	1325	5000	1000	**6000**	3000	700
8	April	3000	1300	1100	700	**6100**	1525	4500	2500	**7000**	3500	900
9	**Items Total**	**10500**	**4850**	**4200**	**2350**	**21900**		**18000**	**7000**	**25000**		
10	**Items Average**	2625	1212.5	1050	587.5			4500	1750			
11												
12	**Items Balance**	**3100**										

Chart1 / Sheet1 / Sheet2 / Sheet3

Figure 8.20: Final Output

 Test Your Knowledge

Students must solve the following assignment.

Multiple Choice Questions:

1. Cell address A4 in a formula means it is a :

   a. Mixed cell reference
   b. Absolute cell reference
   c. Relative cell reference
   d. None of the above.

2. Cell address $A$4 in a formula means it is a :

   a. Mixed cell reference
   b. Absolute cell reference
   c. Relative cell reference
   d. None of the above.

3. Cell address $A4 in a formula means it is a :

   a. Mixed cell reference
   b. Absolute cell reference
   c. Relative cell reference
   d. None of the above.

4. Cell address A$4 in a formula means it is a :

   a. Mixed cell reference
   b. Absolute cell reference
   c. Relative cell reference
   d. None of the above.

5. If the following arithmetic operations are all found in a formula with no parentheses, which one is completed last?

   a. +
   b. *
   c. /
   d. ^

6. To alert Excel that you are entering a formula and not text, type a(n) ______ preceding the formula.

   a. ampersand (&)
   b. equal sign (=)
   c. number sign (#)
   d. asterisk (*)

7. Which function is used to determine the lowest number within a range?

   a. SUM
   b. AVERAGE
   c. MAX
   d. MIN

Fill in the Blanks:

1. In MS-Excel formula starts with ________.

2. In ________ referencing the relative address of the cell gets adjusted w.r.t. the current cell.

3. To Create an absolute cell reference ________ sign is used before the parts of formula.

4. If you enter 12+24 in a cell, Excel will display ________.

State Whether True or False:

1. All formulas start with an = sign in Excel.

   a. True
   b. False

2. When a cell containing a formula is moved, The cells referring the moved cell, Show an error value.

   a. True
   b. False

Write cell references for the following:

1. Reference (Fixed column and Relative row) formed by row 134 and column BD.
2. Mixed Reference (Relative column and Fixed row) formed by row 120 and column IA.
3. Absolute Reference formed by row 45 and column Z.
4. Relative Reference formed by row 19 and column AB.

Suggest the Excel functions that can be used for carrying out following operations:

1. To calculate total marks of a student if his marks in five subjects are given in five different cells.
2. To calculate average sales made by salesman of a company, if sales made by each of the salesman is available.
3. To find out the marks of top scorer in a class, if marks of all the students are available.
4. To find out minimum quoted rate from various quotations available.

What does the following commands do:

1. Cell B8 contains the formula =AVERAGE(B10:D12). What will be the contents of cell B9 if B8 is copied to B9?
2. Cell B8 contains the formula =AVERAGE($B$10:$D$12). What will be the contents of cell B9 if B8 is copied to B9?
3. Cell B8 contains the formula =AVERAGE(B$10:D$12). What will be the contents of cell A7 if B8 is copied to A7?
4. Suppose the cell C8 contains the formula =A1 + $A$2 + $A3 + A$4. The formula is copied to D10. What formula will be found in D10?
5. Given that cells A1, A2, and A3 contain the values 10, 20, and 30, respectively, what value will be displayed in a cell containing the cell formula =SUM(A1:A3)?
6. Given the cell values for A1, A2, and A3 above, what value will be displayed in a cell containing the cell formula =AVERAGE(A2:A3)?

7. Given the cell values for A1, A2, and A3 above, what value will be displayed in a cell containing the cell formula =A1+A3/A1+A2^2?

8. What happens if the equal sign is left out of the formula in question c above?

9. Given the cell values for A1, A2, A3, A4 and A5 above, what value will be displayed in a cell containing the cell formula =COUNT(A1:A5)?

10. Given the cell values for A1 above, what value will be displayed in a cell containing the cell formula =ROUND(A1,2)?

11. Given the cell values for A1 to A4 and B1 to B4 above, what value will be displayed in a cell containing the cell formula =SUMPRODUCT(A1:A4,B1:B4)?

12. Given the cell values for A1:A5 and B1:B5 above, what value will be displayed in a cell containing the cell formula =SUMIF(A1:A5,"eAcademy",B1:B5)?

13. Given the cell values for A1 to A5 above, what value will be displayed in a cell containing the cell formula =SUBTOTAL(4,A1:A5)?

14. Given the cell values for A1, A2, A3, A4 and A5 above, what value will be displayed in a cell containing the cell formula =COUNTIF(A1:A5,"<100")?

15. Given the cell values for A1 above, what value will be displayed in a cell containing the cell formula =SQRT(A1))?

16. Given the cell values for A1 above, what value will be displayed in a cell containing the cell formula =ABS(A1)?

17. Given the cell values for A1, A2, A3, A4 and A5 above, what value will be displayed in a cell containing the cell formula =MIN(A1:A5)?

18. Given the cell values for A1, A2, A3, A4 and A5 above, what value will be displayed in a cell containing the cell formula =MAX(A1:A5)?

19. Given the cell values for A1 above, what value will be displayed in a cell containing the cell formula =UPPER(A1)?

20. Describe the steps required to *display cell formulas.*

Write formulas for the spreadsheet below:

-	A	B	C	D	E	F	G
1	Amount	Discount	Tax	Total		Discount rate	20%
2	$50.00	$10.00	$4.00	$44.00		Tax rate	10%
3	$100	$20.00	$8.00	$88.00			
4	$10.00	$2.00	$0.80	$8.80			

1. Write a formula for B2 which calculates the discount as the amount times the discount rate. Make sure the formula can be copied to B3 and B4.

2. Write a formula for C2 which calculates the tax by multiplying the amount less the discount by the tax rate. Make sure the formula can be copied to C3 and C4.

3. Write a formula for D2 which calculates the total which is the amount less the discount plus the tax. Make sure the formula can be copied to D3 and D4.

Evaluate formulas using spreadsheet given below:

-	A	B	C	D	E	F
1	6	0	5	$50.00	Interest rate (APR)	18%
2		3	4	$47.50	Years	2
3	Book	10	13	$45.00	Amount	$1000.00
4	6	20	8	$43.00	Payment	???

1. =MIN(B1:C4)

2. =MAX(A1:B4)

3. =SUM(B1:C3)

4. =AVERAGE(A1:B4)

5. =COUNTA(A1:B4)

6. =COUNT(A1:B4)

7. =IF(A4<10, IF(A1<20, C1, C2), C4)

8. =UPPER(A3)

9. =T(A2)

10. =ROUND(D2,-1)

Macros and Database Management

Objectives

- Automating tasks you perform
- Uses of Macros
- Creating and Storing Macros
- Database Management
- Excel 2000 database limitations
- Sorting
- Using Filters
- Using Advanced Filter
- Data Forms

Automating tasks you perform

If you perform a task repeatedly in Microsoft Excel, you can automate the task with a macro. A macro is a collection of keystroke that is created, saved and later called by typing an assigned control key or selecting menu item. A macro is a series of commands and functions that are stored in a Visual Basic module and can be run whenever you need to perform the task. When you record a macro, Excel stores information about each step you take as you perform a series of commands. You then run the macro to repeat, or "play back," the commands.

Uses of Macros

A macro automates frequently used operations by converting a few keypresses into a stored series of worksheet manipulations. You may wish to use a macro to guide the data entry process of an inexperienced user. Once a new set of values is typed into a worksheet, such as current sales or cost information, a macro could then print a standard report and a corresponding chart.

Manage your Macros

With the Visual Basic Editor, you can edit macros, copy macros from one module to another, copy macros between different workbooks, rename the modules that store the macros, or rename the macros. For example, if you wanted the text-wrapping macro to also make the text bold, you could record another macro to make a cell bold and then copy the instructions from that macro to the text-wrapping macro.

Macro Security

Microsoft Excel 2000 provides safeguards against viruses that can be transmitted by macros. If you share macros with others, you can certify them with a digital signature so that other users can verify that they are from a trustworthy source. Whenever you open a workbook that contains macros, you can verify their source before you enable them.

Understanding Macro Viruses

A macro virus is a type of computer virus that's stored in a macro within a workbook or add-ins program. Viruses are programs that are written by individuals, usually with the intent to destroy or corrupt data.

When you open an affected workbook or perform an action that triggers a macro virus, the virus can become active, be transmitted to your computer, and be stored in ***Personal.xls***, a hidden workbook, or some other undetectable location. From that point on, every workbook you save can be "infected" automatically with the virus. If other people open infected workbooks, the macro virus can also be transmitted to their computers.

Excel displays a warning message whenever you open a workbook that contains macros. You can then decide whether to open the workbook with the macros enabled or whether to open the workbook with the macros disabled so that you can only examine and edit them. A macro virus can be harmful only if it is allowed to run, so disabling the macros allows you to open the workbook safely.

Creating and Storing Macros

You can create a macro in one of the two ways. The first is to enter the Record Macro mode using the **Tools → Macro → Record New Macro** menu selection.

A Record Macro dialog prompts you for a macro name. You can also assign a shortcut key or add a selection to the bottom of the Tools menu to run the macro. The shortcut key is stored with the current workbook. If the macro shortcut key is the same as a standard Excel shortcut key, it replaces the standard shortcut in the current workbook. Shortcut keys use either Ctrl+x or Ctrl+Shift+x, where x is any letter **a** through **z**.

When using the Record Macro dialog each keystroke is recorded. The word "REC" is highlighted at the bottom of the screen to tell you that the macro recorder is on a Stop button is also displayed in a small dialog. When you finish recording your keystrokes, either click the Stop button or use the **Tools → Macro → Stop Recording** selection. You can view your macro code using the **Tools → Macro → Macros** menu selection and then click the Edit button. This puts you in the Visual Basic Integrated Development Environment (IDE). Once you view or edit your code, return to the worksheet by using **File → Close** and Return to Microsoft Excel.

The second way to create a macro is to begin the Macro Recorder, type a few keystrokes and then click Stop. Then enter the IDE using the Macro dialog's Edit button. At this point you can type your macro commands directly if you understand the Visual Basic language and know how to navigate the Visual Basic Environment.

Running Macros

Just like the creation process, you can run a macro in a number of ways. First display the worksheet for which the macro was designed. Then use **Tools → Macro → Macros** (Shortcut - Alt+F8 key), pick the macro name, and click the Run button. You can also press the shortcut key assigned when the macro was created. Shortcut keys can be added later using the Macro dialog's Options button. You can also run the macro from the Visual Basic Editor while you are editing the macro. To interrupt the macro before it completes the actions you recorded, press ESC. If you are finished with the operation of your macro, you can save the workbook containing the macro in the normal way.

Database Management

A structured collection of related data about one or more subjects. An address book, a Telephone directory, Student database, etc.

A database is not something that is necessary complicated or difficult to create or manipulate. You can think of a telephone directory as a database. It is simply a collection of data that can be organized so that it is easily accessible. If we take the example of a list of names and addresses in an address book, then each complete entry for a person will form a record, while each item of data, such as the name or phone number will form a field within each record.

In Microsoft Excel, you can easily use a list as a database. When you perform database tasks, such as finding, sorting, or subtotaling data, Microsoft Excel automatically recognizes the list as a database and uses the following list elements to organize the data.

- The columns in the list are the fields in the database.
- The column labels in the list are the field names in the database.
- Each row in the list is a record in the database.

Field: A field is a column within an Excel 2000 database.

Record: A record is a row within an Excel 2000 database.

Field Name: In an Excel 2000 database the top row of the database will normally hold the names of each field (column). It is usually descriptive text describing the function of the particular field. Field names are not essential for some of the database functions, such as sorting a list.

Excel 2000 database limitations

- An Excel 2000 database is limited to 65,536 rows and 256 columns.
- Only one user at a time can access an Excel 2000 database.
- The entire database must be held in memory (where as external databases do not have to be held entirely in memory).
- An Excel 2000 worksheet stores additional information (i.e. formulas, graphics and formatting information), compared to information held in external databases, and thus takes up more disk space.

To create an internal database

Enter the information in the normal way to create an internal database as shown in Figure 9.1, keeping in mind to include field names in the top row.

	A	B	C	D	E
1	SNO.	NAME OF THE BOOK	WRITER	PUBLISHER	PRICE
2	1	ADOBE ILLUSTRATORS 8.0 CLASSROOM IN A BOOK		BPB	270
3	2	ADOBE PREMIERE CLASSROOM IN A BOOK: TM		TM	270
4	3	CORE JAVA VOLUME 1: AWL	HORSTMAN	AWL	434.42
5	4	CORE JAVA VOLUME 2: AWL	HORSTMAN	AWL	478.07
6	5	ELECTRONIC COMMERCE: TL	SCHNETDER	TL	960.52
7	6	FLASH 4.0 BIBLE: IDG	REINHARDT	IDG	429
8	7	IIS 4.0 MCSE STUDY GUIDE: IDG	DILLON	IDG	450
9	8	INSIDE ADOBE PHOTOSHOP: TM		TM	399
10	9	INTERNET INFO SERVER 4.0 STUDY GUIDE: BPB	MATHEW	BPB	450
11	10	JAVA 2.0 UNLEASHED: TM		TM	499
12	11	M/S SQL SERVER 7.0 UNLEASHED: TM		TM	360
13	12	MASTERING COLD FUSION 4.5	ARMAN DANESH	BPB	399
14	13	MASTERING MACROMEDIA DREAMWEAVER 3.0: BPB		BPB	299
15	14	MCSE NETWORKING ESSENTIAL STUDY GUIDE		BPB	450
16	15	MCSE TCP/IP NT SERVER 4 STUDY GUIDE	TODD FAMMEL	BPB	450
17	16	PROFESSIONAL SITE SERVER 3.0 COMM ED: SPD	RUBINI	SPD	500
18	17	PURE JAVA SCRIPT	R.ALLEN	BPB	240
19	18	THINKING IN JAVA	ECKEL	AWL	450
20	19	UNDERSTANDING BIZTALK: TM		TM	240

Figure 9.1: A Database of Library Books

Use the **Tab** key or the arrow key to proceed to the next field or **Shift** +**Tab** to go to the preceding field. You can insert or remove rows or columns in the normal way.

In fact, there is nothing special concerning the creation of an internal database, it is just like creating any other spreadsheet type information.

Sorting

Microsoft Excel uses specific sort orders to arrange data according to the value. In an ascending sort, Excel sorts from the lowest value to the highest value. In a descending sort, sort order is reversed except for blank cells, which are always placed last.

- Numbers are sorted from the smallest negative number to the largest positive number.

- When you sort alphanumeric text, Excel sorts left to right, character by character. For example, if a cell contains the text "A100," Excel places the cell after a cell that contains the entry "A1" and before a cell that contains the entry "A11."

- Text and text that includes numbers are sorted in this order: 0 1 2 3 4 5 6 7 8 9 (space) ! " # $ % & ( ) * , . / : ; ? @ [\ ] ^ _ ` { | } ~ + < = > A B C D E F G H I J K L M N O P Q R S T U V W X Y Z

- Apostrophes (') and hyphens (-) are ignored. If two text strings are the same except for a hyphen, the text with the hyphen is sorted last.

- In logical values, FALSE is placed before TRUE.

- All error values are equal.

- Blanks are always placed last.

To sort the data within a database

- Select any cell within the database range.

- From the **Data** drop down menu, select the **Sort** command, which will open the **Sort** dialog box as shown in Figure 9.2.

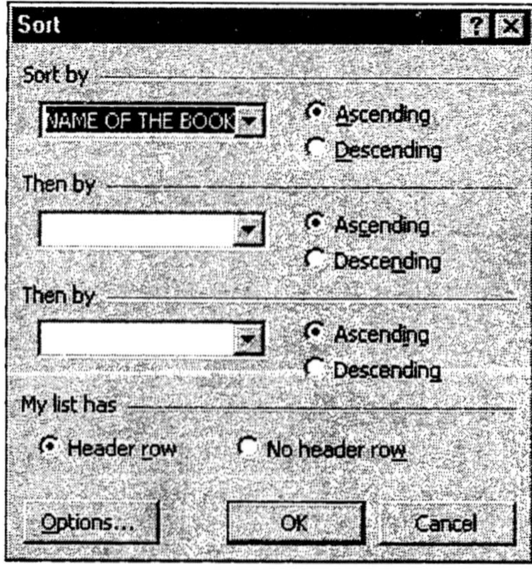

Figure 9.2: Sort dialog box

- As you see Excel 2000 has automatically placed the first field name (**SNO.**), in the **Sort by** box. This was because the active cell was in the **SNO.** field (i.e. column), when the **Sort** command was issued.

☞ *Note: If your database contains a Header Row, but you specify **No header row** in the **Sort** dialog box, then the header will be sorted (and get mixed up) along with the rest of the information contained within the database.*

To sort the database by price

- From the **Sort by** box, select **Price** , and click on the **OK** button.
- To sort the price in descending order, repeat the sorting procedure, but click on the **Descending** radio button, next to the **Sort by** box.

"Then by" Sort option

The optional **Then by** fields allow a total of up to three sort fields to be specified. For instance, you could sort this database by publisher (in ascending order), and then by price (in descending order).

Find data in a list

Microsoft Excel provides several ways to analyze data in a list. You can filter a list to see rows that meet specific criteria by using the **AutoFilter** or **Advanced Filter** command. If you want to find a value in a list by using another value in the list, for example, to find the price of one product from a list of products and their prices, you can use the Lookup Wizard.

Using Filters

You can apply filters to only one list on a worksheet at a time.

1. Click a cell in the list you want to filter.
2. On the **Data** menu, click to **Filter → AutoFilter**.
3. To display only the rows that contain a specific value, click the arrow in the column that contains the data you want to display.

4. Click the value.

5. To apply an additional condition based on a value in another column, repeat steps 3 and 4 in the other column.

6. To filter the list by two values in the same column, or to apply *comparison operators* other than **Equals**, click the arrow in the column, and then click **Custom** as shown in Figure 9.3.

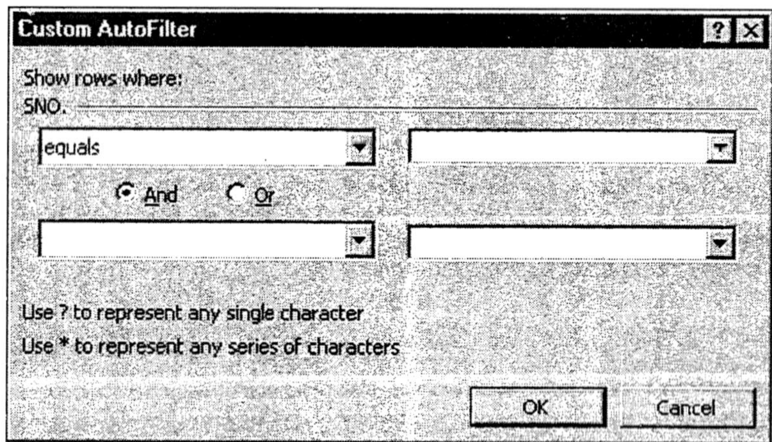

Figure 9.3: Custom AutoFilter dialog box

When you apply a filter to a column, the only filters available for other columns are the values visible in the filtered list.

You can apply up to two conditions to a column by using **AutoFilter**. To apply more complex filters or to copy filtered rows to another location, you can use advanced filters.

Operators	Function
=	Equal to
>	Greater than
<	Less than
>=	Greater than or equal to
<=	Less than or equal to
<>	Not equal to

Table 9.1: Operators available for Custom AutoFilter

Using the And/Or filters

You can use the **And / Or** buttons to impose additional criteria on your filters. For instance, you could display all books costing over Rs. 300, but less than Rs. 900.

Using Top 10 Filter

When you choose Top 10 as your filter criteria, the Top 10 AutoFilter dialog box opens as shown in Figure 9.4.

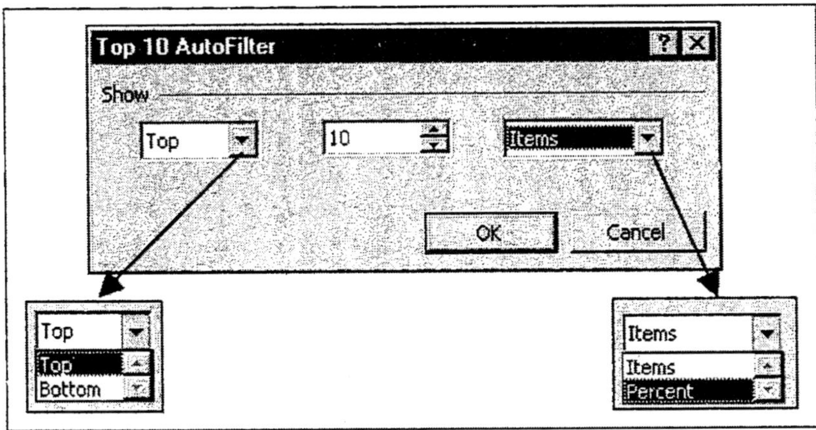

Figure 9.4: Top 10 AutoFilter

In the first box, choose Top or Bottom, depending on whether you want to see the highest or lowest values in the database. In the spin box control, enter a number larger than 0. In the last control, choose Items or Percents. For example, to see the top 10 percent of the scores in a column of test scores, choose Top, enter 10 and then choose Percents.

Creating Subtotals

You can create subtotals based on any field in the database. A subtotal is not necessarily a sum, it can be an average, count, minimum, maximum or other statistical calculation based on a group of records. Subtotal ignores hidden records, whereas Sum does not.

Before subtotalling, you need to sort the database on the field you wish to subtotal on. For example, if you want to subtotal each month's orders, first sort by month. Then select a cell anywhere in the database and take the following steps:

1. First **Sort** the data.

2. Choose **Data → Subtotals** to open the Subtotal dialog box as shown in Figure 9.5.

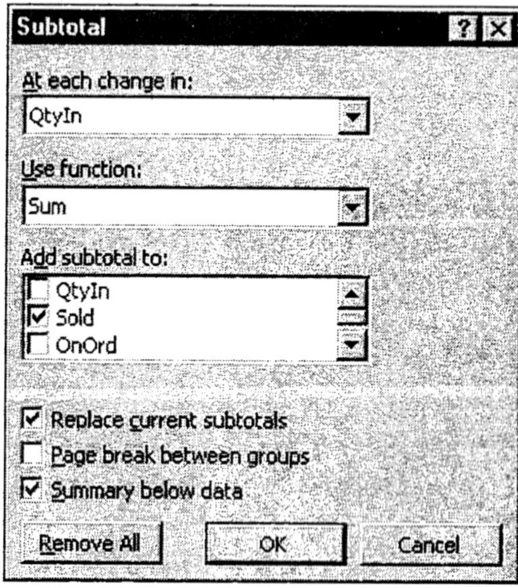

Figure 9.5: Subtotal dialog box

3. Select the numeric fields to be subtotaled when the value of the **At Each Change In** field changes.

4. Select a type of subtotal from the **Use Function** drop-down.

5. In the **Add Subtotal To** select each field you want to subtotal. You can subtotal more than one field at a time, but you have to use the same function, average three fields, sum three fields, etc.

6. If necessary, change the settings for **Replace Current Subtotals, Page Break Between Groups** and **Summary Below Data.**

   - Use Replace Current Subtotals if you have subtotaled earlier and want to replace the former set with new subtotals. If you want both sets of subtotals to appear (for example, sums and averages), deselect this option.

- If you want to print the worksheet with subtotals and each subtotaled set of records to print on a separate page, insert a Page Break Between Group.

- Summary Below Data places a summary (grand total, grand average) row at the bottom of the database.

7. When you have entered the information for subtotals, click the OK button to add subtotals.

Using Advanced Filter

The use of AutoFilter techniques will cover most users requirements when selecting information from an Excel database. The use of advanced filtering techniques allows you to select multiple criteria for the same field and to make selections based on complex formulae.

To use the Advanced Filter

With the parts workbook still displayed, use Data → Filter → Advanced Filter to display all records having the part number N??P, any Description text, and OnOrd values greater than or equal to 0. Note that ?? are wildcards.

1. Enter the values as in A19:C19 as shown in Figure 9.6.

	A	B	C	D	E
17					
18	PN	Description	OnOrd		
19	N??P	*	>=0		
20					
21					
22					

Figure 9.6: Values used in the above example

2. Set up the Advanced Filter dialog box as shown in Figure 9.7 including the Copy to Location button. You can enter each of the cell ranges by clicking the button within the text boxes, dragging the range and pressing Enter.

Figure 9.7: Advanced Filter dialog box

3. Click OK to transfer the matching records to the Copy to range. Compare your results with the following Figure 9.8.

	A	B	C	D	E	F	G	H
1	**PN**	**Description**	**Qtyln**	**Sold**	**OnOrd**	**Cost**	**Price**	**Measure**
2	BGSAE75	Bolt Hex	1050	324	0	0.115	0.2	Each
3	NB6P	Nail, Brt. 6P	300	110	300	0.26	0.5	Each
4	NB8P	Nail, Brt. 8P	200	85	300	0.32	0.55	Each
5	NGSAE75	Nut, Hex	975	392	500	0.065	0.12	Each
6	WFG75	Washer, Flat	1000	950	1000	0.03	0.07	Pound
7	WSG75	Washer, Split	1000	586	500	0.03	0.07	Pound
8								
9	**PN**	**Description**	**Qtyln**	**Sold**	**OnOrd**	**Cost**	**Price**	**Measure**
10	NB6P	Nail, Brt. 6P	300	110	300	0.26	0.5	Each
11	NB8P	Nail, Brt. 8P	200	85	300	0.32	0.55	Each
12								
13								
14								
15								
16		No. of Items	2					2.00
17								
18	PN	Description	OnOrd					
19	N??P	*	>=0					
20								

Figure 9.8: Output of the example

4. This completes the database filtering activities. As you can see, Excel provides some powerful tools for selecting and displaying records matching specified criteria.

Data Forms

Excel 2000 has a built-in Data Form feature which allows you to easily add, view, find, edit and delete records quickly. You can also use the Data Form to display specific records based on a filter criteria. A Data Form is similar to a dialog box and is created by Excel 2000 from the data in your list. For example, if you have a library book list which contains names of several books, along with individual information about each book, Excel 2000 can create a Data Form to display each book title along with individual information. This allows you to edit records in a list individually, rather than having to continually move up and down the entire list.

To add and delete a record

- Select any cell or range of cells in the worksheet.
- From the **Data** menu select **Form** to display the Data Form for the database as shown in Figure 9.9.

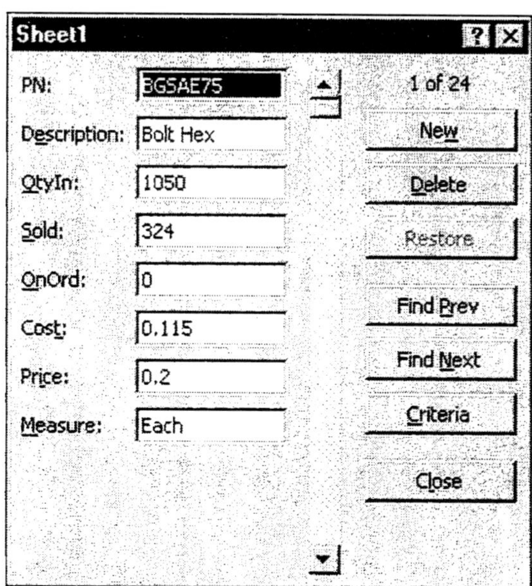

Figure 9.9: Data Form dialog box

- You can now use the Data Form to add, edit, find or delete records in the list.
- Click on the **New** button in the Data Form. A blank record will be displayed.
- Click in the first text box and enter the data required. Press the **Tab** key to move to the next field.
- Enter any other information into the remaining text boxes.
- Press **Enter** when you have finished to move to a new blank record, to keep entering new records.
- To delete the record currently displayed in the data form, click the Delete button to remove the row from the list. A dialog box appears warning that the record will be permanently deleted.
- Select **OK** to delete the record, or **Cancel** to cancel the operation. Any rows below the deleted record in the list will move up.

To edit a record

- Click in the text box containing the data you wish to edit.
- Edit the data as per your requirement.

To navigate between records

- Click on the **Find Prev** button to move back to the previous record.
- Click on the **Find Next** button to move forward to the next record.

Searching records

- Click on the **Criteria** button. A blank, criteria form is displayed.
- Enter the search criteria into the relevant text box controls as shown in Figure 9.10 for one or more fields. Excel joins two criteria with AND, so it will only find records that meet both criteria. You can't search for records that meet either criteria (OR).

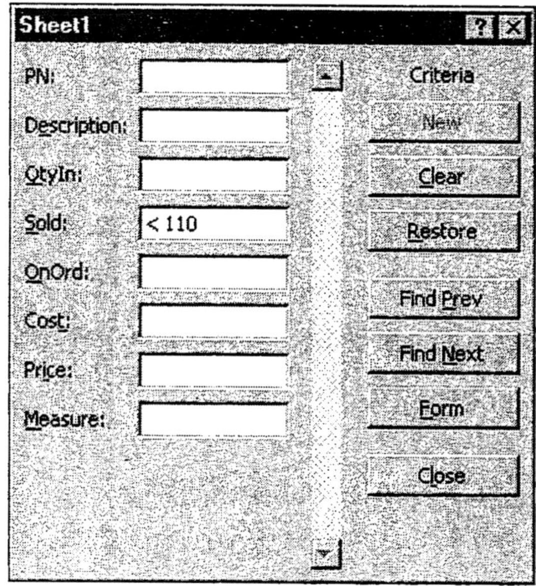

Figure 9.10: Entering records in Data Form

- Click on the **Find Prev** button to find the previous record that meets your criteria, or click on the **Find Next** button to find the next record that meets your criteria.

- Click the scroll bar to view all records in the database.

To close a Data Form

- Click on the **Close** button to return to the worksheet.

Hands on Exercise

Exercise 1: Create a Macro

1. Start Excel and open a blank workbook.

2. Record a macro that enters **"eAcademy"** in the cell C5.

3. Record Additional Macro in the cell C7, enter the address **"F-38, South Extension Part I, New Delhi - 110049"** and in the cell C8 enter **"Tel.: 4655702-05"**.

4. Change the font & size to **Arial**, **14 points bold**, color to **Red** in the cell C5 and make the width to **AutoFit Selection**. Make the cell C7 and C8 flush right and **12 points Times New Roman**.

5. Click on Sheet 2 in the workbook and run the macro created in step 2 to 4.

6. Create a macro button on Sheet 3 and assign the button to the macro created in step 2 to 4.

7. After clicking on the Macro Button the final output comes as shown in Figure 9.11.

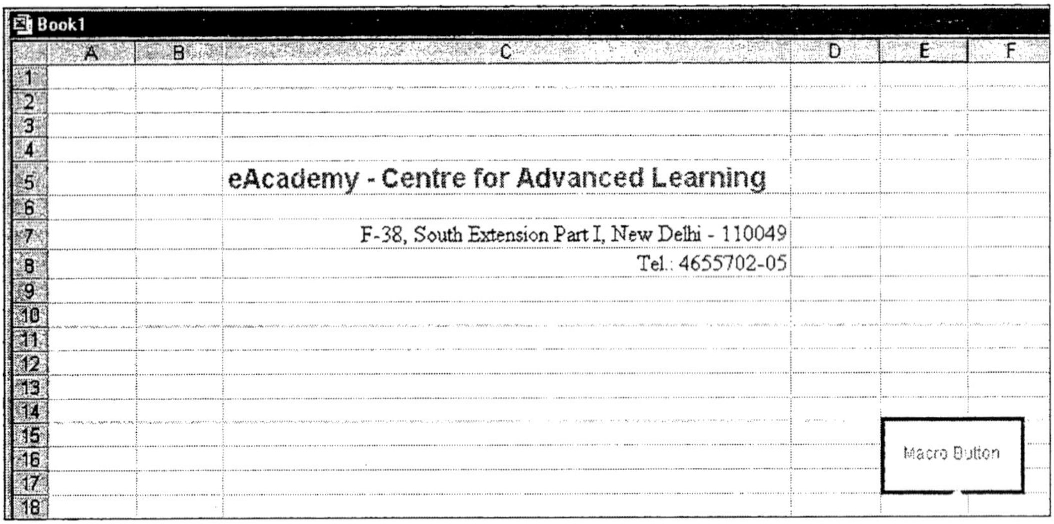

Figure 9.11: Final Output of the Macro

8. Save the workbook.

Test Your Knowledge

Students must solve the following assignment.

Multiple Choice Questions:

1. To get external data from a Web source, you need to click Get External Data from the ______________ menu.

    a. File
    b. Edit
    c. Data
    d. Tools

2. Mark the most appropriate option statement

    a. Mail Merge can be used to print the form letters.
    b. Mail Merge can be used to print the form letters and mailing labels.
    c. Mail Merge can be used to print envelopes.
    d. All of the above.

3. Creating form letters using Mail Merge involves

    a. Creating the main document.
    b. Creating the main document and data source.
    c. Inserting merge fields in the main document and merging the main document with data source.
    d. Both (b) and (c).

State Whether True or False:

1. Merging two documents into single one is called Mail Merge.

    a. True
    b. False

2. It is not possible to merge print letter only for a specific record in a word processor.

    a. True
    b. False

3. Data source file is also known as form letters.

   a. True
   b. False

4. The document containing the common text for all the letters is known as the main document.

   a. True
   b. False

5. It is not possible to include a merge field more than once in a document.

   a. True
   b. False

6. The document containing information that gets changed from letter to letter is known as the data source.

   a. True
   b. False

Tables, PivotTable and PivotChart

Objectives

- Introduction to PivotTable and PivotChart Wizard
- Using Tables
- Creating and Editing Charts
- Creating a Chart with the help of ChartWizard

Introduction

A **PivotTable** is an analytical tool that summarizes information from particular fields of an Excel list, a relational database file. PivotTables are a powerful tool for data analysis. A *PivotTable* summarizes the columns of information in a database in relationship to each other.

To create a table using PivotTable

Open a workbook named PIVOT. This is a tabulation of the number of sales calls made and resulting sales and sales amounts made by the members of the New York area sales team. Each team member has a geographical area in and around the New York City area.

Follow these steps to create a table using PivotTable.

1. Start Excel and open the Pivot file. The table resembles the following screen as shown in Figure 10.1.

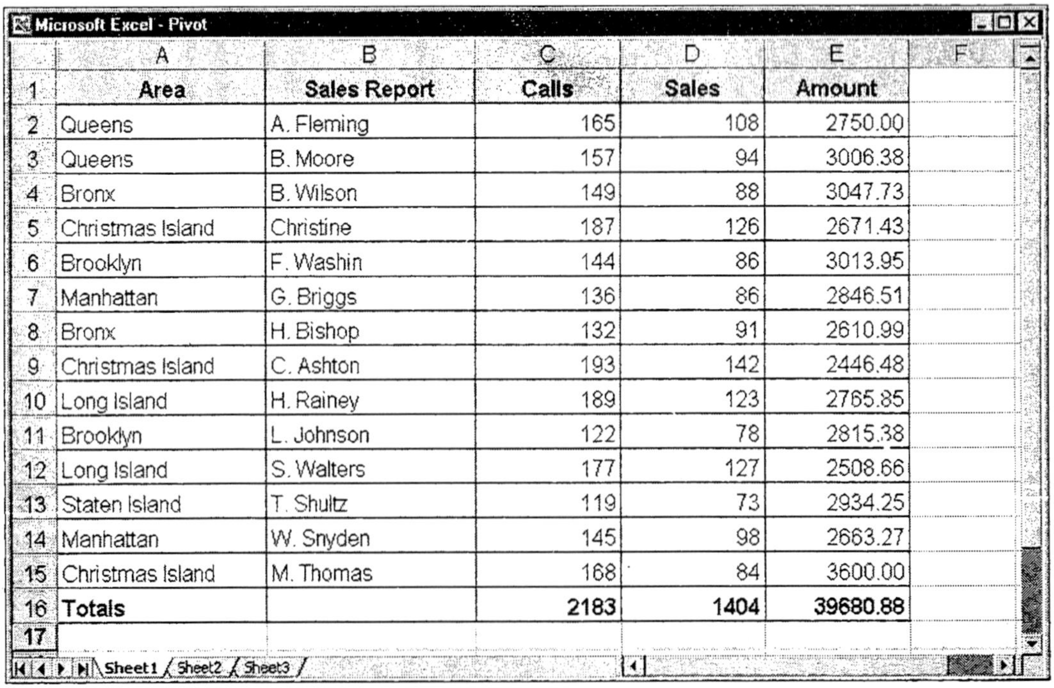

Microsoft Excel - Pivot

	A	B	C	D	E	F
1	**Area**	**Sales Report**	**Calls**	**Sales**	**Amount**	
2	Queens	A. Fleming	165	108	2750.00	
3	Queens	B. Moore	157	94	3006.38	
4	Bronx	B. Wilson	149	88	3047.73	
5	Christmas Island	Christine	187	126	2671.43	
6	Brooklyn	F. Washin	144	86	3013.95	
7	Manhattan	G. Briggs	136	86	2846.51	
8	Bronx	H. Bishop	132	91	2610.99	
9	Christmas Island	C. Ashton	193	142	2446.48	
10	Long Island	H. Rainey	189	123	2765.85	
11	Brooklyn	L. Johnson	122	78	2815.38	
12	Long Island	S. Walters	177	127	2508.66	
13	Staten Island	T. Shultz	119	73	2934.25	
14	Manhattan	W. Snyden	145	98	2663.27	
15	Christmas Island	M. Thomas	168	84	3600.00	
16	**Totals**		**2183**	**1404**	**39680.88**	
17						

Sheet1 / Sheet2 / Sheet3

Figure 10.1: A Pivot file

2. Position the cell pointer in A1 and use **Data → PivotTable Report** to summarize sales information by each area as follows:

♦ [A 1] **<Alt, D, P>**; examine the dialog box in Figure 10.2.

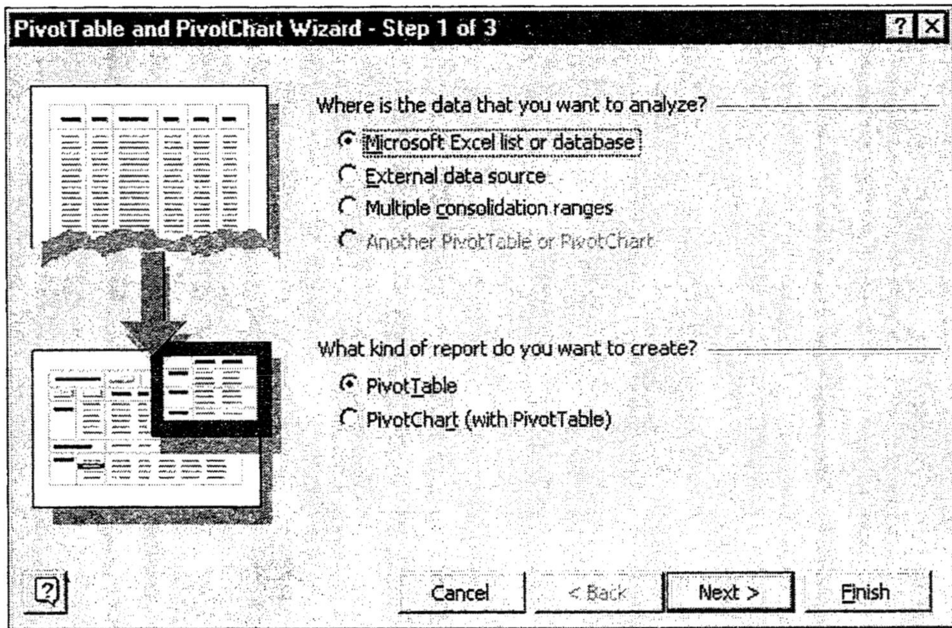

Figure 10.2: Step 1 of the Wizard

♦ Click **<Next>**. A dialog box appears as in Figure 10.3. Notice that the area A1:E16 is selected.

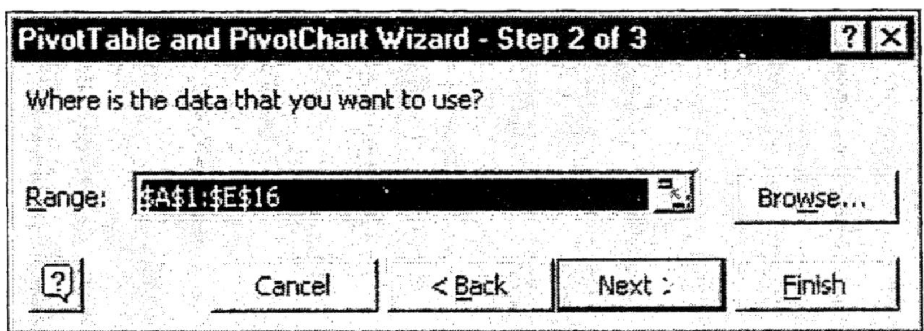

Figure 10.3: Step 2 of the Wizard

☞ *Whenever you want to change the range, just click the text box button, drag the desired range of cells, and press* ***<Enter>****.*

- Click **<Next>** and then click **Layout**. Now drag the displayed title buttons (Area, Calls, Sales and Amount) located on the right side of the dialog box into the row (Area) and column (Calls, Sales, Amount) data areas as shown in the following Figure 10.4. Note that *"Sum of"* is added by Excel.

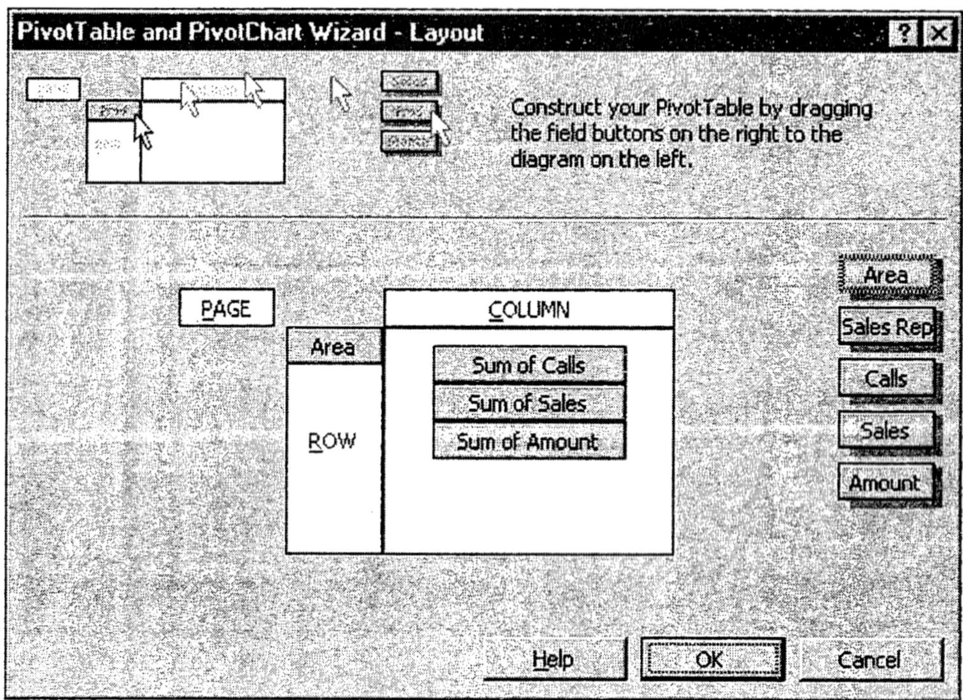

Figure 10.4: Layout Design

- Click **OK** then click **Options**. Use the default options shown in the Figure 10.5. Notice the name of the PivotTable is *PivotTable1*. You can have more than one PivotTable in a worksheet.

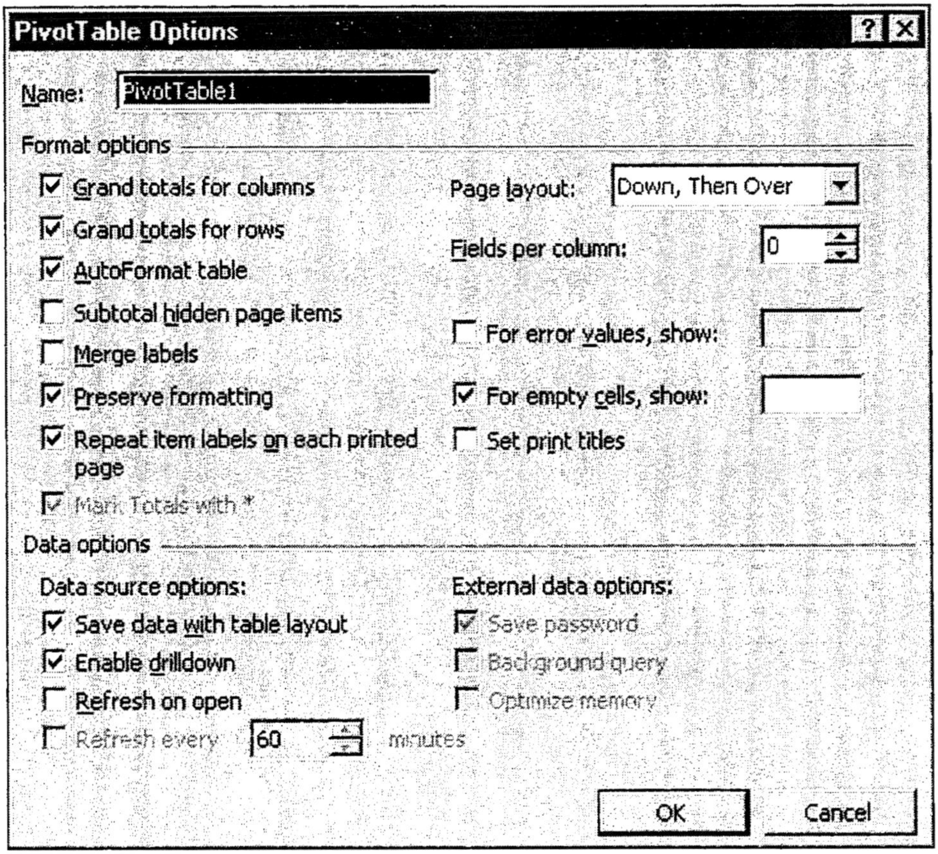

PivotTable Options

Name: PivotTable1

Format options

- [x] Grand totals for columns
- [x] Grand totals for rows
- [x] AutoFormat table
- [ ] Subtotal hidden page items
- [ ] Merge labels
- [x] Preserve formatting
- [x] Repeat item labels on each printed page
- [x] Mark Totals with *

Page layout: Down, Then Over

Fields per column: 0

- [ ] For error values, show:
- [x] For empty cells, show:
- [ ] Set print titles

Data options

Data source options:

- [x] Save data with table layout
- [x] Enable drilldown
- [ ] Refresh on open
- [ ] Refresh every 60 minutes

External data options:

- [x] Save password
- [ ] Background query
- [ ] Optimize memory

OK Cancel

Figure 10.5: PivotTable Options

- Click **OK.** Now examine the following dialog as in Figure 10.6. Leave it as is to place the PivotTable on a new worksheet. This adds *Sheet4* to the workbook that contains the pivottable.

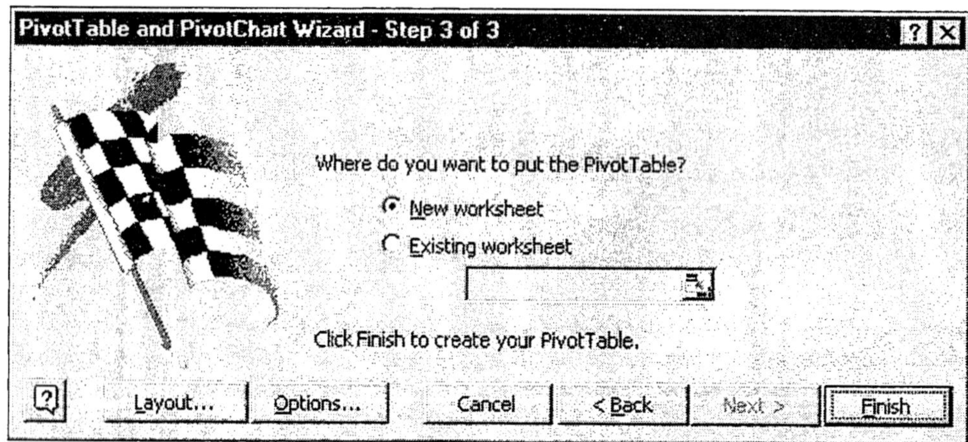

Figure 10.6: Step 3 of the Wizard

- Click **Finish**. Now examine the resulting pivottable to see how each area is summarized as shown in Figure 10.7.

Microsoft Excel - Pivot

	A	B	C	D	E
3	Data	Area	Total		
4	Sum of Calls	Bronx	281.00		
5		Brooklyn	266.00		
6		Christmas Island	548.00		
7		Long Island	366.00		
8		Manhattan	281.00		
9		Queens	322.00		
10		Staten Island	119.00		
11		Totals	2183.00		
12	Sum of Sales	Bronx	179.00		
13		Brooklyn	164.00		
14		Christmas Island	352.00		
15		Long Island	250.00		
16		Manhattan	184.00		
17		Queens	202.00		
18		Staten Island	73.00		
19		Totals	1404.00		
20	Sum of Amount	Bronx	5658.72		
21		Brooklyn	5829.34		
22		Christmas Island	8717.91		
23		Long Island	5274.52		
24		Manhattan	5509.78		
25		Queens	5756.38		
26		Staten Island	2934.25		
27		Totals	39680.88		
28	Total Sum of Calls		4366.00		
29	Total Sum of Sales		2808.00		
30	Total Sum of Amount		79361.77		
31					

Pivot Table Toolbar

PivotTable

PivotTable ▾

Figure 10.7: Final Output and Toolbar

☞ *Note: You can use the PivotTable toolbar to select and group/ungroup two or more region areas. You can also display or hide individual items using the toolbar's Show Detail and Hide Detail buttons. You can also use the toolbar to select data to chart.*

Using Tables

Many types of tables are used in business and finance. Excel lets you create your own table that is based on a formula that contains either one or two variables. You can create a financial amortization table from a formula used to calculate a periodic payment, an interest rate or the balance due on a loan. Similarly you can create a payroll table based on hours worked and different pay rates.

There are two types of data tables:

1. The **one-variable table** operates with a formula having a single variable.
2. The **two-variable table** operates with a formula having two variables.

To create a simple two-variable table

1. Begin with a blank worksheet.
2. Select A1:F15, set the number format category to General: [A1:F15], click the right mouse button, pick **Format → Cells**, pick the **Number** tab and the **General** category, and click **OK**.
3. Enter the information in the worksheet as shown in the following Figure 10.8, including the formula in B5. This formula is used to derive the periodic payment based on the principal amount of a loan, the rate of interest and the number of payments. The formula in cell B5 is displayed by selecting the cell and pressing F2 key.

Microsoft Excel - Amort

	A	B	C	D	E	F	G	H
1	Principal	1000						
2	Interest	0.08						
3	Payments	12						
4			(Monthly Payment Amounts for Different Terms)					
5		=PMT(B2/B3,B3,-B1)	12	24	36	48	60	
6		0.05						
7		0.055						
8		0.06						
9		0.065						
10		0.07						
11		0.075						
12		0.08						
13		0.085						
14		0.09						
15		0.095						
16		0.1						
17		0.105						
18		0.11						
19		0.115						
20		0.12						
21								

Figure 10.8: Creating two-variable table

☞ *Note: Use the command Edit → Fill → Series with Series in Columns and a Step value of 0.005.*

Microsoft Excel - Amort

	A	B	C	D	E	F	G	H
1	Principal	1000						
2	Interest	0.08						
3	Payments	12						
4			(Monthly Payment Amounts for Different Terms)					
5		$86.988429	12	24	36	48	60	
6		0.05						
7		0.055						
8		0.06						
9		0.065						
10		0.07						
11		0.075						
12		0.08						
13		0.085						
14		0.09						
15		0.095						
16		0.1						
17		0.105						
18		0.11						
19		0.115						
20		0.12						
21								

Table
Row input cell: $B$3
Column input cell: $B$2
OK
Cancel

Figure 10.9: Filling Row/Column Input Cell details

4. Select B5:G20 and use **Data → Table** to designate B3 as the Row Input Cell and B2 as the Column Input Cell: Select [B5:G20] **<Alt, D, T>** pick [B3] **<Tab>** pick <B2> click **OK** as shown in Figure 10.9.

5. An amortization schedule fills the table area for interest rates from 5% to 12%.

6. Format B1 and C6:G20 as Currency ($1,234.00) as shown in Figure 10.10. Notice cells C6:G20 are filled with #### because of small column width.

Microsoft Excel - Amort

	A	B	C	D	E	F	G	H
1	Principal	$1,000.00						
2	Interest	0.08						
3	Payments	12						
4			(Monthly Payment Amounts for Different Terms)					
5		$86.988429	12	24	36	48	60	
6		0.05	$85.61	$42.76	$28.50	$21.37	$17.09	
7		0.055	$85.84	$42.87	$28.57	$21.42	$17.14	
8		0.06	$86.07	$42.98	$28.64	$21.48	$17.18	
9		0.065	$86.30	$43.09	$28.72	$21.53	$17.22	
10		0.07	$86.53	$43.20	$28.79	$21.59	$17.27	
11		0.075	$86.76	$43.31	$28.86	$21.64	$17.31	
12		0.08	$86.99	$43.42	$28.93	$21.70	$17.35	
13		0.085	$87.22	$43.54	$29.01	$21.75	$17.40	
14		0.09	$87.45	$43.65	$29.08	#######	$17.44	
15		0.095	$87.68	$43.76	$29.15	$21.86	$17.48	
16		0.1	$87.92	$43.87	$29.23	$21.91	$17.53	
17		0.105	$88.15	$43.98	$29.30	$21.97	$17.57	
18		0.11	$88.38	$44.10	$29.38	$22.02	$17.62	
19		0.115	$88.62	$44.21	#######	$22.08	$17.66	
20		0.12	$88.85	$44.32	$29.52	$22.13	$17.70	
21								

Figure 10.10: Formatting the cells as Currency to 2 decimal places

7. Format B2 and B6:B20 as Percentage; use two decimal places.

8. Highlight C6:G6. Click on **Format → Column → AutoFit Selection.** Notice cells C6:G20 are now filled with monetary values. Compare your display to the following Figure 10.11.

Microsoft Excel - Amort

	A	B	C	D	E	F	G	H
1	Principal	$1,000.00						
2	Interest	8.00%						
3	Payments	12						
4			(Monthly Payment Amounts for Different Terms)					
5		$86.988429	12	24	36	48	60	
6		5.00%	$85.61	$42.76	$28.50	$21.37	$17.09	
7		5.50%	$85.84	$42.87	$28.57	$21.42	$17.14	
8		6.00%	$86.07	$42.98	$28.64	$21.48	$17.18	
9		6.50%	$86.30	$43.09	$28.72	$21.53	$17.22	
10		7.00%	$86.53	$43.20	$28.79	$21.59	$17.27	
11		7.50%	$86.76	$43.31	$28.86	$21.64	$17.31	
12		8.00%	$86.99	$43.42	$28.93	$21.70	$17.35	
13		8.50%	$87.22	$43.54	$29.01	$21.75	$17.40	
14		9.00%	$87.45	$43.65	$29.08	$21.80	$17.44	
15		9.50%	$87.68	$43.76	$29.15	$21.86	$17.48	
16		10.00%	$87.92	$43.87	$29.23	$21.91	$17.53	
17		10.50%	$88.15	$43.98	$29.30	$21.97	$17.57	
18		11.00%	$88.38	$44.10	$29.38	$22.02	$17.62	
19		11.50%	$88.62	$44.21	$29.45	$22.08	$17.66	
20		12.00%	$88.85	$44.32	$29.52	$22.13	$17.70	
21								

Figure 10.11: Implementing AutoFit Selection

9. Change the principal amount to $2,000.00: [B1] **2000 <Enter>**. If necessary, increase the width of column C by dragging the right edge of the C label to the right. Now compare your display to the following Figure 10.12.

Microsoft Excel - Amort

	A	B	C	D	E	F	G	H
1	Principal	$50,000.00						
2	Interest	8.00%						
3	Payments	12						
4			(Monthly Payment Amounts for Different Terms)					
5		$4,349.421454	12	24	36	48	60	
6		5.00%	$4,280.37	$2,138.02	$1,424.86	$1,068.47	$854.69	
7		5.50%	$4,291.84	$2,143.54	$1,428.49	$1,071.17	$856.84	
8		6.00%	$4,303.32	$2,149.06	$1,432.13	$1,073.88	$859.00	
9		6.50%	$4,314.82	$2,154.59	$1,435.77	$1,076.59	$861.16	
10		7.00%	$4,326.34	$2,160.14	$1,439.42	$1,079.31	$863.33	
11		7.50%	$4,337.87	$2,165.69	$1,443.07	$1,082.03	$865.49	
12		8.00%	$4,349.42	$2,171.25	$1,446.73	$1,084.76	$867.67	
13		8.50%	$4,360.99	$2,176.81	$1,450.39	$1,087.49	$869.84	
14		9.00%	$4,372.57	$2,182.39	$1,454.06	$1,090.22	$872.02	
15		9.50%	$4,384.18	$2,187.98	$1,457.74	$1,092.96	$874.20	
16		10.00%	$4,395.79	$2,193.57	$1,461.42	$1,095.70	$876.39	
17		10.50%	$4,407.43	$2,199.17	$1,465.10	$1,098.45	$878.58	
18		11.00%	$4,419.08	$2,204.78	$1,468.80	$1,101.20	$880.77	
19		11.50%	$4,430.75	$2,210.40	$1,472.50	$1,103.96	$882.97	
20		12.00%	$4,442.44	$2,216.03	$1,476.20	$1,106.72	$885.17	
21								

Figure 10.12: Changing the principal amount to $50,000.00

10. This concludes the table activities. Save the file as *AMORT.XLS*: **<File → Save As>**.

Creating and Editing Charts

Charts help you convert numeric data into visual display in which you can identify trends and pick out patterns at a glance. By using lines, columns, bars and pie slices to compare series of data over time and across categories. Charts often provide clear answer to tough questions.

When you create a new chart, Excel allows you to place it on its own chart sheet or to embed a chart object within the worksheet that contains the data you want to chart. Excel automatically maintains links between worksheet data and its graphic representation on the chart. If you change the numbers or text in the data range, the columns, pie slices, and other graphic elements on the chart changes.

Various types of Charts

Creating a chart makes it easier to compare and contrast the figures in a worksheet.

Area Chart

Use this when you want to emphasise change over time. In the example on the right, the contribution of several states to sales is shown from 1994 to 1996. Washington has increased the most over time.

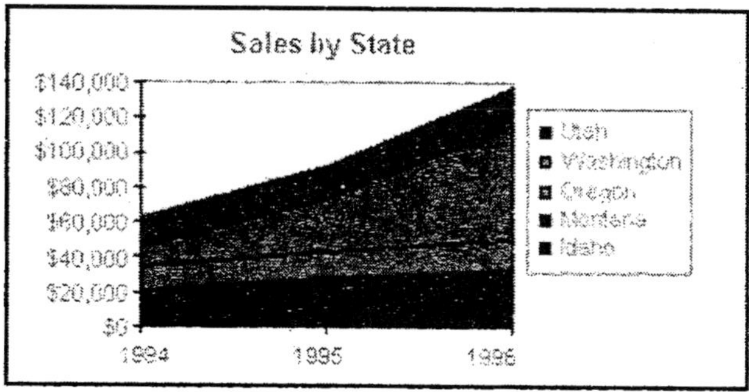

Figure 10.13: Area Chart

3-D Surface 

A surface chart is a bit like a topographic map. Colours and patterns indicate areas that are in the same range of values. In this chart temperature and time are plotted together to show the tensile strength they produce.

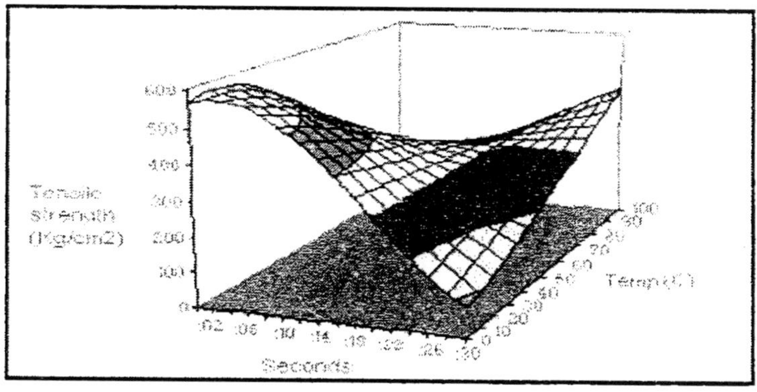

Figure 10.14: 3-D Surface Chart

Bar Chart

A bar chart compares values with each other. The example chart shows expenditure figures over six months.

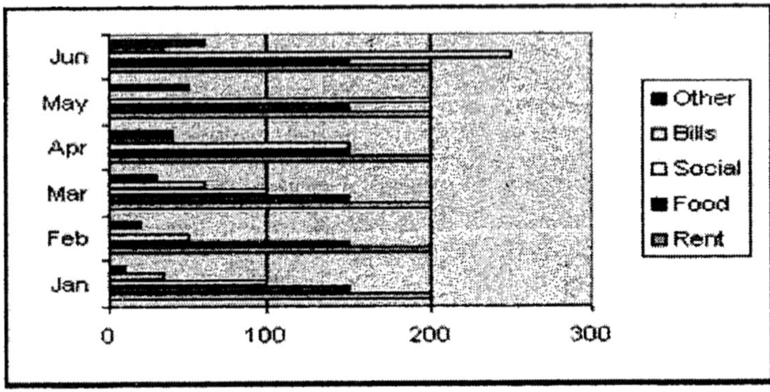

Figure 10.15: Bar Chart

Radar Chart 

In this chart, each category of information has it's own line radiating out from the centre. In the example shown there are three brands of vitamin, each represented by a line. The further the line reaches out from the centre the more vitamins it has in it.

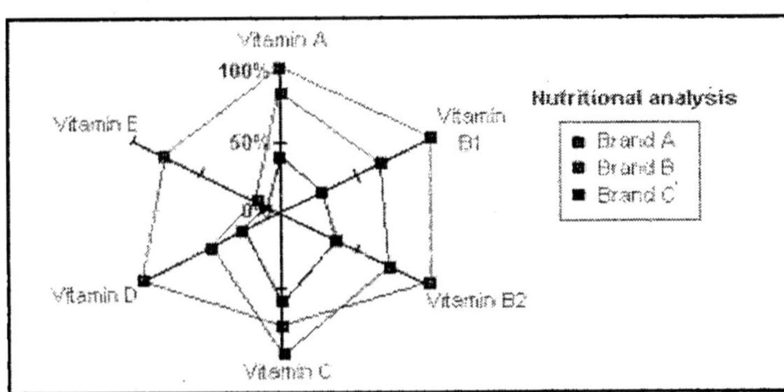

Figure 10.16: Radar Chart

Column Chart

A column chart is very similar to a bar chart, except the bars reach vertically instead of horizontally. The example chart compares expenditure figures over six months.

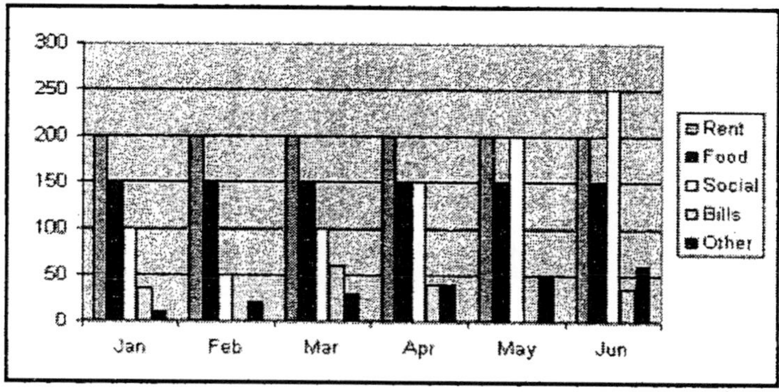

Figure 10.17: Column Chart

Bubble Chart

A bubble chart shows three sets of variables, represented by the two axes and the size of the bubble. In the example chart market share is plotted. The axes shows the number of products and the sales, and the size of the bubble shows the market share.

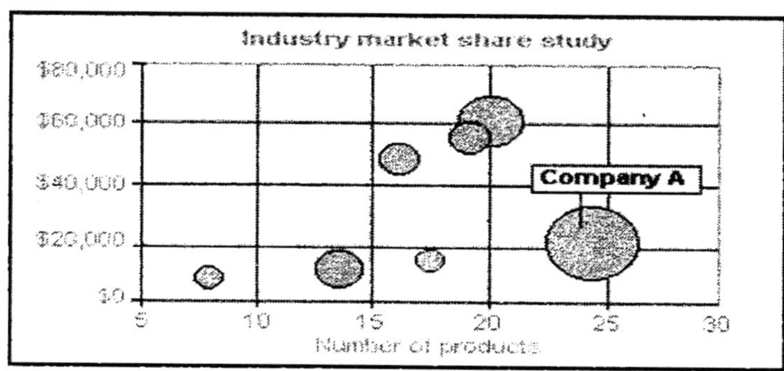

Figure 10.18: Bubble Chart

Line Chart

A line chart is useful for comparing trends. In the example chart, expenditure figures are shown over six months.

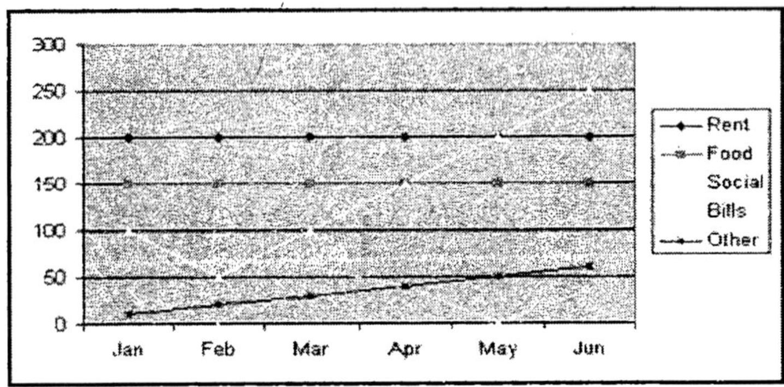

Figure 10.19: Line Chart

Scatter Graph

A scatter graph is useful for comparing a set of values with the average or predicted values. In the example chart, one set of dots show predicted temperatures, and another set of dots show the actual temperatures around it. This type of chart is commonly used for scientific data.

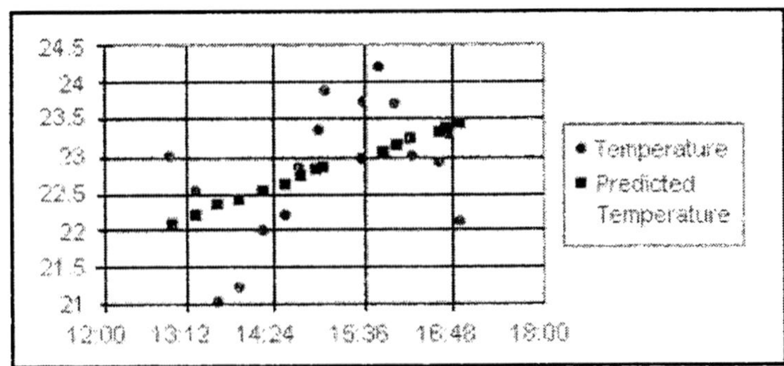

Figure 10.20: Scatter Graph

Pie Chart 

A pie chart can compare one set of figures. In the example chart, expenditure in January is shown.

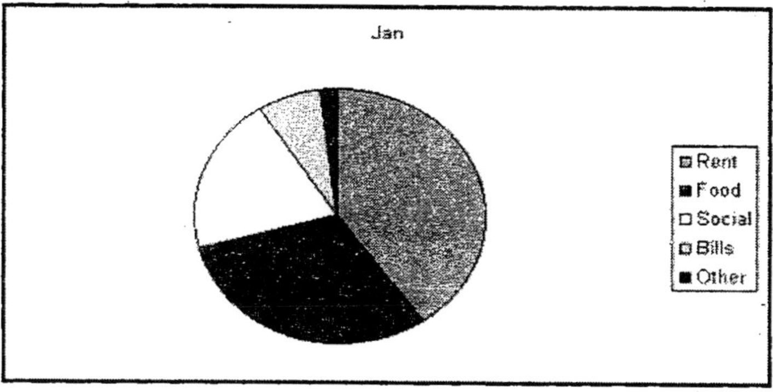

Figure 10.21: Pie Chart

Doughnut Chart 

A doughnut chart is very similar to a pie chart, except that it can show more than one set of figures. Each ring of the doughnut represents a set of figures. In the example chart, one set represents Gasoline revenues and the other property revenues.

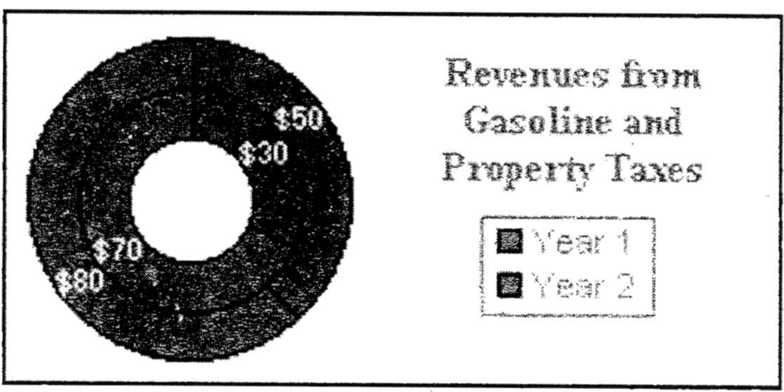

Figure 10.22: Doughnut Chart

Two basic techniques for creation of Charts

- Click the Chart Wizard button on the Standard toolbar and adjust all its options in four easy steps.
- Create a chart on its own chart sheet using the default chart type, chart options and formatting, open the worksheet that contains the data you want to make a chart. Select the range that contains the data you want to chart and then press F11.

Creating a Chart with the help of ChartWizard

- Select the cells you want to include in a chart. If you want to highlight a non-contiguous range, highlight the first range with the mouse, and hold down the **Ctrl** key and click on any other cells you want to select.
- On the **Standard** toolbar, click on the **Chart Wizard** icon.
- Step 1 of the **Chart Wizard** dialog box is displayed as shown in Figure 10.23.

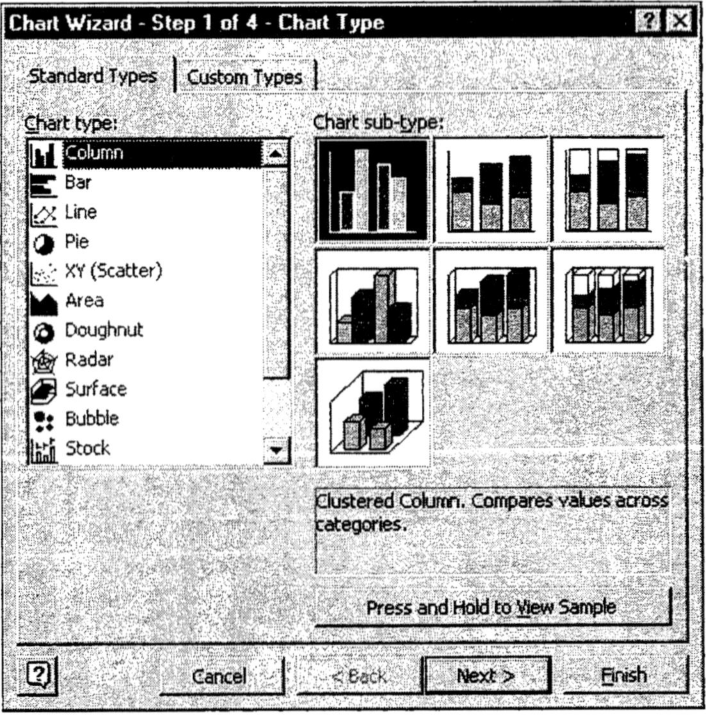

Figure 10.23: Chart Wizard

- Continue making your choices via the Chart Wizard until you reach the final step of the **Chart Wizard**.
- Select **Finish** and the chart will appear on your screen.

Moving and Sizing a Chart Object

When you create a chart on a worksheet, the position and size may not suit you. If you want to make changes, you can move and resize the chart.

- Click on the chart you wish to move, so that small black squares called handles are displayed around the border of the chart. This indicates that the chart is selected.
- Place the mouse pointer inside the chart area and drag the chart to the desired location.
- Release the mouse button when you have placed the chart where you want it.
- Move the mouse to one of the corner selection handles and drag and drop. The chart is re-sized in the same way that any graphic is re-sized within the Microsoft suite of applications.

Changing a Chart Type

After you have created a chart, you can change it to another chart type. When a chart is selected on a worksheet, or if a chart sheet is the active sheet, the commands displayed on each menu change to reflect commands that are used for charting.

1. Activate the chart sheet or double-click the chart on the worksheet. A dashed border outlines the chart on the worksheet.

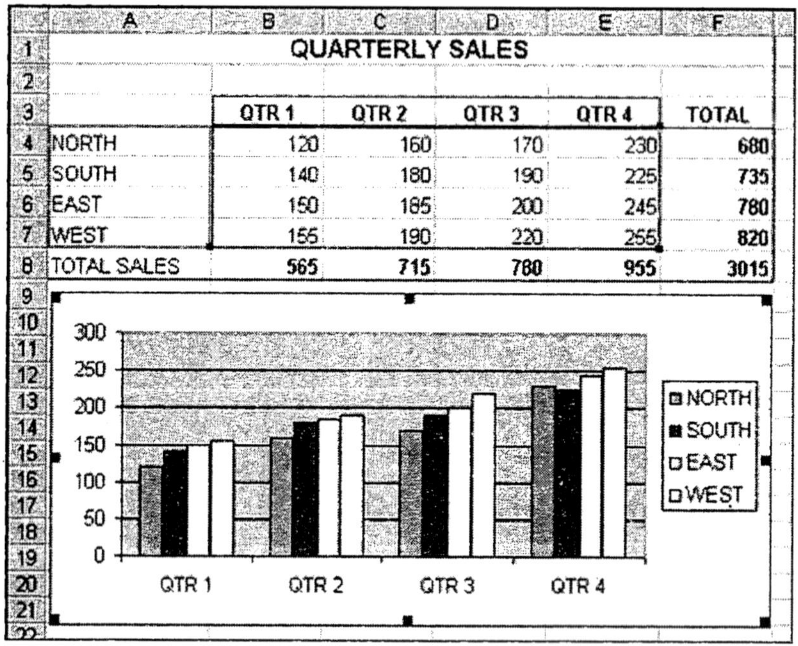

	A	B	C	D	E	F
1	QUARTERLY SALES					
2						
3		QTR 1	QTR 2	QTR 3	QTR 4	TOTAL
4	NORTH	120	160	170	230	680
5	SOUTH	140	180	190	225	735
6	EAST	150	185	200	245	780
7	WEST	155	190	220	255	820
8	TOTAL SALES	565	715	780	955	3015

Figure 10.24: Data and corresponding chart

2. Choose the Format Chart Type command
3. Select the type of chart you want.
4. Choose OK.

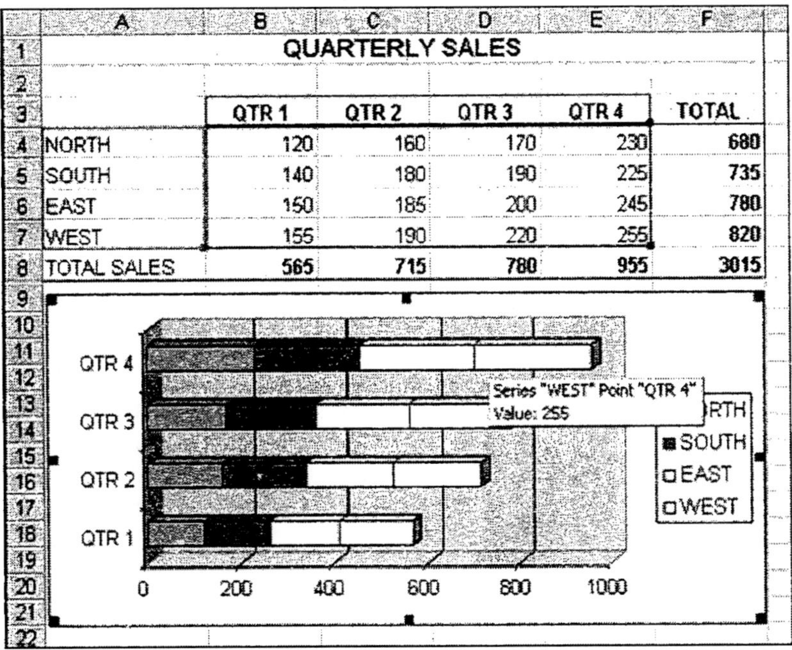

	A	B	C	D	E	F
1		QUARTERLY SALES				
2						
3		QTR 1	QTR 2	QTR 3	QTR 4	TOTAL
4	NORTH	120	160	170	230	680
5	SOUTH	140	180	190	225	735
6	EAST	150	185	200	245	780
7	WEST	155	190	220	255	820
8	TOTAL SALES	565	715	780	955	3015

Figure 10.25: Changing from Column chart to Bar chart

Why Insert Pictures?

You can put in pictures for various reasons: to illustrate a point, to put in a company logo or simply to brighten up your worksheet.

Inserting a Picture from File

Use this method to insert a picture you have stored at an earlier date

1. Click in the cell where you want the top right corner to be.

2. Click on the Insert menu.

3. Click on Picture.

4. Click on from File. You will get a box as shown in figure below.

5. Browse to find your picture.

6. Select your picture.

7. Click Insert and your picture will be inserted in your document

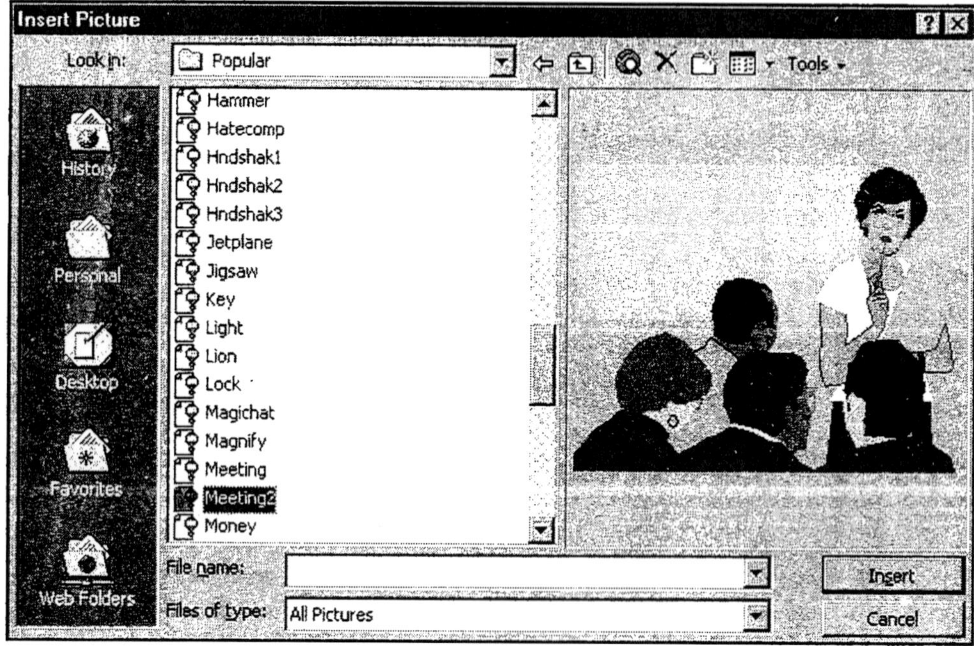

Figure 10.26: Insert Picture from file dialog box

Inserting ClipArt

Microsoft Office includes a series of pictures you can insert in a document to brighten it up or illustrate a point. These are called ClipArt.

To Insert ClipArt

1. Click in the cell where you want the top right corner to be.

2. Click on the Insert menu.

3. Click on Picture.

4. Click on ClipArt. You will get the Insert ClipArt as shown below.

5. Click on a category. You will get a series of pictures.

6. Select a picture. You will get a small box.

7. Click on the icon to Insert ClipArt. Your ClipArt will be inserted.

8. Close the dialog box.

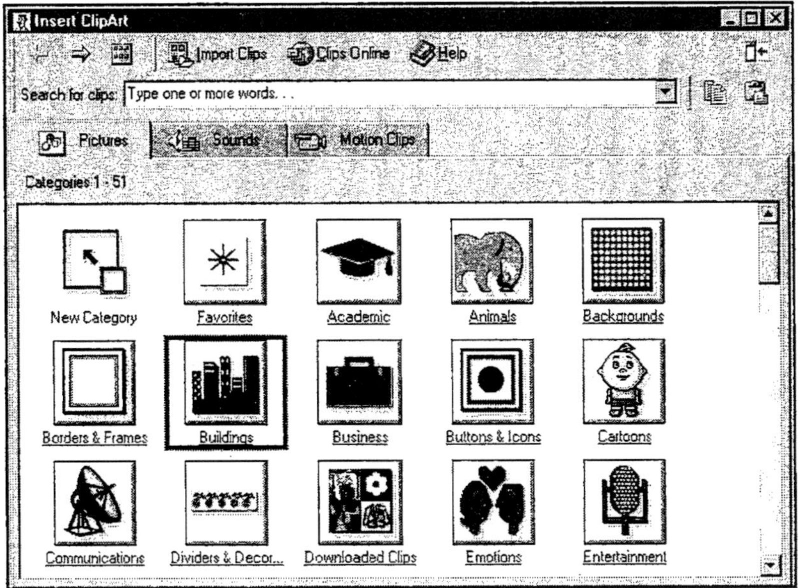

Figure 10.27: Insert Picture from Clipart dialog box

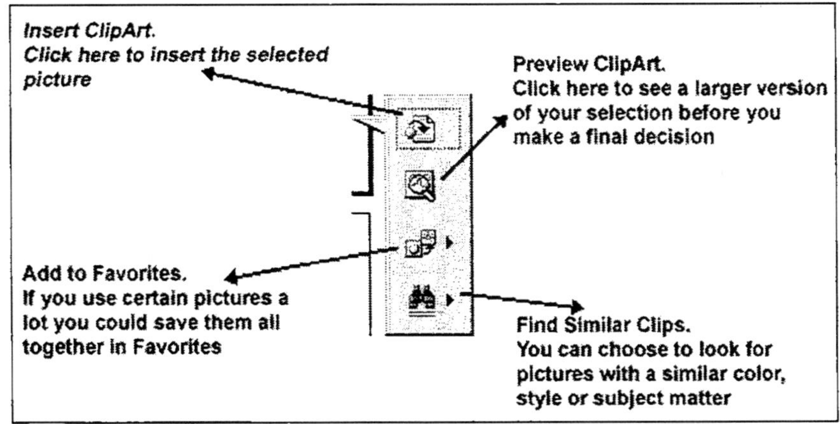

Figure 10.28: Insert picture drop down menu

 Hands on Exercise

Exercise 1: Create a Regional Sales and Expense worksheet and chart

1. Type the title and row and column titles as shown in Figure 10.29. Use the Increase indent button.

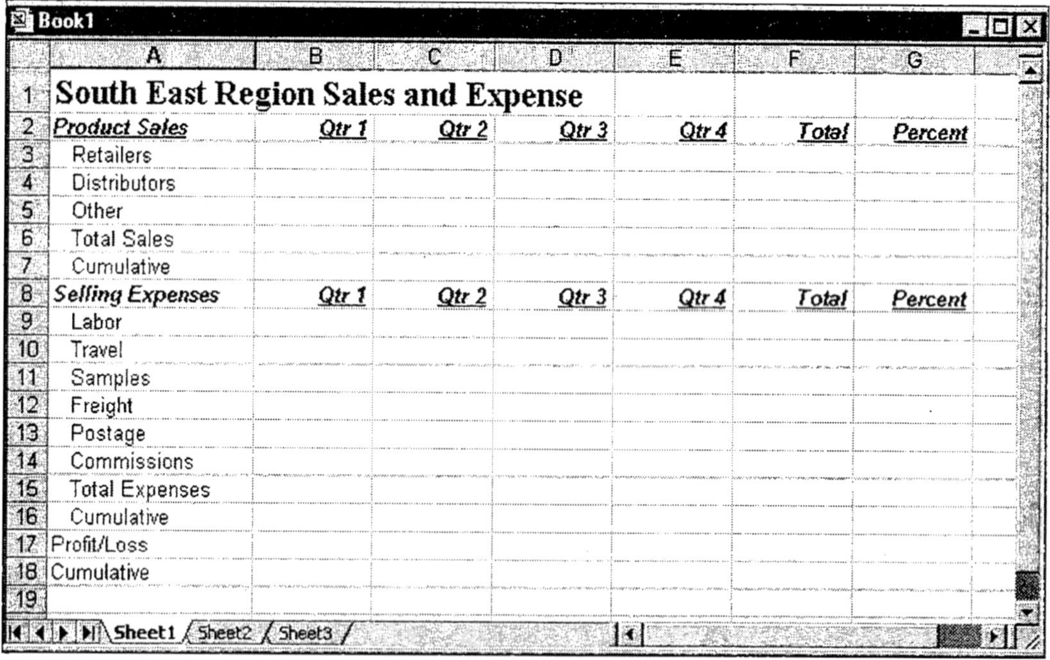

	A	B	C	D	E	F	G
1	South East Region Sales and Expense						
2	Product Sales	Qtr 1	Qtr 2	Qtr 3	Qtr 4	Total	Percent
3	Retailers						
4	Distributors						
5	Other						
6	Total Sales						
7	Cumulative						
8	Selling Expenses	Qtr 1	Qtr 2	Qtr 3	Qtr 4	Total	Percent
9	Labor						
10	Travel						
11	Samples						
12	Freight						
13	Postage						
14	Commissions						
15	Total Expenses						
16	Cumulative						
17	Profit/Loss						
18	Cumulative						
19							

Figure 10.29: Creating a sample worksheet

2. Change the font in cell A1 to Times New Roman 16 point bold, flush left.

3. Widen column A to 18, and column B through F to 10 characters.

4. Set the column heading in B2:G2 flush right, Arial 10 points, Bold, Italics and Underline. Bold, Italics and Underline the text in cell A2 and A8, Arial 10 points.

5. Then copy the column headings in B2:G2 to B8:G8.

6. Enter a Total Sales formula in B6 by using the Autosum function.

7. Copy the B6 formula in C6:F6.

8. Enter the Cumulative formulas in B7:E7. In cell B7, press =B6 and in cell C7, press =B7+C6. Copy the C7 formula in D7:E7.

9. Enter the Total Expenses formula in B15 by using the Autosum and copy the B15 formula in the cells C15:F15.

10. Copy the cumulative sales formulas in B7:E7 to B16:E16.

11. Now enter the Profit/Loss formula in B17:F17. In the cell B17, press =B6-B15. Copy the cell B17 and paste it into cells C17:F17.

12. Enter the Cumulative profit/loss formulas in B18:E18. In the cell B18, press =B7-B16. Copy the cell B18 and press enter after selecting the cells C18:E18 to paste.

13. Now enter the row total formula for F3:F5. In the cell F3 click the autosum button, select B3:E3 and press enter. Copy the F3 formula and press enter after selecting the range F4:F4 to paste.

14. Copy the F3 formula and press enter after selecting the range F9:F14.

15. Now enter the percent formulas. In cell G3 enter +F3/F6 <F4> Enter. Copy the G3 formula and press enter after selecting G4:G6 and G9:G15 to paste.

16. Format the value areas B3:F18 to 2 decimal places.

17. Format the percent column to show percentage sign and upto 2 decimal places.

18. Now compare your worksheet with the Figure 10.30.

	A	B	C	D	E	F	G
1	**South East Region Sales and Expense**						
2	***Product Sales***	***Qtr 1***	***Qtr 2***	***Qtr 3***	***Qtr 4***	***Total***	***Percent***
3	Retailers					0.00	#DIV/0!
4	Distributors					0.00	#DIV/0!
5	Other					0.00	#DIV/0!
6	Total Sales	0.00	0.00	0.00	0.00	0.00	#DIV/0!
7	Cumulative	0.00	0.00	0.00	0.00		
8	***Selling Expenses***	***Qtr 1***	***Qtr 2***	***Qtr 3***	***Qtr 4***	***Total***	***Percent***
9	Labor					0.00	#DIV/0!
10	Travel					0.00	#DIV/0!
11	Samples					0.00	#DIV/0!
12	Freight					0.00	#DIV/0!
13	Postage					0.00	#DIV/0!
14	Commissions					0.00	#DIV/0!
15	Total Expenses	0.00	0.00	0.00	0.00	0.00	#DIV/0!
16	Cumulative	0.00	0.00	0.00	0.00		
17	Profit/Loss	0.00	0.00	0.00	0.00	0.00	
18	Cumulative	0.00	0.00	0.00	0.00		
19							

Figure 10.30: Applying formulas

19. Now select the cells B3:E5 and B9:E14 click **Locked** check box to remove the check mark in the menu **Format → Cells → Protection**. To protect the worksheet press **Alt+T+P+P** and press enter. If required enter password otherwise leave it blank.

20. Save the workbook as South East Sales.xls.

21. Type any numbers you want in the data entry cells to see how the workbook operates as shown in Figure 10.31.

South East Sales

	A	B	C	D	E	F	G	H
1	**South East Region Sales and Expense**							
2	***Product Sales***	***Qtr 1***	***Qtr 2***	***Qtr 3***	***Qtr 4***	***Total***	***Percent***	
3	Retailers	56.30	60.20	58.40	65.40	240.30	51.81%	
4	Distributors	59.40	38.70	44.50	41.20	183.80	39.63%	
5	Other	4.50	9.50	11.20	14.50	39.70	8.56%	
6	Total Sales	120.20	108.40	114.10	121.10	463.80	100.00%	
7	Cumulative	120.20	228.60	342.70	463.80			
8	***Selling Expenses***	***Qtr 1***	***Qtr 2***	***Qtr 3***	***Qtr 4***	***Total***	***Percent***	
9	Labor	4.50	4.50	4.80	4.80	18.60	4.01%	
10	Travel	3.60	4.00	4.10	3.90	15.60	3.36%	
11	Samples	0.50	0.60	1.10	0.80	3.00	0.65%	
12	Freight	0.70	0.90	0.70	1.00	3.30	0.71%	
13	Postage	0.30	0.40	0.30	0.50	1.50	0.32%	
14	Commissions	8.40	7.60	8.00	8.50	32.50	7.01%	
15	Total Expenses	18.00	18.00	19.00	19.50	74.50	16.06%	
16	Cumulative	18.00	36.00	55.00	74.50			
17	Profit/Loss	102.20	90.[illegible]	95.10	101.60	389.30		
18	Cumulative	102.20	192.60	287.70	389.30			
19								

Sheet1 / Sheet2 / Sheet3

Figure 10.31: Final output after inserting data

22. Produce a chart using the values in A2:E5. Unprotect the worksheet using the **Tools → Protection** menu. Select A1:E5, click the Chart Wizard button and follow the steps 1 to 4 and finally click finish to get the chart as shown in Figure 10.32.

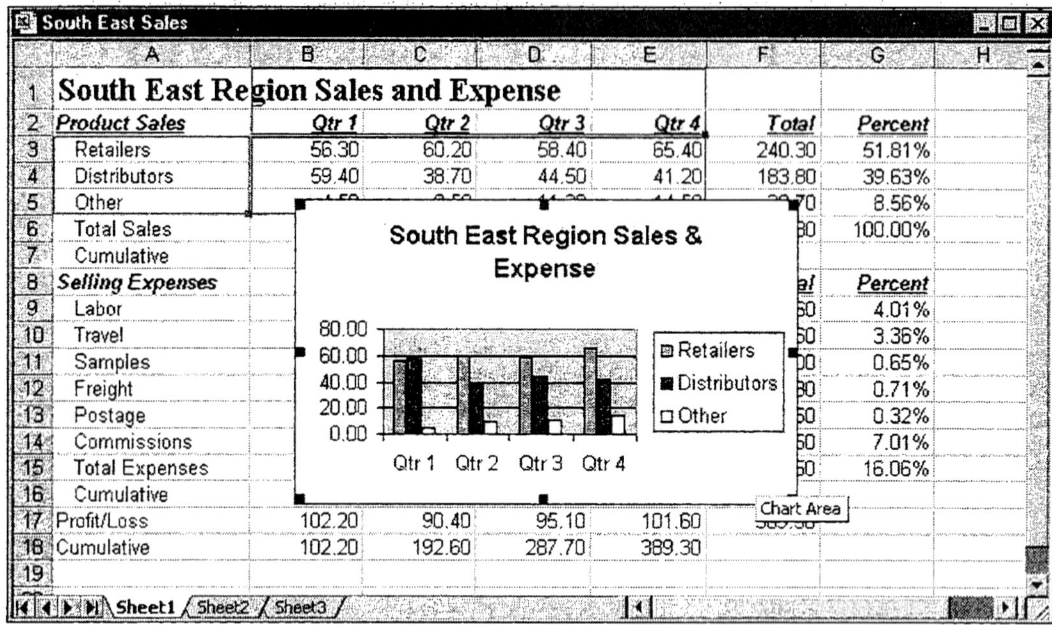

Figure 10.32: Creating a chart from the selected data

23. Save the workbook.

 Test Your Knowledge

Students must solve the following assignment.

Fill in the Blanks:

1. A ________ is a graphical representation of worksheet data.
2. In ________ chart, only one data series can be plotted.
3. A chart placed in a worksheet is called a ________ chart.
4. Scatter chart is also known as ________ chart.
5. A bubble chart shows three sets of ________.
6. The ________ operates with a formula having a single variable.

State Whether True or False:

1. Scatter chart is also called Doughnut chart.

   a. True
   b. False

2. A chart object placed in a worksheet alongwith data is called chart sheet.

   a. True
   b. False

3. A chart object placed in a worksheet alongwith data is called embedded chart.

   a. True
   b. False

Short Questions:

1. What is a PivotTable?
2. What are the various types of charts. Name them and write short notes of each of them?
3. What are the two techniques for creation of Charts?
4. Write down the steps involved to insert a ClipArt?

Assignments

Objectives

- Microsoft Word Assignments
- Microsoft Excel Assignments

Microsoft Word Assignments

Assignment # 1

Open a New Word Document and design a page similar to shown below and save on your desktop as **Assignment1.doc.**

 VOICES

"I have always considered myself a swayamsevak (volunteer) of India and her people and shall remain so forever".
ATAL BIHARI VAJPAYEE, prime minister, clarifying that there had been "unwarranted interpretation" of his speech in New York.

"Every day you come and disrupt assembly proceedings. If you persist in your behaviour, you will not be seen in the next assembly".
N.CHANDRA BABU NAIDU, Andhra Pradesh, Chief Minister, to Congress MLAs who continuously blocked legislative business.

"These chaps in the Task Force twiddle their thumbs and wait till Veerappan strikes. I would have pitched a tent inside the jungle".
K.P.S. Gill, former Punjab Police chief, lambasting the tactis used by the Special Task Force to nab Veerappan.

"When I should be concentrating on training the hockey team, I am running from pillar to post looking for accommodation".
RANJIT SINGH, penalty corner coach of the Indian hockey team to the Sydney Olympics, lashing out at team manager Jothikumaran.

 VIS – A – VIS

"I wish we had taken Mamta Banerjee seriously when she complained earlier. The situation is really bad".

"Fernandes' remarks are motivated. How can he say such a thing after hearing only one side?"

Assignment # 2

1. Open a New Document and type the following text in 11 points Arial font, Normal, Heading Arial 14 points bold.

   ## Computer Generation

   In 1946 Lee De Frost invented the thermoionic value which was the most significant invention in the field of calculating device. The valves were able to amplify or switch electric signals electronically. These valves resemble ordinary bulbs except that they are generally smaller and more elongated. Still we can see some of them in old radios and T.V. sets.

   In 1938 Claude Shannon, an electrical engineer invented that the circuits could be employed to perform logic and arithmetic by the use of electronic switching circuit.

   Computer Generation refers to the advancement of computer technology over the years. The development of electronic computer technology can be classified into four chronological categories.

2. Insert the following text after the third paragraph.

   They are as follows:

   - First Generation Computer
   - Second Generation Computer
   - Third Generation Computer
   - Fourth Generation Computer

3. Save the document as **Assignment2.doc** on the desktop of your system.

4. Move the second paragraph to the end of the document, using drag and drop feature.

5. Restore the original status of the document.

6. Now provide a header 'Historical Background of Computer' in 13 point bold, italics, top right aligned and in Times New Roman.

7. Your name, in *italicized 12 points Times New Roman font,* centered on a line at the bottom of the page as footer.

8. Move the second paragraph in the end of the document using cut, paste operations.

9. Undo the above actions.

10. Now Redo the above actions.

11. Go to end of the document (in one step).

12. Go to the beginning of the document (in one step).

13. Search the word "computer" in your document with options Match case, Find whole word only.

14. Replace the word "computer" with "Computer".

15. Format the above written paragraphs and give the options as follows:

Alignment	Justified
Indentation	Left 0.2" Right 0.2"
Spacing	Before 6 pt. After 6 pt.
Special	First Line by 0.4"
Line spacing	1.5 Lines

16. Set the margins to 1.25".

17. Insert the following table at the end of your document.

Type	Typical MIPS	Typical megabytes	Example Machine	Example use
Personal Computer	1	1	IBM PX/2	Word Processing
Mini Computer	2	4	PDP-11/84	Real-Time Control
Supermini	10	32	SUN-4	Network file server
Mainframe	30	128	IBM 3090/300	Banking
Super Computer	125	1024	Cray-2	Weather forecasting

18. Try to put the following text at the end of the document in the format as shown below:

ABS 65 001
CHAIN 85 003
COMMON 17 005
DEF FN 12 007
END 109 009
ERR 21 011
GOTO 69 013
INT 18 015
LLIST 35 017
MERGE 56 019
NEXT 6, 34 021
PAINT 98 023
PSET 72 025
RIGHT$ 26 027
SPACE$ 123 029

BEEP 24,63 002
CLEAR 87 004
CVD 60 006
DELETE 86 008
ERASE 73 010
FIX 8 012
INP 11 014
LEFT$ 36 016
LOF 97 018
MKS$ 87, 88 020
OPEN 54 022
POKE 25 024
RENUM 83 026
SAVE 143 028
STOP 52 030

SYSTEM	95	031	AND	176	032
BLOAD	39	033	CHDIR	89	034
CLOSE	9	035	CONT	76	036
CVI	59	037	DEF SEG	81	038

19. Print a hard copy of your document.

20. Save and close the document.

Assignment # 3

Open Word 2000 and write a short report on a topic on which you are an expert. The report should contain:

1. A title, formatted in 18 points Arial font, bold centered at the top of the page.

2. Your name, in *italicized 12 points Times New Roman font,* centered on a line below the title.

3. At least two paragraphs of information about your topic, left aligned, in 12 point Times New Roman font, with a space between the two paragraphs.

4. A bulleted list in one of the paragraphs.

5. Insert two-three small graphic somewhere near the bottom of the page.

6. No spelling errors (use spell-check).

7. Save your work as **Assignment3.doc** on the desktop of your system.

8. Print a hard copy of your document.

Assignment # 4

Create your BIO-DATA in Word. Save your work as **Assignment4.doc** on the desktop of your system.

Assignment # 5

Design a letter in Word in which thank your teacher for the efforts/pains he/she takes for you. Save your work as **Assignment5.doc** on the desktop of your system.

Microsoft Excel Assignments

Assignment # 1

1. Make a worksheet using the following Employee names, their Joining Dates and Basic Salary.
2. Save your work on the desktop as **Assignment1.xls**.
3. Print a hard copy of your work and close the file.

Employee Name	DOJ	Basic Salary
Manish Soni	12/01/95	8500
A. Hariharan	02/05/97	7500
Rohini Sharma	30/04/98	7300
Kushagra Mehta	26/06/99	8500
Dinbandhu Dinanath	05/11/98	5700
Mandira Singh Bedi	01/08/01	4500
Tulsi Rathore	30/12/98	6700
Steve Nicolson	26/04/99	10000
Rumki Datta	15/10/00	4000
Shivani Sood	20/07/93	9000

4. **Important Instructions:**

   Dearness Allowances (DA) is paid @ 33.33% of Basic Salary.
   House Rent Allowances (HRA) is paid @ 15% of Basic Salary + DA combined together.
   City Compensatory Allowance (CCA) is paid @ 7.8% of Basic Salary + DA + HRA combined together.
   Provident Fund (PF) is deducted @ 8.99% of Basic Salary + DA + HRA + CCA combined together.
   Income Tax (I. Tax) is deducted @ 10% of Basic Salary + DA + HRA + CCA combined together.
   Net Salary is summation of Basic Salary + DA + HRA + CCA less PF and I. Tax.

Assignment # 2

1. Make a worksheet of Student Grading Chart using the following student names.

   Vivian Richards
   Ericka Ashton
   Yolanda Yalgar
   Andrew Abrahms
   Danny D'Souza
   Kamal Trenton
   Rocky Thrush
   Steve R. Alvarez

Robert Balsa
Corinne Yahudi

2. Add math grades for the tests as indicated.

	Test 1 (25 questions)	Test 2 (25 questions)	Test 3 (25 ques) (25 questions)	Test 4 (20 questions)
Vivian Richards	24	25	24	20
Ericka Ashton	14	19	18	14
Yolanda Yalgar	17	19	23	18
Andrew Abrahms	22	24	24	19
Danny D'Souza	17	16	19	11
Kamal Trenton	25	24	25	19
Rocky Thrush	23	20	22	17
Steve R. Alvarez	21	23	21	17
Robert Balsa	19	18	16	16
Corinne Yahudi	25	22	25	18

3. Compute the percentage for each student's total. Show the total score and the percentage for each student.

4. Create a header for the chart. Include your name.

5. Save your work on the desktop as **Assignment2.xls.**

6. Print a hard copy of your work and close the file.

Assignment # 3

Create an appropriate title for your grading sheet. Center and bold the title and select an appropriate font size.

Select an "AutoFormat" style of your choice.

Sort the students alphabetically, by last name, in ascending order. To do this

- Select the columns and rows containing the student names and grades
- From the toolbar, select Data, Sort
- Make sure the Sort by says Column A and that Ascending is selected
- Select OK

Check that the information was sorted correctly. If you made an error, try to determine where you made an error and then use the Undo feature to restore the worksheet to its original order. Correct your error and redo the sort.

Assignment # 4

Your company, Southwestern Publishing Corporation pays a commission based upon books sold. Prepare a revenue and commission statement based upon the following information:

Salesperson	Number of Soft Cover Books Sold	Number of Hard Cover Books Sold
Allen DeBois	1200	200
John Coopersmith	1753	315
Sally Green	1122	285
April Chapman	955	238
Craig Mann	522	680

Assumptions:

Price	Hard Cover Books	:	$22.95 each
Price	Soft Cover Books	:	$6.95 each
Commission	Hard Cover Books	:	8.5%
	Soft Cover Books	:	12%

Prepare a spreadsheet showing your calculations to determine the

1. Revenue (Hard Cover Books and Soft Cover Books)
2. Total Revenue
3. Commission: (Hard Cover Books and Soft Cover Books)
4. Total Commission
5. Create a Chart (any style) showing the above information.

Turn in an original page (with lines and shading) as well as a formula page. (The entire formula must show).

Use "=round(,0)" where applicable so all columns will add correctly.

Assignment # 5

You work in the Finance Department for **LDC Corporation Inc.** Your job is to prepare a list of outstanding notes receivable each month. Please prepare a spreadsheet based upon the following information for the Month of November, 2000.

Use the following financial information:

Face Value	Interest Rate	
0	12.0%	Late Penalty: 12.5%
500	9.6%	Report date: November 30, 2000
1000	9.2	Days/Year: 365

Note Number	Face Value	Period Days	Issue Date
1	$615	60	8/15/2000
2	$700	90	9/22/2000
3	$265	45	7/1/2000
4	$900	30	6/1/2000
5	$1500	120	5/30/2000

Show the Interest Rate, Days outstanding, Interest Earned, Late Penalty and Total due - Use appropriate Lines and Shading to make the report interesting and easy to read! Use two decimals where appropriate. Prepare a chart to show the above information.

Assignment # 6

1. Complete the labels as shown below:

	A	B	C
1			
2			
3			
4		REVENUE	January
5		Catalog Sales	2800
6		Internet Sales	3400
7		Total Sales	
8			
9		EXPENSES	
10		COGS	1600
11		Salaries	1700
12		Rent and Utilities	1000
13		Office Supplies	600
14		Total Expenses	
15			
16		NET PROFIT	
17			

2. Point to the border between columns B & C, and double-click to AutoFit column B.

3. Click on cell C4, point to the AutoFill handle in the lower-right corner, and drag it to columns D and E. Highlight cells C10:C13 and do the same thing. This is what the screen should then look like.

REVENUE	January	February	March
Catalog Sales	2800	3300	
Internet Sales	3400	4000	
Total Sales			
EXPENSES			
COGS	1600	1600	1600
Salaries	1700	1700	1700
Rent and Utilities	1000	1000	1000
Office Supplies	600	600	600
Total Expenses			
NET PROFIT			

4. Type 3300 in cell D5 and 4000 in Cell D6. Highlight cells C5:D6, then drag the AutoFill handle to column E. You should get 3800 and 4600 for March.

5. Click on cell C7. Click on the AutoSum button on the Standard Toolbar.

6. Hit the Enter key to accept the AutoSum.

REVENUE	January	February
Catalog Sales	2800	3300
Internet Sales	3400	4000
Total Sales	=SUM(C5:C6)	

7. Select cells D7 and E7. Click the AutoSum button. Highlight cells C14:E14, then click the AutoSum button.

8. Click on cell C16. Type the formula that subtracts Expenses from Revenue.

9. Use the AutoFill handle to copy this to columns D & E. Here is the resulting spreadsheet.

REVENUE	January	February	March
Catalog Sales	2800	3300	3800
Internet Sales	3400	4000	4600
Total Sales	6200	7300	8400
EXPENSES			
COGS	1600	1600	1600
Salaries	1700	1700	1700
Rent and Utilities	1000	1000	1000
Office Supplies	600	600	600
Total Expenses	4900	4900	4900
NET PROFIT	1300	2400	3500

10. Highlight the titles in column B and row 4. Remember, hold down the Ctrl key to highlight multiple ranges.

11. Change the font to whatever you like, with a font size of 14.

12. Highlight all of the numbers. Click on the currency button.

13. Click the Decrease Decimal button twice to get rid of the decimal points.

REVENUE	January	February	March
Catalog Sales	$2,800	$3,300	$3,800
Internet Sales	$3,400	$4,000	$4,600
Total Sales	$6,200	$7,300	$8,400
EXPENSES			
COGS	$1,600	$1,600	$1,600
Salaries	$1,700	$1,700	$1,700
Rent and Utilities	$1,000	$1,000	$1,000
Office Supplies	$600	$600	$600
Total Expenses	$4,900	$4,900	$4,900
NET PROFIT	$1,300	$2,400	$3,500

14. Highlight cells B4:E6. Click on the Chart Wizard button. Go with the defaults on each one. You will make a column chart.

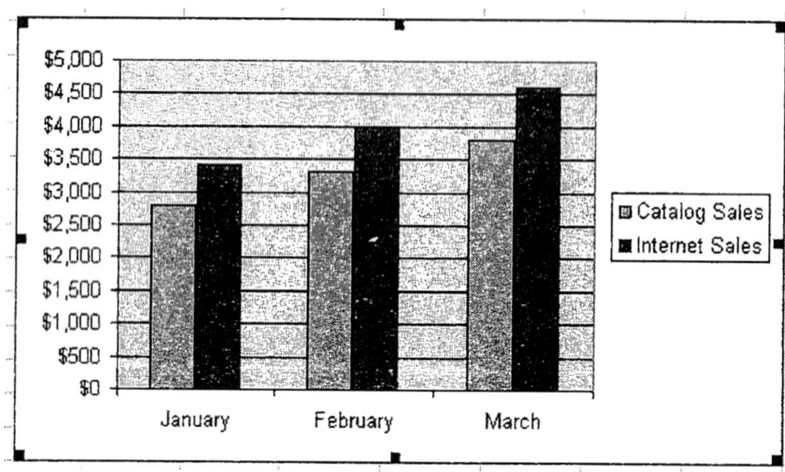

Assignment # 7

1. Create a worksheet as shown below:

	A	B	C	D	E
1	Quarterly Sales Analysis				
2					
3	**Salesman**	**Qtr 1**	**Qtr 2**	**Qtr 3**	**Qtr 4**
4	A001	83454	27825	57349	97435
5	A002	66347	26243	99466	98164
6	A003	33878	97246	56485	72343
7	A004	77235	48265	99458	33654
8	**Total**				

2. Name the range B3:B6 as 'Qtr 1'

3. Similarly define the names for the other ranges C3:C6, D3:D6 and E3:E6.

4. Now find the sum of the range Qtr 1 in the cell B7.

5. Also find the sum of the other ranges Qtr 2, Qtr 3, Qtr 4 in cells C7, D7 and E7 respectively.

6. Create a stacked column chart depicting the relation of Salesman A001 in all the four quarters.

7. Create a Area chart depicting the sales in all the four quarters.